# MARKOS VAMVAKARIS
# THE MAN AND THE BOUZOUKI
# AUTOBIOGRAPHY

Markos Vamvakaris, born in 1905 in Syros was a pioneer of *rebetiko*, the urban folk music of Greece. The *bouzouki* was a disreputable instrument but he paved its path to glory. He spent many years, first as a stevedore in the port of Piraeus and then as a butcher in the slaughterhouse. During this time he fell in love with a tigress, his first wife, he learnt to smoke hashish and to play the 'sacred' instrument: 'I had a great passion. My life was all *bouzouki*. It took me over - but it also took me up in the world, way up ...'

This is the first ever translation into English of the Autobiography compiled by Angeliki Vellou-Keil in 1972. It opens a window onto a time of extraordinary creativity in the history of Greek music, an explosion of song writing in the interwar period. Its composers wrote about themselves and each other, the rituals of hashish smoking and the landmarks of a now vanished city.

Markos the repentant sinner and living legend, looks back at childhood idylls in Syros, the arrival of the Asia Minor refugees, the terrible years of the Nazi Occupation, the ceaseless love affairs and disappointments, and the triumphs of the *bouzouki*. He offers a rare insight into the lives of toiling workers and the lowlife of one of the world's most ancient ports, where East meets West. Out of this melting pot he produced the classic songs that Greeks of all ages still love and know by heart.

## THE TRANSLATOR

Noonie Minogue is a London based writer and artist. She was an English literature scholar at Newnham College Cambridge and studied Ancient Greek and Latin both at Cambridge and later at Birkbeck College London University. Publications include 'Nero the Singing Emperor' (Short Books 2005). She lived briefly in Greece and has studied the language, literature and music of Modern Greece ever since. She has played rebetiko on cello, guitar and baglama with a number of bands.

## GREEKLINES

Greece has a very rich musical tradition. While the whole world talks about Cuban Salsa, Argentine Tango, Portugese Fado, Spanish Flamenco, Indian Ragas, Jazz and Blues very few people know about *Rebetika*, *Epirotica*, *Mantinadhes*, *Nisiotika* and *Pontiaka* ... the music of Greece. There are many passionate enthusiasts among those who have discovered it.

Greeklines has been set up with the idea of making this music better known by publishing key texts from Byzantium to the present day. Markos Vamvakaris' Autobiography tells the story of the 'Greek Blues' directly through the eyes of its founding father. At this challenging time for Greece we are keen to promote awareness of the country's rich and diverse cultural heritage.

**Pavlos Melas**
**Greeklines.com**

# Markos Vamvakaris
## The Man and the Bouzouki
### Autobiography

Edited and Translated by Noonie Minogue
Published by Greeklines.com

# GREEKLINES.COM

Copyright © Greeklines.com and the Vamvakaris Family
First edition published 2015 by Greeklines.com

All rights reserved. No part of this publication may be reproduced, stored in a retrieval system, or transmitted in any form or by any means, without the prior permission in writing of Greeklines.com and the Vamvakaris family.

A catalogue record of this book is available from the British Library.

ISBN 978-0-9932633-0-9

Designed and set by Greeklines.com
Edited and translated by Noonie Minogue
Greek text compiled by Angeliki Vellou-Keil
Title-page illustration by David Prudhomme
Cover and photos edited by Georgia Konsta

Although every precaution has been taken in the preparation of this book, the publisher and author assume no responsibility for errors or omissions. Neither is any liability assumed for damages resulting from the use of this information contained herein.

# CONTENTS

| | |
|---|---|
| *List of Illustrations* | ix |
| *Glossary* | xi |
| *Introduction* | xv |
| *Translator's Note* | xx |
| *Prologue by Angeliki Vellou-Keil* | xxv |

## PART I: SYROS

| | | |
|---|---|---|
| 1 | Syra, Your Upper Chora | 1 |
| 2 | I Wanted to Be Heracles | 26 |
| 3 | Ermoupoli | 37 |

## PART II: PIRAEUS

| | | |
|---|---|---|
| 4 | Coal and the Harness | 48 |
| 5 | Manghia | 58 |
| 6 | Refugees | 62 |
| 7 | Slaughterhouse | 66 |
| 8 | The Army | 76 |
| 9 | Wreckage | 87 |
| 10 | Bouzouki and the Tekes | 94 |
| 11 | All the Rebetes of the World | 103 |

## PART III: GOLDEN YEARS

| 12 | The Famous Quartet | 116 |
| 13 | I Don't Want you Anymore | 132 |
| 14 | Tours and Glories | 135 |
| 15 | Your Blue Windows | 143 |
| 16 | Votanikos | 149 |

## PART IV: WAR YEARS AND AFTER

| 17 | I've Seen a Lot | 169 |
| 18 | In this Bad World | 197 |
| 19 | I like Hearts Like Mine | 218 |
| 20 | The Music, the Words, The Songs | 244 |

*Appendix: Introduction to Greek Edition*     273
*Acknowledgments by Angeliki Vellou-Keil*     289

# LIST OF ILLUSTRATIONS

| | | |
|---|---|---|
| 1 | Yovan Tsaous and friends at Piraeus | 62 |
| 2 | Markos, worker at the slaughterhouse | 67 |
| 3 | Markos, 1929 | 102 |
| 4 | Lemonadhika | 103 |
| 5 | The Famous Quartet | 116 |
| 6 | Markos and Vangelio, newly weds | 179 |

# GLOSSARY

A note on spelling and prounciation: **Dh**, as in *dhimotiko* should be pronounced like a soft: **th as in -*the*** - the definite article. This is a transliteration of the Greek 'Delta': Δ, δ

**(a)manes**, (pl. (a)*manedhes*) - vocal improvisation; so called because of the mournful interjection '*aman aman ...*' - a little like the English 'Alas ...'

**antartis** (pl. antartes) – an insurgent or rebel. A term used for Greek resistance fighters, mostly members of *ELAS*, the 'Greek People's Liberation Army', the predominantly communist military wing of EAM, the 'National Liberation Front'.

**arghile** – Ottoman style water pipe, hubble bubble or hookah used for smoking tobacco or hashish.

**barba(s)** - respectful term of address for speaking to older men, similar to 'uncle', used in villages mostly, but also in Piraeus.

**chasapiko** - the butcher's dance, originally from Constantinople, in 4/4 or 2/4 metre.

**café aman** – a fasionable musical café with a platform, orchestra and dancers. It takes its name presumably from the fact that *amanedhes* would be on the programme. Typical dances would be: *zebekiko*, *karsilamas*, *chasapiko*, *chora*, *serviko*, and *tsifteteli*. The café aman was found in the more progressive and cosmopolitan cities like Smyrna, Aivali, Volos, and Thessaloniki.

**chasiklis** (pl. chasiklidhes) - hashish smoker, hashish addict.

**chasiklidhika** - the large body of songs devoted to the rituals of hashish smoking and the pleasures of the *arghile*.

**dervisis** - a 'dervish'. A very superior sort of *mangas*, extra cool, quiet, dignified, reserved, someone people looked up to.

**dhimotika** – the rich culture of traditional Greek folk music that emerged from a largely rural culture: dances such as the *tsamikos* and *kalamatianos*. The younger generation of Greek musicians often refer to this in English as 'demotic' music but it has been left as *dhimotiko* in this text as 'demotic' is not the kind of word Markos would use.

**douzeni** – a special tuning for the *bouzouki* or *baglama*.

**dhromoi** – literally, 'roads' i.e. scales, modes, maqams.

**gaida** – bagpipes.

**kleftis** - 'bandit'. The *klefts* were mountain 'brigands' who resisted the Turkish occupation through many generations from their lairs in mountainous remote areas. Figures of romance in the popular imagination they danced warrior dances like the *tsamiko*, and played an important role in the Greek war of independence in 1821.

**kleftika** - the songs of the klefts, belonging to the oral folk tradition. They began to be collected and written down in the early 19$^{th}$ century. See above. These songs glorified the ethos of personal freedom, *palikariá* (see below) and *leventia* - manly grace, beauty and nimbleness.

**koutsavakis** (pl. Koutsavakidhes) - a tough, knife-carrying type who spoke a particular slang, and walked with a characteristic swagger. '*Koutsa koutsa*' is how the crab walks in the famous rebetiko song *Ta Kavourakia* of Vassilis Tsitsanis. They wore distinctive clothes - often a jacket with the right sleeve empty, and twirling moustachios; generally a slightly more dangerous kind of *mangas*. Markos mentions several *koutsavakidhes* whose exploits were legendary but bloody. He also says that they dance the *zebekiko* and *chasapiko*.

**laika** - popular urban music, in contrast with traditional rural folk music or *dhimotika*, (see above). 'Our music', as Markos calls it: '*laiko* song was born in the hearts of the poor who toil, the workers. *Laiko* song is what the working man likes'.

**mangas** (pl. manghes) - a man who is a master of himself, and has little respect for any authority beyond his own inclinations and personal principles. He enjoys the beautiful things in life. He talks little and does not cause trouble unless challenged. For more on *manghes* as a social group see A.V.K's 1972 Introduction in the appendix.

**manghia** – the ethos of the *mangas*, a way of life to be found in the underworld of cities or ports, with its own code of honour, language and hierarchies, peopled by *manghes, koutsavakidhes, daidhes* (hell-raisers), *mortidhes* (devil-may-care diehards) and dervishes (see *dervisis* above). These are words that appear constantly in *rebetiko* songs.

**oke -** a measurement of weight = 1.24 kilos

**palikari** – brave young man, one who exemplifies the qualities of *palikariá* - the courage, chivalry and derring-do of the warrior. Markos applies this word to various legendary *koutsavakidhes* and to *manghes* who didn't give information to the police.

**penia (pl. penies)** – The stroke of the *penna* (plectrum) on the strings of an instrument.

**rebetiko** – Greek urban folk: songs written mostly by composer-instrumentalists, mixing traditional folk roots with Asia minor influences, sometimes drawing on European style dance tunes. This music developed in the second half of the 19th and the first half of the 20th centuries as the mostly rural population of Greece concentrated in increasing numbers in the cities, particularly the great ports of Asia Minor and the Greek Mainland, islands like Syros, Lesvos and Samos, and the diaspora in America – where in fact some of the earliest recordings of *rebetiko* were made. In the early thirties, after Markos made his first recordings of bouzouki in Athens, the bouzouki came to dominate the scene. *Rebetiko* exploded in Piraeus and gained popularity all over Greece. There is a large overlap between *rebetiko* and what Markos means when he talks about laiko song.

**rebetis** (pl. rebetes) - a free-spirited type who embodies the bohemian life of the subculture that produced *rebetiko (see above)*. Markos uses this word in his songs eg: *Oloi Oi Rebetes tou Dounia,* ('All the *rebetes* of the World') but outside the songs, it appears rarely in this Autobiography. He talks more about *manghes.*

**rebetissa** – the female version of rebetis.

**smyrneika** – songs from Smyrna, (now Izmir), the cosmopolitan Greek city in Asia Minor which went up in flames in September 1922. Typical instruments would be violin, oud, santouri, kanonaki, tsimbalo, *politiki lyra*, and clarinet.

**taliro** – a 5 drachma coin or note, roughly equivalent to a dollar.

**taximi** - instrumental improvisation, usually in the mode of the song that follows, but also played on its own.

**tekes** - originally a Turkish word meaning an Islamic monastery or retreat for Dervishes, which later came to mean a hashish den, usually a simple shack or side room off a *kafeneion*, where *chasiklidhes* went to smoke the *arghile.*

**teketzis** – the owner of the tekes who would probably be a *chasiklis* and very possibly a *koutsavakis*, (see above).

**tsifteteli** - Greek 'belly dance' in 4/4 metre.

**zebekis** - legendary Anatolian guerilla fighters who, from late 17th to early 20th century, protected villagers from government tax collectors and bandits in the Aegean areas under the Ottoman empire. They performed a special warrior's dance, the *zebekiko..*

**zebekiko** - the warrior's dance of the zebeks, in 9/8 or 9/4 metre, normally danced solo and freestyle.

# INTRODUCTION

Whatever title you give him - 'pioneer', 'trail blazer', 'patriarch', or 'Commander in Chief' of *bouzouki*, Markos Vamvakaris stands, a towering craggy presence in the history of *rebetiko* music. It's enough to refer to him by his sturdy apostolic first name. He needs no epithets or patronymics. 'Markos' he muses, with a touching mixture of pride and wonder: 'it's a big name ... a street is named after me in Syros'. The name evokes the heavyweight solidity of a man who toiled and sweated, 'the working man, by whom and for whom *laiko* song was created.'

Born in Syros in 1905, he started helping his father feed the family at an early age. They had no money for a mule, so 'barefoot and in rags' they carried heavy loads of withies for basket weaving from the rivers up to the village of Upper Chora. In 1912 he had to leave school and go to work in a cotton mill. At the age of fifteen he dropped a boulder through the roof of somebody's house and stowed away in a boat to Piraeus. By then he'd already worked as a factory hand, a mule driver, drummer boy, butcher's boy, grocer's boy, newspaper hawker and bootblack. One of his most famous songs has the title: *Markos, Jack-of-all-trades.*

Over the next five years in Piraeus he was a stevedore loading coal on and off ships. Being unusually tall and strong he earned extra pay in the team that carried the heaviest loads. He left this backbreaking work to become a skinner and slaughterer in the Piraeus slaughterhouse. For a man who frequently said 'flowers, letters and music are what I like - and add to that fine clothes', it was bad luck to be destined to so many years in the most strenuous and filthy jobs imaginable, first grimy and black with coal dust, then red with the blood and filth of the abattoir.

He was born though, with an aptitude for rhythm and rhyme, and an appetite for beauty. His inner 'dervish', as he called it, his 'aristocratic streak' was crying out for a different kind of life. It carried him off on what his despairing parents called 'the downward path'. This took him to the underworld of the '*piazza*', the bordello and the hashish dens or *tekedhes*. This was the world of '*manghia*' - an alternative moral universe, where exhausted workers sat in shacks or caves, side by side with old jailbirds, thieves, and murderers, talking in arcane slang and smoking their *arghiledhes*, either in stoned companionable silence or playing and singing on their stringed instruments: the *tsivouri*, the *bouzouki*, the *gonato*, *baglama*, or *tzouras*.

Even as a boy, Markos had begun to soak up '*manghia* by the ladleful' in Ermoupoli, the port of Syros. Now in Piraeus he lived and breathed *manghia* but his sins were women and hashish, not killing or stealing. He was 'the best kind of *mangas*', tough, sensible, a man of gravity and few words - in other words a dervish: 'What I mean by 'dervish'is that I was a *mangas* who could hold my head up high. I didn't stir up trouble. People respected me and I respected them ... We made our money by the sweat of our brow'. More than anything else, Markos was a man with a genius for writing songs that Greeks of all ages still know and love, and an overpowering passion for the *bouzouki*.

Markos fell in love with the *bouzouki* when he heard an old convict, Nikos Aivaliotis play. It was a *coup de foudre* and he learned to be a 'wild beast' on the *instrument* in just six months. He learned by listening to the old men of the *tekedhes*. Soon crowds began to form wherever he played. He began writing songs when he was doing military service in 1925, a time which he spent mostly in the barracks jail – 'a dreamy place for me', as he said, quiet and peaceful. What makes Markos a trailblazer is that he took the *bouzouki* out of the *tekedhes* and set up the first *laiko* band, playing at a small dive in Piraeus. This was the *Xakousti Tetras* (The

Famous Quartet), with Yiorgos Batis on baglama, Stratos Payioumtzis the singer and Anestos Delias.

Markos' first recordings in the early thirties shot both him and the *bouzouki* to stardom. So began the golden years of the Piraeus-*bouzouki* strand of *rebetiko* music. The arrival of the Asia Minor refugees had already enriched the musical life of Athens and Piraeus and now the interwar years saw an explosion of musical talent, a golden age of songwriting. Composers ranged from accomplished and cosmopolitan musicians like Peristeris and Tountas, both from Smyrna, and both recording directors, one at Odeon/Parlophone, the other at Columbia, to relatively uneducated people like Markos. Piraeus became 'a nest of singing birds'. The day-to-day life of people round the port, the sacred rituals of hashish smoking, the landmarks of a now vanished city, were immortalized in these songs. The translation of lived experience into song was unusually direct. Many songs were little snatches of life in which the composers mentioned themselves and their friends by name. This autobiography is interspersed with the songs Markos wrote out of his own life.

Before long Markos was persuaded to sing as well as play at the recording studios. He didn't think he could sing but that scratchy, mean-old-man voice turned out to be 'exactly what they were looking for'. Now the radio was broadcasting Markos Vamvakaris all over Greece and he shot to fame. The *bouzouki* which to start with had brought him low, now lifted him high. 'The *bouzouki*, like I told you, is what the hardened criminals laid hold of, killers with life sentences, the guys on death row ... Nowadays, as you see, just anybody picks it up. A guy's not even likely to think what he's got his hands or to say I've got a *bouzouki* and it's a sacred thing, because it's come out of that world ... that's why the police were hounding it and that's why the police were chasing *me*. They didn't want the *bouzouki* to spread. But still, it *did* spread ... ' The *bouzouki* was, in the end, the means by which Markos managed to keep his whole family alive through the difficult, hungry years of the occupation.

    Although Markos set the *bouzouki* on its path to glory he didn't make the fortune out of it that a younger generation of players did. 'All these great and famous *bouzouki* players are ungrateful ... they should have kept a candle burning every day at the feet of Saint Markos! Because I can tell you, if it weren't for me where would these millionaires be? ... I was the first who spread the table for the feast and said Come on, sit down, let's eat ... I *am* your teacher. I led the way.' This was a grievance. Markos had in fact made more money than he ever dreamed of but it never stayed long in his pocket. His cult status now, may well be due to the feeling that since he didn't make those millions, for him the *bouzouki* never lost its 'sacred' nature. He didn't compromise or swing with the times. He didn't elaborate into more western-style modes or stray from the 'roads' or the *taximia* he'd learnt in the *tekedhes*. He achieved his songs with deceptively simple ingredients: 'I'm a straight *bouzouki* man. The genuine article. The old guys used to play it thirty, forty, fifty years ago. That's my kind of *bouzouki*. Same with Papaioannou and Keromytis. The working man's Instrument. Me and these guys, we keep it simple.'

    This image of the unswerving monolith needs to be leavened with another image. We have to remember the dervish. In the old recordings you will sometimes hear one of the musicians shout '*Yiasou Marko mou, Dervisi!*' - 'Yay! Markos, you dervish!' The resourcefulness, the adroitness and the inner fire, that fuelled the music, the endless love affairs, and survival through the bleak years of neglect in the fifties, are encapsulated in Markos' spectacular ability to dance the *zebekiko*. In this he combined machismo with precision and grace. 'Such a big man, and not to fall over!'

He kept things 'simple', he was a heavyweight, centred in one place but he whirled on it like a spinning top.

Reading the Autobiography in Greek it's impossible not to be struck by the vivid sense you get of a man talking aloud. The mood swings and wild inconsistencies – the jostling unresolved facets of Markos' character – are precisely what make this story so recognizably human and engaging. The soulful confessional vein of the opening page gives little indication of the diatribes to come, against the first wife, the 'tigress' Zingoala, or against those 'faggots' who 'strut about nowadays with their *bouzoukia* reaping in the millions'. We enter a world very different from ours and it's not one in which modern sensibilities will always be perfectly comfortable. Markos' views on various matters, especially women, are unlikely to accord with what people these days would like him to think. As Markos' fame grows outside Greece, the mythologizing process is well underway. His songs and his music seem to speak so directly to people there's some danger they may then cast him in their own image. It seems like the right time now to let him tell his own story to the English speaking world in his own voice – or at any rate, the nearest I could get to it.

## TRANSLATOR'S NOTE

The Greek text of this autobiography was compiled in the early seventies by Angeliki Vellou-Keil. The story of how this came about and how she interviewed Markos for three weeks intensively in 1969, is to be found in the extract from her Prologue to the first edition, which I've translated and included here. The introduction which she wrote for that edition, first published in 1978, is also included at the back as an appendix, in her own English version. Her work in assembling the book from the mixture of recorded material and hand written exercise books in the dimly remembered age of cut and paste and typewriters, was undoubtedly heroic. However, it soon became clear that this text would not work in English without some radical editing and reorganizing. It's much easier now than it was forty years ago, to coax the story into a more logical sequence.

For instance various digressions on the musical life of Syros in Markos' childhood have now been moved from the Piraeus years of part II into the childhood section of Part I, which in its turn has also been reorganized into a more chronological order. The original chapter and section headings have been replaced by new titles. In Part II the army chapter has been brought back to follow immediately on the Slaughterhouse chapter instead of coming at the end. Another digression, originally from Part II has been moved to the end of the final chapter where Markos talks about the effect of censorship in his songs. His digression on the subject of the 1936 crack down on hashish, the decline of the *tekes* culture and the questions his young son Stelios kept asking on the subject of his past life as a hashish smoker, fitted well with what he had to say about the censorship of hashish songs - the *chasiklidhika* - under the Metaxas dictatorship. The two things obviously went hand in hand so it seems more helpful to encounter them all in one place. The reluctance Markos had in talking to his sons about his past life as a *mangas* also seemed to round things off nicely by bringing us back to the Markos that we meet in the opening pages; the repentant sinner and family man. Never mind the fact that between the opening pages and the final ones we encounter numerous other versions of Markos where he is neither a family man nor repentant.

I have cut some passages where Markos goes into lengthy detail about the *arghile* and the cannabis plant, also the questions and answers on technical matters about the music that were in chapter seven of the original text. If these could be united with the recorded tapes of Markos talking and actually playing the *taximia* and *douzenia* that he talks about, they would be far more illuminating. It may be that at some future point this material could be put together into some kind of supplement online. Smaller changes, beyond the obvious pruning of repetitions, have involved moving lines around within a paragraph to sharpen the momentum of an anecdote; or moving a paragraph up or down so as to unite interrupted trains of thought. In cases where one paragraph repeated another, I ran the best parts of both into one. Various random sentences that looked pale and wan among strangers had to be scooped up into a temporary orphanage, then reinserted where they made more sense.

In mopping up these stragglers and trying to clarify the obscurer passages I've done my best not to tidy Markos beyond recognition. The preservation of an authentic voice was paramount in all the efforts to shape a more readable narrative. He is still allowed enough digressive freedom, I hope, to keep that freshness, that sense of a man telling his story out loud in the order that his thoughts come to him, not as a worked over written text. The question has arisen over nearly every word or phrase: 'Is this Markos?' Would a man with little more than two years of schooling and who lived that kind of life use this or that word? I threw out many words that seemed too elevated. But on the other hand one has to bear in mind that Markos loved letters, he was bright and he loved the little schooling he had. He tells us that he listened out for interesting words to put into his songs. He uses fancy French phrases for instance like *enfants gatés*. That consideration offers some leeway for the occasional use of more highflown words. When it came, for example, to the famous episode of the calf that cried when he went to slaughter it, no substitute could be found for 'inconsolably'.

The language Markos speaks is not always clear or grammatical, and it is steeped in the *argo* of lowlife Piraeus between the wars. In order to create a voice that would convey the vernacular flavour of the original I have drawn on whatever colloquialisms sprang to mind, wherever they came from. It is of course difficult to be colloquial without locating Markos in a specific place and I've tried very hard not to land him in the mobster underworlds of Cockney London, Chicago or the Mississippi delta. But all colloquialisms have to come from somewhere. English readers may therefore be affronted by Americanisms and similarly Americans may find English phrases unfamiliar. One consideration to keep in mind is that Markos spoke in a language and an argo that is sometimes obscure to a younger generation of Greeks. Many words are not to be found in any lexicon and therefore have to be investigated by 'asking around'. The right people to ask tend to be octogenarians. So the occasional sense of an unfamiliar idiom may replicate what a native Greek speaker feels when reading this text in Greek. Generally I've tried to use turns of phrase that would fit the epoch Markos lived in, especially since his mindset is very much of its time.

The harder I looked at the songs the more obvious it became that blank verse translations fell flat and that Markos loved rhymes. They were an essential part of his panache.

Sometimes he puts multiple rhymes even into one line of a song. Many of his songs have a satirical punch or a devil-may-care jauntiness about them that cannot be conveyed without the inherent gaiety and gusto of rhyme. For all Markos talks about tortures, troubles, and sorrows many of the songs reveal a great verve and zest for life. Even when he has written a thoroughly gloomy song the effect of his rhymes is to clinch that sense of bitterness with laconic emphasis. Once I'd rhymed one song there was no looking back! Starting out with the fear that this would require taking liberties and a possible loss of word-for-word accuracy, it seemed as if, by some mysterious process, not only the mood but also, quite simply, the meaning came out more clearly in rhyme and rhythm than it did before. The Greek versions are printed beside the translation so anyone with a command of both languages can judge if this claim is justified.

Some of the words that crop up throughout this autobiography are untranslatable in one simple word. I've left them in the original Greek and many of them could be regarded as part of the essential terminology that goes with *rebetiko* or *laiko* music. The book therefore opens with a glossary. Greek or foreign words that recur are printed throughout the book in italics and they will be explained in a footnote the first time they appear.

The songs printed here are not always exactly the same version as those recorded by Markos in the 30s or 40s. The differences are slight but sometimes a verse here or there may be missing. They are as Markos remembered them in 1969 so I have simply translated them as they come in the original Greek edition.

I have to thank the musician and composer, Pavlos Melas, for having the idea and offering me the difficult but enjoyable task of translating Markos into English. Without his vision, intelligent editing, accuracy checks, and good humoured patience, not to mention energy and efficiency in all its practical aspects, this project would neither have got off the ground nor reached the finishing post. We're also grateful for the warm support and helpful comments of Angeliki Vellou-Keil and Charles Keil, as well as the kind cooperation of the Vamvakaris family.

**Noonie Minogue**

# EXTRACT FROM PROLOGUE TO THE GREEK EDITION OF 1978 BY ANGELIKI VELLOU-KEIL

Edited and Translated by Noonie Minogue

I first got to know Markos Vamvakaris at his house at 35 Odhos Ofriniou, in Aspra Chomata in Kokkinia, in the autumn of 1967. Mingos Christou had sent us from Thessaloniki. When he heard that my husband and I were interested in learning the 'roads' of the *bouzouki* and the *taximia*, he introduced us at once. 'Go and find Markos Vamvakaris in Piraeus.'

Markos received us warmly in his semi-basement studio, his workshop, and for some time he answered our questions, sometimes playing, sometimes talking, sometimes singing. It gave him particular pleasure that we were from America and that in the few days we had in Greece we'd found time to come and see him. He fondly remembered his glory days when he was the great 'Markos' and the whole of America wanted to see him. 'And yet they didn't let me go and earn money with my *bouzouki* because my name had a black mark on it from the times when I used to get busted for smoking hashish.'

He showed us his Autobiography which he'd started by himself. More recently some students from the university, Nearchos Georgiadhis and Angeliki Kalamaras, had been helping him to write it, acting as secretaries. Since the political situation had just changed, Markos didn't want to submit the story of his life to a repressive censorship. He was sure its publication would be forbidden. 'Why don't you take it over there to America where there's more freedom?'

His faith in me, the simplicity with which he entrusted to me his life's work - because back then that's how he regarded this book, didn't leave me much room for manoeuvre.

'Let me see ... but how can it be done? I'll have to translate it first ... let's see.'

'Take it kid, and bring it out. I want to see it as a book before I die.'

I liked Markos' story. His language is the kind of Greek that we speak, that we hear and think, but don't find in books, the sort of language that you read and it seems like you can hear someone talking. So a plan began to take shape, by which Markos' Autobiography would be completed and prepared for publication. I came to Greece in September 1969 for three weeks. I brought the text and about a hundred and thirty questions as well as an interviewing technician, a musicologist drafted in by the anthropologist and worshipper of *laiko* music, Yannis Andromidhas. For two weeks I enjoyed the hospitality of the Vamvakaris family in Nikaia. Morning and evening Markos and I settled down to the conversation which I was recording. I put to Markos as many questions as I could and did my best to cover the numerous gaps in the story. This work that we did yielded more than thirty hours of recorded interviews and it was often tiring for Markos but his passion to see the book finished and complete was the one thing that gave him strength and courage to bear this taxing daily routine.

From the moment I got back to America, and with many interruptions due to prior commitments, I started working through all this material. The interviews provided material which, though always interesting, had the free association of thought that one has in conversation. Markos often referred in the same breath to events that belonged to different times and which were, perhaps, responses to my question and to my palpable presence. This made the written narrative confusing and hard to follow. Some of these bits were reallocated to the parts of the narrative where they belonged chronologically. However the text as it's presented here, still has many such digressions into the past and future. This is entirely natural in an oral narration. Apart from certain connective phrases or words the entire text is in Markos' own words, as he wrote it down himself or dictated it to various 'scribes' at different times or as he told it to me. The book consists of an assemblage of paragraphs taken directly either from Markos' own exercise books or from tape recordings of the interviews.

Markos wrote his story knowing that the world knew and loved his work and his story was the life through which the songs came into being. Markos regarded it as fundamental that he should write down mainly his sorrows: the agonies of poverty and deprivation, the bitterness of the ingratitude of relatives and friends, the undying pain of betrayal, the passion for hashish, the ceaseless bewilderment of love affairs one after the other, along with the little glories and memories of the daily wage-slave. The story remains not the exceptional story of one creator but a story representative of all the people who as a class gave birth to and loved *rebetika* and *laiko* song. To a large degree it's the history of our cities as it was lived by the exiled islander, farmer, or skilled worker who became a general labourer and paved the way for the urbanization of Greece with his ill paid toil.

Markos, both by temperament and by conviction was a man of few words. He'd say something and that was that. The whole meaning in two or three words, for instance 'beautiful woman'. What does it matter what kind of beautiful woman? Since to Markos she was beautiful, that was enough. All the usual effects of beauty flow from the fact that Markos found her beautiful. This economy of expression and especially his faith in the subjective truth was a fundamental element in the composition of his songs.

**Angeliki Vellou-Keil**

# PART I: SYROS

## Chapter 1

### SYRA, YOUR UPPER CHORA

I am driven to tell the story of my life. I want to see it written and to read it from beginning to end as if it were someone else's. I think this will give me some relief from all the sufferings that have filled my heart till it's ready to burst. So many sorrows that nobody would want in his own life. This story of mine I plan to make known to the world.

The kind lady who's acting as my scribe says the first Christians used to confess their sins aloud and then everybody forgave them. That's how they got it off their chests. But now the world's a rotten place and I know plenty of people will think I should be ashamed to own up to the things I'm about to tell you. But I'll find the courage and take no notice of those people. A man, if he's to be called a human being, has to be able to step into the shoes of his fellow man.

The wrongs I've suffered and the wrongs I've committed are the same. My faults are also my sufferings. I wasn't born wicked and I never thought of being happy if somebody else was sad. I wasn't born wicked and I wasn't born to live the life I lived. That's why I'm brave enough now to show my sins to the world, to the people whose joys and sorrows, wealth and poverty, lost families and exile I was the first to sing.

I want this world to be my confessor and I believe all these people I've written for and will go on writing for, hundreds of songs, will forgive me as this is the reason for looking back over my life. To be understood and to be forgiven. That's why all of you who read my story, friends or strangers, but especially those who know me, come now and shake my hand with a heart-felt greeting. Tell me what's done is done and all these things belong to the past. Tell me that if you'd lived the life I did you'd have done the same.

Of course it's over and done with now and I remember my old life like a bad dream, the sort that makes you leap out of your bed in a fright. That's pretty much how I leap out of mine when I run my past life before my eyes and remember its bad moments. These days my life has settled down. I live quietly, a family man with a good and dear wife and my three sons, Lord love them. I honestly adore my children and take a lot of trouble with all three so that in the future they'll be moral and useful members of society. I will see them and feel proud and pleased with them. I want to be proud of my children even if I wasn't able to make my parents proud of me. At least I'll do my duty as a father.

I was born in the capital of the Cyclades, in beautiful Syros in a poor neighborhood of Upper Chora called Skali in 1905 on Wednesday 10th May, third hour of the morning, to very poor parents. I was the first-born son and two other boys followed, Leonardhoss and the third, Frangiskos. My father's name was Dhomenikos, my mother's Elpidha, born Provelengiou. They fell in love and got married, penniless both. Until 1912, when I was seven, my parents, me and my two younger brothers lived a poor life pretty much like all the villagers, but a peaceful one and carefree as far as I was concerned. Our parents did all they could to get by and raise us. My mother was pretty and cheerful. She made jokes, sang nicely and was full of life. As for my father, the whole of Upper Chora loved him, the whole of Syros did - he'd never harmed a soul. He was a hardworking unskilled labourer; sometimes he worked as a coal-shoveller refuelling the ships of Palios, Tsiropinas, Psyachis, Panteleas, Embirikos, Goulandris and others.

Being the oldest son, I started to go along with my father on different jobs. I loved my father and I followed him round like a little dog. Maybe what bound us together so close was his *gaida*.¹ I don't know who my father learnt the *gaida* from, but I do know that there were three brothers and they all played the *gaida*. One was my uncle Antonis. He played it very well but he was a heavy drinker and got into fights. He died. Another was my uncle Morfinis who also played the *bouzouki* a little. Morfinis was a bit stuck-up, for no good reason, and he was a tease. He died in America, left in 1912 and didn't come back. His children are in New York - there's another Markos Vamvakaris there, same name.

I didn't know my dad's father, but it sounds like he was called Markos and also a composer. He used to write songs, poems, that sort of thing, and in his village people used to say 'the boys of *barba* Markos Rokos'. He was a good, tough man, a hardworking farmer from a village on Syros called Danakos. He married Rosa Lionta, my grandmother, a beautiful, sturdy woman from the same village. I met her. When my grandpa died, Rosa moved to Ermoupoli and married again. Their property at Danakos went to the dogs. There was this half-wit guy over there, latched onto it. Then some relatives who had their heads screwed on took it over and got it for free, they didn't pay a bean. My father and uncle couldn't care less about claiming back their property.

My mother's father was Leonardhos Provelengios. I never met him but I know he was a Catholic and a tailor. His wife was Mariyitsa. They had Frangiskos, Nikolaos, Yorghis, Koula, Irini and Elpidha, my mama. The three sons - my uncles - were Catholics and tailors like my grandpa. The Catholic tailors who made suits had a great reputation in those days. Nikolaos was hard as nails, but the other two were good and by and large we had a helping hand from them. I know that one of them was also a keen amateur player on the squeezebox.

---

1 Bagpipes made from goatskin.

Frangiskos started out as a tailor but later he gave up tailoring and became a food merchant. He had market gardens as well at Pateli. Twice when my father was away in the army he fed us. We were always shopping on credit. He wrote it down but where was the money going to come from? He didn't get anything. I mean he turned a blind eye and we conveniently forgot. We were in the shop every day. He had a wife though, called Katerina who didn't want to see us at all. This woman wanted only her own folks around her and they were a bad lot. Her brother was a crook and a swindler; nothing he hadn't got up to in Syros. These were the kinds of people she liked. But our uncle gave us a lot of stuff secretly, behind her back. He was scared of his wife.

My grandma Mariyitsa lived at Frangiskos's house. He was well set up, not just with one good house but five or six. Some in Upper Chora for his own use, some for storage, some for the grocery business, some for renting and others he gave to his kids when they got married. He was a good provider. Grandma was with him in the evenings, but she came to our house during the day, most days. Whatever Frangiskos had spare, my grandma brought to our house for us kids. She had other grandchildren, but it was us she was sorry for. We needed it. Mama was her youngest daughter.

Yiorgos was the poorest brother. With all the tailoring he died young - about the age of thirty-five. I went for a while to learn tailoring with him but I didn't manage it. Great job, tailoring. I still remember even now my uncle saying to me 'Sit down now and make button holes.' But I didn't take to it in the end. This uncle Yiorgos I'm telling you about, out of all my mother's brothers he was the one I loved a lot. He took an interest. So did the old rich one, Frangiskos. *He* did too. But Yiorgos was poor. He only just managed to make ends meet for his own family.

The one who was despicable and an utterly miserable old geezer was Nikolaos. When he found out I'd gone to Syros for the first time as a grown man, and heard that I was Markos - the radios were blaring out Markos Vamvakaris and nothing but Markos Vamvakaris - I went to see him; but what a cold fish! I said to him 'How you doing uncle?' I mean, I was prepared to make an effort. What? Was I going to be prickly and hold a grudge? I knew what kind of a pathetic individual he was so I just let him be like that. He said to me 'How are you Markos, what news eh? Are you well?'

'I'm fine.'

'Well done, my boy.'

He'd told me to come to his house and have a bite to eat, but no. There wasn't a crumb. He was, all the same, the best tailor in Syros. Such a clientele! He belonged to the biggest men's outfitters in Syros. All those boys were tailors. One made jackets, the other trousers, the other waistcoats, but this Nikolaos did everything. He sewed for all the quality folk in Syros. He had a house and a good job. The best. Never took a single day off. He was earning pots of money. It's about ten or fifteen years since he died. But if he had his patron saint in front of him he wouldn't give him so much as a glass of water.

All our family are Catholics, Frankosyrans[2] they call us. All the villages in Syros are Frankosyran. Danakos, the village of my granddad Markos, was Catholic and the Upper Chora where we lived was Catholic too. Only down in Ermoupoli they're Orthodox. The Orthodox came from somewhere else, Mykonos, Andros, Santorini ... now of course they've become Syrans, but actually they're not the *original* Syrans. The true Syrans are undoubtedly these Catholics I was talking about. Even if Ermoupoli has filled up now with Catholics, still, everyone knows who's Orthodox and who's a Catholic. But when I was a boy in

---

2 Frankish Syrans: The island was conquered by the Venetians after the sack of Byzantium by the Venetians and Franks in the Fourth Crusade in 1204. It remained part of the Duchy of the Archipelago until 1522, which is why most of the inhabitants were Catholic.

Syros the Orthodox lived in the lower Chora[3] near the sea and we, the Franks, lived in Upper Chora. Our house was at Skali[4] high up in the Chora, but it didn't have steps even if it *was* called Skali. Where I lived was a mountain pretty much, where they'd built houses out of the stones. Solid well-built houses, with narrow little streets. There wasn't space for orchards or big courtyards but they had stone benches along the outside walls where people used to sit. We had a song back then:

| | |
|---|---|
| I'll go no more to Piskopio | Δεν πάω πια στο Πισκοπιό |
| To sit on the stone bench, | να κάτσω στην πεζούλα, |
| Since they told tales about me, | γιατί μου βγάλαν αβανιά, |
| That I love a serving wench. | πως αγαπώ μια δούλα. |

Our house had three rooms, two bedrooms where we slept, a kitchen where we cooked and ate and a cellar underneath where my father did his basket weaving. He was a maestro when it came to weaving these baskets. He'd set up this line of work and had good connections with the big fruit and vegetable stores in Syros: Koutzoupis, Kostonaki, the Karavidhes and Balabanis; there were loads and they all loved him; went to him rather than anyone else. They had these baskets which they called *arkadhes,* very good baskets from Constantinople. You could put fifty or sixty *okes* worth of stuff into them, you name it, eggplants, okra, tomatoes, potatoes, just about anything. But they weren't strong. You'd use them for one or two months and then their bottoms dropped out. My father had worked out a technique by which he put the bottoms back in and made them unbreakable. He used to mend up to twenty a day.

---

3 The capital town of any island is generally called Chora. Historically the chora would be a high up place away from the sea due to the danger of pirates or other invaders. But Ermoupolis was a bigger port than Piraeus in the 19th century. It became the capital of the Cyclades and it supplanted the old Chora, now known as Upper Chora. The two are very close to each other.
4 Skali means 'step'.

When he had a lot of work he'd take on a helper he'd specially trained.

My mother had us kids to look after at home. She cooked all different kinds of food. Could be money went a bit further in those days but still we were a poor family. I mean, sometimes my father had work and sometimes he didn't. He'd go to the fields and work as a digger for a day's wages, or else he might go and gather bundles of kindling from dry twigs or strips of lentisk root. When he did day labour in the fields we went through lean times.

The weather in Syros was very good. In those days it rained regularly, not like now with these heavy downpours we have in between long droughts. Back then it rained at decent intervals - light rain which kept things well-watered, good for the vegetable plots in the villages. They don't want to have to pump water over there because it's hard work; all done with hoisting winches, donkeys or mules going round in circles to draw it up.

In winter the weather's heavy, black and cloudy. It gets cold and you wrap up warm with a flannel vest and a jacket. In spring the earth gets green, there's figs, pomegranates, almond trees, carobs, a lot of lovely things. Not that much fruit though. Figs mostly. By the rivers there are loads of oleanders, bay trees, willows and mastic trees too, which smell good when they're in season. I used to know all about these things because I often went to the rivers with my father to gather canes for basket weaving. In Syros they have the best sage tea. It's a miracle. There's no sage tea like that anywhere else. I drink it over here every day. Chios has it, they do have it in other places but this one I'm talking about is *the sage tea of Syros,* not like anywhere else.

Mama used to cook beans, baby marrow, tomatoes, and eggplants, which my father brought back from the villages where he worked. In the evening the diggers who worked in the market gardens and orchards brought home all kinds of stuff for their families. Beans in those days were the staple food. Poor man's grub but there was loads of it and we ate our fill. We went and gathered snails as well and there was meat once a week on Sundays. They bought one or two *okes*, if that, on Saturday. My granny Mariyitsa used to bring us homemade barley bread because she had a brother in Pao where they grew barley. She brought us dried figs too, grapes, greens when it was the season, and sometimes loads of tomatoes which we pulped. Her brother and sister gave her stuff and she passed it on to us. That's what we boys grew up on, all three of us.

Downtown Syra, I mean Ermoupoli was more beautiful than Upper Syra, more spacious and open with magnificent well-built houses where the shipping-line tycoons and manufacturers lived. There were lots of those kinds of people down there. We had some public buildings in the upper town but nothing like the amenities they had down below. Their main square for example is the size of a football pitch! All smooth tiles underfoot and the law courts all around, but I can tell you, the Upper Chora was *cleaner*. When it rained our paving stones had a thorough sluicing. The housewives whitewashed their houses and everything shone.

We used to go down into Ermoupoli from Upper Chora most days. In the market down in Syra they had big well-stocked fruit and vegetable shops. We did our shopping and brought it back up, twenty minutes on foot. Now of course there's public transport. Bam! With a bus you leave from the market place down there and you get to the upper town at Pantelaki. There's a market in Upper Syra too but we kids longed to go down there. We couldn't wait to grow up so we could go down and work in a shop, a fruit and veg or grocery store. And of course it seemed like that time would never come.

From an early age, we kids had a whole load of chores to do, but all the same, if four or five of us pals got together we used to sing, tumble about on the ground, chuck stones around, get into fights and fall in love. Going out of Skali the road led to Portara and we used to go and play up there on a slope where there was some open ground. The kids higher up rolled stones onto those below. Sometimes the result was bandaged heads but nothing much worse than that. The mamas yelled at us of course. But there was a crazy nutcase from Persino, above Portara and he used to join in the fun. When he appeared the mothers would scream 'Pick up your kids!' A complete lunatic! He rolled down huge boulders, weighing half a ton. It was a steep slope. The minute you let go of the stone, off it went. We used to tease him and call him 'Loony'.

From there we used to go to Plati, where the women went to do their washing in the river and fetch water. Another road led to Piyi. That's where the famous water was - fresh water, clean and cold. We used to go up there, and also to Rematia where there was an Orthodox church, the Virgin of the Life-giving Spring. It had a yearly festival when the Orthodox folk used to come up from Lower Chora. Lots of people came. The women filled their pitchers with water and carried them back down. Some came from Plati on their way to Skali. Others came from Piyi on their way up to Danelaki, to Pourna and San Georgy. These are the districts where they lived, all of them round Upper Chora. Then there was Sifneika where they sold jugs, plates and earthenware pots. It was from there we went to the village of Kini. We took the path to a barren spot called Voulias and from there you went by a shortcut to Yerou Yanni. This took us straight down to Kini. In those days that was the only way to get there. But now there's a big road goes from Della Grazia through Finika to Kini. The buses go, and taxis.

In the summer we headed off to the sea for swimming and Kini was the place where we went every Sunday with or without our parents' permission. My brother Leonardhos very nearly drowned there. He didn't know how to swim and he went in deep. Only God saved him. I don't know how he was saved but saved he was. The same thing happened to me another time at Nisaki in the harbor. It was Sunday afternoon, a fine day and the sea was calm. Three of us came down from the Chora, my cousin Joseph Daelis and another kid Yiorgos Voutsinos larking about all the way there, running, pointing, always busy with something or other, chucking stones around, the kind of stuff kids do. You kick something along the road, you run into folks along the way and do cheeky stuff, that kind of thing. The boys I was with knew how to swim but I didn't. They said 'Wherever it looks dark, don't go there, it'll be deep.' How did that slip my mind? I went out of my depth, sank to the bottom and bobbed up again three or four times. They fished me out half drowned, or rather *one* of them did. The other panicked and ran away. It was my cousin pulled me out, more dead than alive. He put me face down on some rocks in front of the little island by the gate where the boats come in. I coughed up and revived. After a couple of hours I still felt terrible but we got up and went home. My parents saw the state I was in and gave me a beating because I'd sneaked off. They told Joseph's mother the whole story. If it hadn't been for him, if he'd got in a funk like the other one, I'd have drowned. Bravo Joseph for pulling me out!

All this was when the grapes and figs were beginning to ripen. In the summer people went back to their villages. For instance, some people left the Upper Chora and went down to Kini, Della Grazia, Parakopi, or Finika. There was a place called Pateli too, which I put in that *Frangosyriani* song. If they had a house down there they stayed all through the summer. I used to play with the kids of all the other families. We ran about all over the place filching figs and cutting grapes on the sly.

I had an uncle there, one of my mother's brothers, who had some land with figs and vines. I was such a scamp, I used to pilfer his figs and grapes and took my chums along too, the whole gang of us. We used to go to Plati as well. There they had plums, cherries, figs, grapes, lemons, and passionfruit. Up in Piyi we'd get water figs, the ones that grow in watery ground, not as nice and delicious though, as the proper ones; real figs were better. We found lots of those, white figs, *maronia*, *loubardhika*, *gaitania*. These were all different kinds of figs. The *maronia* were white, the *loubardhika* and *gaitania* were black, The *loubardhika*, the sweetest were the king of figs. There were capers too. We picked them and brought them back home to pickle.

I remember summer in the village when I was a child. In front of the village was a big field. The river Platis ran between us and the field. There was a threshing floor there. Oh boy, it was happy days at threshing time! The river came out of Piyi further on up and in our village it had the name Platis. What they called it downstream I wouldn't be able to say. It went through Santorineika and flowed into the sea. We used to go and play there in the river, me, Petros and Dimitrios Delasoudhas, another Petros Provelengios, a whole bunch of kids from the neighbourhood of Skali. There were hollows in the rock where the water got deeper and we made little toy boats out of paper or tin. This little river back then always had water even in the summer.

We used to go out into the fields with hollow canes and stuff earth into them to make them into 'guns' for hunting the birds you get that time of year, the fig and grape season. That's when we hunted *kefaladhes*.[5] Sometimes we even caught these little birds in our hands, little tiny birds but they flew up in the air and you hunted them with canes. The *faneta*[6] were little birds a bit like sparrows. The *skarthia* were

---

5 Probably the red-headed shrike, lanius collurio, found in Greece between April and October.
6 Linnets.

tiny. We caught those in our hands. Migrating birds too, *kardherinia*[7] and *lougra*. There were quails and turtledoves but for these we needed a weapon. My dad used to take me with him when he went hunting so I got to know them. I knew turtledoves, quails, and hoopoes by sight. I knew lots of other birds too, all different kinds.

We used to hunt around in the thyme bushes for a kind of insect we called *metaxadhes*. They were gold with green faces. We collected them and put them in matchboxes, males and females together along with some food. Then we left them alone and they'd multiply. We'd say 'They're going to have babies' but I never saw them making babies or having them! It was just something we used to say.

Another thing we did was make kites from sheets of paper, *Stefanota* we called them. We stuck them together with reeds and flew them all over the place but mostly at Portara which had more open space. We were all crazy about the kites. When there was no school we kids from Skali used to go round all these neighbourhoods and play maybe leap-frog or sometimes marbles, which we collected and sold for a bit of pocket money. I'm old enough to remember the drachma coin and it was worth something back then. Fifty cent pieces too, the old ten cent coins and even the twenty cent silver coins which date from Otto's[8] time!

We had squabbles as kids do. One would say 'Why d'you pinch my marbles?' Second kid: 'Why did you bust my kite?' Another: 'Why did you go fig picking in my folks' fig trees?' And so on. A million different things. I had a fight with the son of Tsipouros. We often quarreled. We'd be playing marbles, then he'd come along and we'd beat each other up, wrestling, swearing, head-butting, the usual silly childish stuff. I wouldn't back down. Then we'd have the mamas on the warpath, trying to stop us fighting and cursing. Everyone

---
7 Goldfinches.
8 Otto, a Bavarian prince who became the first modern king of Greece, 1832 - 1862.

up there in the Chora was family. So and so would be a godfather, the next person would be a cousin, or a third cousin, a relative on the mother's side, or the father's side and so on. All one big family.

We older kids did jobs round the house. My mother would give me a small pitcher and say 'Off you go and fetch some water.' We got our water from Plati where the springs were. For the best water though, we went to Piyi where the church was, Saint Dionysus I think or else the Virgin of the Life-giving Spring.[9] The river there had enormous plane trees. We used to cut the leaves and put them on top of the sponges.[10] Another of my jobs was to go to the grocer's and do the shopping. In the shop it would be me measuring out the goods as I was the oldest. We all did errands as we got older like for instance: 'Go to Lower Chora, to Ermoupoli, you'll go to this shop, you'll see that man and you'll give him that, he'll give you this ... ' We were kids and we did what we were told.

The person we feared most was our mama. Of course we feared our dad as well. Papa never whipped us but our mother used to give a stinging whack with her stick. She used to yell at us but still we were in awe of our dad. That was something else. You didn't want to let things get to that point with him! Our mother used to hide us but the one who rescued us the most was our grandma. She'd scoop us up and we were gone! She took us off to uncle Frangiskos' house. We'd stay there and she gave us dried figs.

The evenings in our neighbourhood, we all used to play hide-and-seek in the cellars or narrow little alleyways. Or we sang the songs that were doing the rounds at that time. We beat out the rhythms with tin lids and rusty old cans that we found in the fields. Forgotten most of them by now but I do remember one from that time.

---

9 *Zoodochos*.
10 Possibly the sponges were used as stoppers to keep the water from slopping out of the pitchers.

After all the things
   you've done to me,[11]
I don't want you any more,
I don't like you any more.

You've blackened my guts,
I don't want you any more,
I don't like you any more.

And here's another:

To the desolate ravine,
To the den we used to play in,
Our ill-fated hearts
Brought us once again.

Από τα πολλά που
   μου'χεις καμωμένα
Δε σε θέλω πια
Δε μ'αρέσεις πια.

Τα σωθικά μου
τα'χεις μαυρισμένα
Δε σε θέλω πια,
Δε μ'αρέσεις πια.

Στην έρημη τη ρεματιά
στην παιδική φωλιά μας,
μας έφερε ξανά
η άμοιρη καρδιά μας.

That one was a waltz. There was another song too which came from the theatre.

I want you Doc,
To take a look.
I hurt I suffer,
I'm not well.

For ten days
I've been coughing,
And when I cough
I cough like hell.

Ήθελα γιατρέ μου
λίγο να με κοιτάξεις
Πάσχω, υποφέρω,
δεν είμαι καλά.

Εδώ και δέκα μέρες
που μ'έπιασε ένας βήχας
και όταν πα'να βήξω,
βήχω δυνατά.

There were theatres in Syros where of course I didn't go, but the songs used to reach us. We got to hear *them* at least. Down in Ermoupoli of course there were lots of musicians and there still are. There was a place called 'The Beer of Koliopoulou' I remember. It had a band that played every evening: violin, *santouri,* piano, and *oud,* no *bouzoukia.* These guys knew their stuff; read music and wrote it. They played everything, whatever the customers wanted. There

---

11 *Apo ta Polla pou Mou'cheis Kamomena.*

was always an orchestra in Syros, at least one if not two. There may have been a European style orchestra too in the square at the Koliopoulou place.

Our local players were proper musicians too of course. They used to do weddings, christenings and name days, all over the place. Women didn't usually go to the *kafeneion* in those days. Honour was a very big deal back then. Families were funloving but they had their parties at home. They got the musicians to come and play in their houses. *We* didn't of course because we were poor. The best we could manage was the *gaida* and drum playing *syrtokalamatiana*.[12]

One time I remember four or five of us went to the house of an old woman, a relative of mine called Maria. I'd made up a little song for her and we sang it, beating out the rhythm as usual with our sticks and tin cans.

| | |
|---|---|
| *Hey, Maria Staxou* | *Για μια Μαρία η Σταξού* |
| *She keeps a tidy hovel!* | *είναι καλό λατάρι.* |
| *She gets up every morning* | *Σηκώνεται κάθε πρωί* |
| *And sweeps it with a shovel.* | *σκουπίζει μ'ένα φτυάρι.* |

We were just a bunch of scamps and we sang this song. Even then I had a knack for making them up.

All of us in Upper Chora loved God. The village had the Monastery of the Holy Virgin or *Kioura,*[13] as it was called, Saint George and Saint Antonis, all Catholic churches and at Skali we had Saint Sebastian. We went there to church every Sunday, mamas and papas with all their kids. The *Kioura* had fifteen to twenty brothers and that's where we did the 'brotherhood'. They gathered the children there, gave us toys and taught us the Paternoster, the Catholic prayers, some in Greek and some in Latin. The *Kioura* had a large terrace

---

12 Syrtos and kalamatianos are circle dances, the most popular and common throughout Greece and the diaspora. Both have similar steps but syrtos is 4/4 and kalamatianos is in 7/8 rhythm.
13 A local name for *Kyra*, i.e. The church of 'Our Lady'.

with a climbing frame, a rocking horse and some swings. It was a place where we played and let off steam.

I used to go there all by myself. Wherever the kids got together, that's where I'd go and hang about too. We had a great time playing with our toys, climbing trees, making swings out of ropes. An hour's playtime at the *Kioura* was how they rewarded kids who'd been good at school. After school was over, the priests gave us *ayiakia*, little cards with holy images and saints, Christ, the Holy Virgin, Saint John, Saint George, and Saint Sebastian. Being kids you see, we collected all these holy things and kept them in our schoolbook.

A big festival in Syros and not only in Syros but wherever there were Catholics, was Saint Dorea. This was when the boys and girls took First Communion. It was a huge festival this Saint Dorea. Those of us who were going to take first communion went to the Church of the Holy Virgin for Catechism, to learn the prayers and chant the liturgy: the *Lord's Prayer*, the *Creed*, the *Act of Contrition*, all those things we Catholics have. We were just kids then and we loved God. I was very regular then but I barely remember even the half of it now.

In Catholic churches they have something that looks like a sentry box, called a Confessional. Same time every Saturday I used to go to confession all dressed up in my best. You go in there and sit down, the priest on one side and you on the other. You don't see the priest. You only hear him speak. I wasn't scared. I used to go and make my confession so that I could take Communion. We told the priest what our mothers had told us to say, plus a few other things we remembered ourselves and the priest asked us some questions too. I used to take Communion once a fortnight. They gave us the Host, which is something like a large flat pill that dissolves in your mouth like flour - completely tasteless. I used to pay attention because I liked all this business. But when I grew up I gave up church. As soon as I got married for the first time I forgot all that rigmarole. Our parish was Saint Sebastian and the priest in charge of it was called Don Yannis Almansis. You can't imagine how much he loved me when I went back to Syros for the first time and wrote *Sabastia*.

| **Syra your Upper Chora** | **Σύρα η Απάνω Χώρα σου** |
|---|---|
| Syra, your Upper Chora, | Σύρα η απάνω χώρα σου |
| Set upon its lofty perch | με την ανηφοριά σου, |
| With steep old steps all up and down | με τα πολλά σκαλάκια σου |
| And St Sebastian's Church | και με το Σαμπαστιά σου. |
| | |
| From out your bowels and your heart | Μ'έβγαλες απ'τα σπλάχνα σου |
| You brought me forth, your young, | μεσ'από την καρδιά σου |
| Because of me, Oh Syra mine, | και ξακουστό σου το'κανα |
| Your name's on every tongue. | Σύρα μου τ'όνομά σου. |
| | |
| Twice I've come to visit you, | Είκοσι χρόνια δυο φορές |
| Twice in twenty years, | ήρθα να σ'αντικρύσω |
| Along with my bouzouki | και με το μπουζουκάκι μου |
| To sing songs of love and tears, | γλυκά να τραγουδήσω. |
| | |
| So that Syrans get to hear | Ν'ακούσουν όλοι οι Συριανοί |
| The heart-felt songs I sing, | τραγούδια με μεράκια |
| Remember their old happy days, | να θυμηθούνε τα παλιά |
| Forget time's poisoning. | να σβήσουν τα φαρμάκια. |

Don Almansis knew me and my parents from when I was just a scamp. They had to chase us back then to make us sit quiet in church. If we didn't they chucked us out. He was fond of me and whenever I went back as a grown man I always went to see him. In our parish there was also Don Michalis. *He* was a musician too. He played the organ in the church. He left Syros and later I found him over here in Piraeus, in Ayios Dionysis.

When the big holy days came along, like Easter, there was evening church. People didn't say 'Let's go to church', they said 'Let's go to Compline.'[14] We kids used to go and sing Compline and it lasted from eight in the evening till ten or eleven. Then there were the *Tenebrae*.[15] We made the *Tenebrae* before we went to church. We went to a carpenter to get the wood cut, high as your elbow and a span wide. We screwed two sheets of metal, one on each side of the wooden frame. When the priest was finishing the service he struck the *Tenebrae* inside the church and as soon as the service was over, we kids ran outside and tried to stamp on Saint John the Capuchin. Only the small kids played *Tenebrae*. We had two teams. Those of us in the parish of Saint Sebastian were called *Dezooeetes*[16] and the parishioners of Saint John were called *Capuchins*. *Dezooeetes* is a French thing. I don't know what it comes from or what it means. We *Dezooeetes* would run along banging our *Tenebrae* so as to go and stamp on St John the Capuchin.

*Got there, got there*          Ἴσαμε ἴσαμε,
*Stepped on Saint John fair and square!*          τον Αι Γιάννη πατήσαμε!

That's what the *Dezooeetes* chanted to the *Capuchins* and the *Capuchins* in their turn used to chant:

*Got there, got there*          Ἴσαμε ἴσαμε,
*Stepped on Saint Seb fair and square!*          το Σαμπαστιάν πατήσαμε!

All those things happened before Easter, when they got out the *Epitaphios*. It still happens. It'll go on happening too. It's religion this thing. No way do they change that Catholic

---

14 The night prayer and final service of the day in monasteries before the great silence till morning.
15 Latin for shadows or darkness: a rite that took place in Holy Week and involved the gradual blowing out of candles after each of nine psalms until the church was plunged into darkness. Markos uses the word to mean the square gongs which they made for the *strepitus* - the 'great din' symbolizing the earthquake which followed Christ's death on the cross.
16 Jesuits. To Markos *Dezoeetes* was simply a French sounding name that had no meaning. A brotherhood of Capuchin monks settled in Syros in 1633 and the Jesuits came and built their monastery a century later.

stuff. It's just the way it's always been. They take orders from the Pope.

On Good Friday they got out the *Epitaphios*.¹⁷ It's a big thing for us, this *Epitaphios*. It pulls together all the spiritual stuff and all the symbols of Christ's passion like the ladders they hung him up on, the ropes they dragged him with, the gall they gave him to drink and the bloodstained robes they stripped off him. Every Christian who follows behind the *Epitaphios* carries the weight on his back. All the sufferings of Christ are paid up and done with. Clean slate. Then everyone sings psalms. All the *Epitaphios* tunes were sad. We kids went and listened to the church service with lanterns and candles and waited for the *Epitaphios* to come out. It was decorated with the first flowers of the year. All the housewives in Syra picked flowers and brought them to the church for the *Epitaphios*.

On Easter day everyone gathered in the churches again for the Resurrection. Everyone had a good time at Easter. They dyed eggs red and made all sorts of *koulouria*¹⁸ with different names, *psathouria, kolykia, lazari*, big doll shaped loaves, Easter bread. My mother used to make special things too, sweet *koulouria*. She made them at Christmas time. Of course the well-off people made more of these fancy doodahs while the hard-up folks made things only if they had the stuff to make them with. If the cupboard was bare we ate plain bread and that was that. At New Year they made *vassilopitta* - a sugary bread with silver hidden inside; we put in a franc or fifty cents. In Syros back then there was a kind of drum, the *toubi* or *toubaki*, an arm's length across the top and the same in height. We kids used to take them and go carol singing.

---
17 An ikon showing Christ after his deposition from the cross. It was carried on a bier in procession on Easter Saturday.
18 Ring shaped bread or biscuits that the Greeks still make on festive occasions.

We sang the same carols as now:

| | |
|---|---|
| Good evening masters, | Καλήν εσπέραν άρχοντες |
| By your leave I'll sing | κι αν είναι ο ορισμός σας, |
| To all your house | Χριστού τη Θεία γέννηση |
| The birth of Christ our king. | να πώ στ'αρχοντικό σας. |
| | |
| For Christ is born | Χριστός γεννάται σήμερα |
| In Bethlehem this day, | στη Βηθλεέμ την πόλη, |
| Glory in Heaven, | οι ουρανοί αγάλλονται |
| The world is bright and gay. | χαίρεται η φύσις όλη. |

Then a week later there'd be the carols of Saint Vassilis:

| | |
|---|---|
| Saint Vassilis | Αγιος Βασίλης έρχεται, |
| From Caesaria's walking, | από την Καισαρεία. |
| He holds an ikon and some paper, | βαστά εικόνα και χαρτί |
| Paper and some ink | χαρτί και καλαμάρι. |
| The ink was writing | Το καλαμάρι έγγραφε |
| And the paper talking. | και το χαρτί μιλούσε. |

When it came to carol singing the Catholic kids sang to Orthodox folk and the Orthodox kids used to climb up and sing in the Catholic villages too. People used to give us a drachma, maybe a two-drachma piece or some sweets, that sort of thing. We carried a basket to put the sweets in.

There was Carnival in February and that lasted forty days. Everyone celebrated it with eating and drinking, treats and games. Everyone in Syros loved dancing and so did I. There were bagpipe dances, carnival dances which the *Zebeks*[19] learned and dances from Asia Minor, the Turkish ones, from Constantinople and Thrace. But we Syrans were very famous for our *Zebekiko*.

I can't dance any more now. I'd take one step and fall flat on my face. That's not because I'm an old man and haven't

---

19 The men and boys of the village who dressed up as *Zebeks* - legendary Anatolian guerilla fighters who, from late 17th to early 20th century, protected villagers from government tax collectors and bandits in the Aegean areas under the Ottoman empire. They performed a special warrior's dance, the *zebekiko*, freestyle with arms outstretched like a hawk.

got it in me. No - it's the illnesses I've had. Me and dancing. Ah, if you could have seen me even fifteen years ago you'd have been blown away. Hey! Such a big man, how could he do those things? A spinning-top and right on the mark! How could he not lose it and tip over? *Zebekiko, chasapiko*,[20] *serviko*, those were the three dances I danced. But most of all *zebekiko*. The *zebekiko* which they danced in Syros wasn't danced anywhere else. They had daggers that they put crosswise on the ground. They knelt on the ground and danced. The village of Koulouri is famous for its *chasapiko*. I went back to Koulouri years later to play *bouzouki* and I danced *zebekiko*. They all grumbled at me. 'What's this thing!' they said. The Syrans just couldn't dance *chasapiko* the way the Koulouriots did. But then the Koulouriots couldn't dance the Syran *zebekiko*, pah no way!

When I was dancing as a little boy you can't imagine the stick I got from the organ grinders. I was so crazy about the music that when they stopped playing and left the instrument on the stool, what did I do? I used to press my ear against the barrel organ hoping for more, and then bam! The organ grinder would start kicking me for fear I'd knock it over. But for all they used to kick me, later, they took me on for publicity reasons. 'Come on *Frango*[21] dance,' they'd say and as soon as I was dancing their jaws would drop. They'd say to my poor father, God rest him, 'Your son is one hell of a dancer!'

At carnival time over there, that's when the *zebekia*[22] happened. Up to forty individuals got together and set up a dancing school. Two months before carnival they opened the school and the *Zebeks* began to learn the *chasapiko, serviko, chasaposerviko* and *zebekiko* In this room all kinds of people

---

20 The butcher's dance, originally from Constantinople, in 4/4 or 2/4 metre, danced in twos or threes with arms over shoulders.
21 A common way of addressing a *Frankosyran*, i.e. a Catholic Syran.
22 *Zebekia* refers to a sequence of dances performed each year at Carnival enacting the drama of the 'Captains' and the abduction of the houri. The dancers were called *Zebeks* and the dance itself, a freestyle dance in 9/8 rhythm, was called *zebekiko*.

learned dancing, whoever didn't know how to dance and whoever was going to dress up as *Zebeks*. Then on *Clean Monday*, the first day of Lent, we'd go out dancing and the school was over. People paid money to be *Zebeks,* twenty five to thirty drachmas, a lot in those days. They made silk costumes and got dressed up in *touzloukia*, a kind of boot made of heavy felt which went round your shins and covered your shoes; the *kontogouni,* a short fur-lined jacket with sleeves hanging down behind; the *stithia,* decorated shirt fronts embroidered with sequins and gold thread; baggy britches, like what the Cretans wear, and beautiful caps with sequins and gold but no tassels. The whole shebang. Silk handkerchiefs too. I can't begin to tell you! The whole thing seems to me like a dream now. I don't know if it's still like this but that's how it was then.

They started learning the dances forty days before Carnival. The 'First Captain' was in charge. The *Zebeks* knew that such and such a person would be 'First Captain this year', and he'd be one of the good dancers. They were all boys, no women at all. There were three 'Captains': 'First Captain', 'Second Captain' and 'Third Captain', the *Hanoumissa* - the 'Captain's' houri, you know, and the 'Hunter'. There were many roles. The 'Captain's Son', which I played one year, would be a little boy. Then there'd be the two 'Arabs' who had to steal the *Hanoumissa* from the 'Captain'. The *Hanoumissa* was a man in woman's clothes. They painted his face to make him look like a beautiful woman.

During the forty days, every Sunday we'd pay for a barrelorgan to be played and we'd dance in some open space. On ordinary days we had the *darbouka*, that's what this drum was called and with that they played the *'zebekia'* which we used to dance. The *darbouka* was made of clay, an open funnel on one side and a big drum-top on the other. Pretty much all of us knew how to play *darbouka*. Anyone who danced knew how to play it. We danced *zebekiko* one by one, *chasapiko* three or four of us at a time, same as *serviko*. *Arapiko,* which was danced by our two 'Arabs', was a bit like the *tsifteteli*. People watched us but we didn't collect money. When we went and signed up to be *Zebeks* it was *we* who paid 25 drachmas, and on Clean Monday they pooled this money to pay for the barrelorgan. I was the only one in my family who danced with the *Zebeks*. I don't know if these things happen in Syros now, but when people started coming over here it caught on in Piraeus too. They did *zebekia* here. I didn't get to see it myself but I heard for instance about Vassilis the coal hauler, 'Captain of *Zebeks*' from Syros.

These things I'm telling you now about Syros were the things every neighborhood did. They did it in Upper Chora. Same again in Lower Chora. Kampoussa had it too. There were three or four areas that did *zebekia*. Each dancer stayed in his own district with his own 'Captains', all in their proper place. We had to show respect to our 'Captain', do as he said and learn the dances the way he taught us. Then we danced and everyone was proud of us. What would you prefer to see, carnival masquerades or these things I'm talking about? Beautiful silk costumes, jackets, felt boots, really top quality stuff! I don't know how the *zebekia* began. They started in Syros. Upper Chora, Lower Chora? I don't know.

The barrel organ didn't play Carnival music. It played waltzes, quadrilles, *syrta*, *kalamatiana*, *chasapika*, *zebekika*, *servika*, tunes that were going round at the time. Syros had a lot of barrel organs. They were everywhere. They brought them over from The City.[23] Papikos and Armaos were both barrel organ manufacturers who came over from there to Piraeus. There *were* other instruments and bands, but at that

---

23 *I Poli,* meaning 'The City', is how many Greeks referred to Constantinople.

time barrel organs were all the rage. Each *laterna*[24] played about ten tunes and they were beautifully decorated. I can't begin to tell you the fancy decorations they put on them. Every Tom Dick or Harry was introducing a new barrel organ. Karpouzas, Tsipilis, Titos ... We had a barrel organ called Markos. Not on my account as I was nobody then, but it was the best. A top of the range instrument, though of course they were all good. There was one guy in Syros, who had a *kafeneion* and he owned forty-five barrel organs!

My father was a very good player on the bagpipes and from the age of six I used to follow him around playing the drum. We went down to Ermoupoli at carnival to play in the *tavernas* and make some extra money. My dad was poor and he needed it. All sorts of people sat there drinking wine and there'd be my father on the bagpipes and me beating in time with my drumsticks on a dog-hide drum: *syrto*,[25] *ballo* and *Cretan*. Those were the bagpipe songs. If I had a drum now I'd do you all the rhythms. I played at carnival with my father for three or four years and we weren't the only ones. In Syra there were lots of bagpipe players who played in pairs with a drummer, usually a father and son. We played for about thirty-five days going from one *taverna* to the other from the first Sunday in Carnival until Clean Monday when it ended. Only the bagpipes did that, not the bands. In those days things were cheap and the most anyone could expect to earn in a day, whether in the fields or anywhere else, was three and a half drachmas. You'd pay three drachmas to get a pair of shoes made and five drachmas for a suit of clothes. Things were cheap. So you see by playing on Saturdays and Sundays during Carnival, my father and I together made about thirty, forty, maybe even fifty drachmas in tips. It was always the *syrto* that these *gaidas* used to play, the very same

---
24 Markos refers to these barrel organs interchangeably as *organaki,* i.e. 'little instrument' or *laterna.*
25 A traditional island dance in 4/4 metre, with many regional variations, danced in a circular line holding hands.

ones that we still hear. Maybe I remember them because I started learning the *gaida*. I got the hang of it and played it, but not the way my father did. There was no singing, just bagpipes and drum and people used to get up and dance. When Carnival was over the workers went back to their usual daily grind, basket weaving or humping coal, whatever manual labour they normally did.

## Chapter 2

## I WANTED TO BE HERACLES

When I was four or five in 1909 I was pretty smart for my age and in those days they didn't bother much about your date of birth, so my father sent me to school. I loved learning. At that time small kids wore calico pinafores. We wore calico and cotton drill. Our teacher Mr Tsangouros was very strict, but I kept on the right side of him because I was a quick learner. I owe him a lot. I spent two years with him and then the next two I spent with a teacher who was a fellow Frankosyran, Mr Prindezi. Tsangouros loved me because I was a good pupil. He treated me well so long as I knew my lesson. What else did he need? I wasn't naughty. The other boys used to tease him and he'd beat them! They called him silly names like 'Nut Case'. I didn't pay attention to such things. I was keen to learn my letters, even if I didn't learn much. I loved history, the olden days, the ancients, Xerxes, Artaxerxes, the battle of Salamis, those sorts of things. I'll never know why I liked them so much. Even now I still like them, Byzantium, the taking of Constantinople ... if I find books about these things I read them. This shows up in my songs, especially in *Ithela na'moun Iraklis*.

*I Wanted to be Heracles*

I was a mangas once,
With blue blood in my arteries,
But now a teacher I shall be
Like the wise man Socrates.

I'd like to steal fair Helen away
And be like handsome Paris
And leave poor Menelaus
With his heart burnt out in ashes.

*Ήθελα να'μουν Ηρακλής*

Ήμουνα μάγκας μια φορά
με φλέβα αριστοκράτη,
τώρα θα γίνω δάσκαλος
σα το σοφό Σωκράτη.

Ο Πάρης θα γινόμουνα
να'κλεβα την Ελένη,
ν'άφηνα το Μενέλαο
με την καρδιά καμμένη.

| | |
|---|---|
| I wanted to be Heracles, | Ήθελα να'μαι ο Ηρακλής |
| The first time that I spied ya, | όταν σε πρωτοείδα |
| So that I'd cut off your head, | να σου'κοβα την κεφαλή |
| Just like the Lernaean Hydra. | σαν τη Λερναία Ύδρα. |
| | |
| What else d'you want me to become | Τι άλλο θέλεις να γενώ |
| Before you'll love and say you do? | για να με αγαπήσεις; |
| With your big head it seem like only | Εσύ με το κεφάλι σου |
| Xerxes is the man for you. | τον Ξέρξη θα ζητήσεις. |

You could say I made the most of the little book learning I had at school. I liked letters so much I even ended up as a newspaper seller later on so that I could read the headlines on the newspapers I was selling.

At the school we went to there was a Catholic priest who came every Wednesday to teach us prayers. I remember one who used to come called Don Markos Aldouvas. We were a bunch of yelling, cheeky little rascals but he meant business. He sure whipped us this guy. He was tough but I wasn't afraid of him. I was a good learner but the others whistled and shouted the minute he appeared. He used to beat them till they went nuts, either with his hand or with the ruler. He had to because they were wild and if he let them alone they'd lynch him. They tortured him, they really did. He was a tall, bookish man. He had that look in his eye that showed him to be a man of letters. In fact we lived in the same neighbourhood. He lived in Skali next to where my uncle Frangiskos had his grocery store.

Catholic kids went to Catholic schools. We had beautiful hymns, Catholic hymns, but I didn't have time to learn them. As soon as I'd learnt some letters and knew how to read I left because we had to earn our bread. That was in 1912 before I finished the fourth year. They took my father into the army and I left school so my mother and I could go to work. She had three small children, me, Leonardhos and

Frangiskos. I was the eldest and I had to do something to help make ends meet.

Some years before 1912, my father had stopped working as a coal hauler. He'd found something better. He started weaving baskets, panniers and hampers. Since he was hard up he had to gather the materials for his work by himself and bring them back home for weaving. The two of us together used to go round the rivers collecting willow switches, reeds and carobs. There were two rivers we used to go to, the Paos and the Galissas, and at some point they both flowed into one. You could smell the reeds. My old man used to do the cutting and I'd soak them under a fig tree. After soaking the switches we made them into bundles that weighed about forty *okes*. Those were the ones my father took; the bundles I carried would be more like fifteen to twenty *okes*. Barefoot and hungry, we carried this load all the way from the village of Galissa to Upper Chora - a two and a half hour trudge. I was a strong boy but still my father was sorry for me. He was afraid I'd suffer from carrying such a heavy load. But then I was sorry for *him*. He was groaning under his load as well and if I could have carried more to lighten his load I would have. We had to make a living somehow and raise the kids you know, there was Leonardhos and Frangiskos. One time I remember, my father was fretting about me. He'd made me a bundle, loaded it on my back and kept turning round to ask 'Are you tired, are you tired?' I was trying to cheer him up and I'd say: 'No Papa, I'm not tired, I'm fine.' I felt so badly for him. You just can't have any idea how sorry I felt for him. *He* was sorry for *me!* But what did I have on my back? Nothing like what *he* had. We didn't have the means for a donkey so we could put it on the animal's back and walk along behind.

So, like I said, 1912 came along and they took my father off into the army. Then my mother enlisted *me* and off we went to get work in Deliyiannis' cotton factory. My mother was pregnant with her belly way out. She started working in the dye section of the mill and I was packaging the thread. She was getting three and a half drachmas a day and I was getting three and a half drachmas a week. Even a couple of drachmas a week was a big deal. Three drachmas a week was an achievement. Bread then was thirty-five cents an *oke*. For sixty-five, seventy cents you'd get a double loaf, two *okes*. They were cheap round white loaves, top quality cheap bread. When life began to get more expensive that's when they began to make black bread. We had to be earning money all the time, no two ways about it, and of course I was the eldest.

A few months after we went to work at Deliyiannis' cotton mill, mama gave birth to a little girl. Later I worked on the threads, running them through the looms. There were lots of young girls in there and I used to tease them no end, nip them, pat them, grab them, a little kiss here and a little something there. They'd be hard at work and with the iron tool that I used on the threads I tweaked their clothes. Some of them liked it and some didn't. Sometimes I got a kiss and sometimes a slap. If one of them wanted me and was fond of me she'd take me off secretly to the cotton sheds and I'd sit there petting her. But I was just a kid while she was grown up so of course this wasn't serious love business. All the same, I got to know a Cretan girl there who tormented me night and day. She used to hug me; she looked for chances to pounce and kiss me: 'Grow up dammit so I can have you for my husband.' Well, you can be sure I did what I could! I was quite a lad, tall kid with long legs - they called me Spindle-shanks.

My mother couldn't say anything as by now I was a big boy. I was a very hard worker and whatever I earned I brought home to her, whether my dad was there or not. I was earning proper money, specially later when I was selling newspapers, and I sure did my bit for the family. My mother worked too in the factory as a laundress washing towels. The guys in the factory had the hots for my mother. She was twenty-eight years old, a beautiful woman. They used to sing: 'Elenaki Elenaki you've watered me with poison. My heart was like a garden, my little grumbler.' I worried and I used to get furious. She tried to calm me: 'Hey, pipe down, kid'. I yelled, I swore at them like blazes. In the end I came very near to throwing one of them into the cistern. This was a huge tank where the factory took in water for the machines. I went crazy, I cussed this guy, made filthy gestures, said a whole bunch of bad things and then I stormed off.

But mama was right. I mean I was watching her but she didn't need guarding. She was a respectable woman. I made her very anxious with my bad behaviour - she didn't want to see her son talk and carry on like that. The wild side of my character was telling me it was time to get away and so I bunked off without telling my mother anything. When it got dark I thought of not going home because I was scared of her. But what else could I do? I went home. My mother was waiting for me, out of her mind with worry. The minute I got in she gave me hell. I got a good thrashing.

About ten days went by, but this couldn't go on. I had to help as much as I could because we needed the money, so I went back to the cotton factory. But very soon I felt like I didn't want to stay any more. If I *had* to work, I wanted to earn more money. So I quit again. When I went home in the evening mama began to grumble: 'How could you leave work when your father's in the army and we were getting that three and a half drachmas a week?' Five or ten days went by with me wandering about like an urchin. I went at night time to sleep at my Granny Mariyitsa's house and she gave me some food.

In the end my mother handed me over to a cousin of hers, the son of my granny Mariyitsa's sister. He'd married a widow called Veroga, a nasty woman, and since I was her husband's relative she didn't want me in her place at all. They lived in the village of Parakopi but my uncle kept a green grocer's in Syra's main town, in Ammos. There was a market there too where the villagers came down every morning to sell their produce. The Syrans called him '*Mouyia*'[26] since he worked as a grocer; that was his nickname.

When my uncle heard what had happened he took me on as odd jobs boy. It was torture. Every evening when I'd finished in the shop I took the donkey up to Prokopi where my aunt's house was. There I ate and slept. In the morning I got up, loaded the donkey with all kinds of vegetables from the plot and went back down to the shop. It seemed to me like very hard work but I had no choice. It was food and lodging and every so often my uncle got me shoes, which I'd never worn till then. He also gave me a small monthly wage. I took it straight to my mother. But I wasn't happy, because quite apart from the sweat and toil I had a big nightmare and this nightmare was none other than my aunt. She didn't look kindly on me. Maybe I was a bit cheeky or maybe it was because she had young children and they were jealous. She didn't get off my back for one second. Every evening when I came in dog-tired, she set me to work sweeping, cleaning the stables, lugging water and loads of other chores.

She cussed like a fishwife and with five rooms in her house she still didn't let me sleep in there with the family but gave me a blanket and sent me three hundred yards away to a dry stone outhouse on top of a little hill where they kept straw and other kinds of animal fodder. I headed off there every night all alone like a stray dog, an outcast. These kinds of huts aren't plastered and the cold comes right through. Veroga had a cousin called Dhomenikos who sometimes slept in there too but he was often away. All these miseries

---

26 Cypriot dialect for 'fly'.

and the terror I felt every night alone in that hut weren't enough. On top of that every evening when my uncle came home to sleep my aunt would sit there complaining. I'd spoken rudely to her or not done what I was meant to do. She said a whole lot of mean things to make him chuck me out. They often beat me too but I put up with it. I knew it was my fault for leaving the factory where I worked with mama. I'd forced her to hand me over to strangers, far from home, away from my brothers and sister, far from a mother's love. At an age when other kids had nothing in their heads except playing, I was slaving from morning to night, no Sundays or holidays, and on top of that, beating and scolding for my reward.

One night something happened. Scared the shit out of me. I set off alone to my straw bed just as I did every evening when it got dark. At the door I was about to strike a match to light the lamp but suddenly I heard this whirring flapping noise in the hay. I froze like I'd turned to stone, nearly went nuts. Not just one or two but thousands of birds startled and flew up into the air all at once. Gave me the shock of a lifetime. I tried to be brave, not to run out screaming and wake everyone up; but I was in a cold sweat until I figured out what it was. That day a flock of these tiny birds must have got into the outhouse. In Syra we call them *yannatsidhes* or *tsimpoyannoi* and they have a habit in the evenings of getting into dry stone huts or hayricks. At last I pulled myself together, I lit the lamp and since I'd brought a sack I began to whack them and kill them because they're edible. I killed three or four hundred birds. In the morning around half past five I got up and went to the house. I had a sack load of dead birds and I took them to my aunt so she could make *meze*.[27] But I told her I wasn't going back to the hut any more to sleep. 'Try sending your own kids to sleep there,' I said. What could she do to me anyway? Old

---

27 Titbits to eat with drinks like Spanish tapas.

baggage, fifty years old and her husband a fine young man of thirty! She had four children from her first husband and she'd had three more with this second one. Fine, maybe I was there because I was poor and unlucky but I wasn't going to be pushed around by *her*, like hell I would!

I can't begin to tell you the beating I got from my uncle for being lippy to his wife. Needless to say she told it him as *she* wanted to tell it and he didn't ask *me*. So I upped and left, but since he was giving me thirty drachmas a month and feeding me, my mother talked me round and told me to be patient: 'We need help, kid, since your father's away soldiering.' She took me by the hand and brought me back again. I agreed to sleep in the out-house like before, only now I went there earlier because they'd bought some piglets and I had to feed and clean them.

Every morning they loaded up a mule with two large baskets, a hundred *okes* of vegetables. My job was to take them down double quick to the shop in the plateia in Ammos. Middle of the night, four in the morning, I'd set off, me and the donkey. Some way along the path there was a stream called Vourlaki. The donkey, don't ask me why, whether it was something he saw in the water or whether he was afraid of the sound of the water, his legs went rigid, his ears shot up and he started going 'Hee haw!' Having climbed onto the saddlepack on top of the load, I now had to scramble down, catch the bridle and drag him across. But no way would he go forward. He was backing up and braying all the time. Then suddenly, with me still holding the reins, he bolted, swept me off my feet and dragged me helter skelter along the road all tangled up in the ropes. By the time I'd got him to stop I was scraped and bleeding from the rocks on the road. The beast was all done up too. At last with a huge effort, my heart pounding, I managed to get him near the place he was meant to be. In a rage I'd gashed his ear with my penknife. He was bleeding from the wound and all in a lather of sweat. Just at this moment he had another sudden change of heart and shot off again like a hunted beast, left me standing and got to the shop first. I came running up behind him. My uncle, the old goat, started slapping me round the head and didn't even ask what had happened to me though he could see I was covered in blood. 'How did you get the donkey into that state?' As if *I*'d done it! But you know what? The old folk used to say they'd seen goblins in that place by the river. I didn't know how far the inhumanity of this bastard who wanted to be called my uncle was going to go, so I opened my mouth and let fly at him the worst words any man can hear and after that I ran away home.

When I got there my mother hadn't got back from work. It was just my grandma at home and when she saw the pitiful mess I was in she was shocked and began to cry. I told her what had happened and she began to shout and curse my uncle. Then she cleaned up my cuts. They were hurting badly - so much, I just couldn't get comfortable. When my mother got home and saw the state I was in she began to cry like my Grandma and I joined in too. We all cried. When I told her what I'd been through she hugged me and kissed me and said I'd done right to get away from that brute. Enough days went by for my cuts to heal and just as I was getting better and ready to throw myself into some kind of job, I was laid low all of a sudden, very sick with double pneumonia. For a couple of weeks it was all doctors and medicines. I was at death's door and almost a month went by before I recovered and got up again.

After I got up I began to wander about all over the place not knowing what to do because I didn't have a job. I made a nuisance of myself; didn't leave anyone alone. My mother saw this and worried because she could see I wasn't heading along the right path every mother wants for her child. But as soon as I'd made up my mind to get a job I struck lucky at once. They took me on as a helper at Moutzouropoulos', the cloth mill. The pay was ten drachmas a week. It didn't take me long to start getting cheeky. Soon I was teasing all the girls in the factory and they began to tease me back. They kissed me, they pinched me and I never missed a chance to get even.

Over in Syros I didn't have love affairs. I was too young. Until the age of fifteen or sixteen we didn't do that sort of thing. We played with those little girls. We teased them, but it wasn't like we could go very far with them. It was here in Athens, aged seventeen or eighteen that I fell in love, bam, with my first wife. I married her for love. I remember one girl in Syros though. I don't know if she was interested because there wasn't any monkey business like there is now. Some guys take young girls, they get round them. I didn't do those things back then and this girl wasn't the sort to throw herself about. She went away to Santorini and became a nun; shut herself up in a convent. She disappeared and I never saw her again; lost all trace of her. She was a beautiful girl, but I was still young. That was before I developed my later passion for women and love affairs. I used to talk to her on the way to school. They loved me, her folks at home. Her father had a wholesale grocery store and my dad used to work for him making baskets. I've remembered this thing ever since. She's still in my head this nun, Rozina. Later I used to go to the islands to play and sing, but I didn't go to Santorini. If I went there and asked around I wonder if I'd find this girl.

In the cloth mill I became more of a pest with every passing day so they went and complained to the boss. He called me in and cautioned me from time to time and threatened to chuck me out, but I didn't heed warnings or anything else and so one day after some new complaints he fired me. I'd worked about four months in his factory. When my mother came back in the evening from work and I told her they'd thrown me out, she began yelling at me saying I didn't take my proper share in our money troubles and so on and so forth.

## Chapter 3

## ERMOUPOLI

After this I went down to Ermoupoli to take whatever work I could find. I went to work in a butcher's shop with someone called Louis Kanelis, a tough guy who'd killed someone in Syros. People had been very shocked by that first act of violence between two Catholics. I left because I was scared of him and went as apprentice to another butcher, Ioannis Miga. He swore like the blazes - on a short fuse you might say, but very straight in his dealings. I didn't stay long there either.

A journalist and publisher called Zoula had a local newspaper *Parartima*[28] and he was looking for young boys to sell his papers. I lost no time, I went to find him and the minute he saw me he took me on. That's how I started on my new 'profession' as newspaper boy. There were about thirty other kids all selling papers like I was. Our publisher dressed us all in uniform and he provided food and a place to sleep for whoever wanted it. I slept there most nights with the other boys, all together in one room like a barracks and in there you'd see and hear all kinds of things you'd never have imagined!

My mother understood this business wasn't going to do me any good, and she scolded me every day, telling me not to go on with it and above all not to sleep every night with this seedy bunch of boys. I didn't take her seriously because this kind of life had begun to draw me in and with hindsight you could say I was kind of cut out for it. So I went on with this work for about two months - long enough to give me a big head and start me on the path I'd be chained to for most of my life. I began to see and get to know close up the rackety life, the underworld, shady dealings, cards and all the

---
28 'The Supplement.'

crap fate deals out. Not that I took part in it. I was too young. It was risky for a young boy not being at home but in a place where there were smaller boys and bigger ones together. What was I doing there! Bad stuff, bad folk. All kinds of ... begging your pardon but they were buggering each other. Some of them went right off the rails later. I mean this place was a bordello. That didn't bother Zoula. What did he care? These people were looking at money and they made lots of it. All the big time crooks gathered at Zoula's. Plenty of times the police came and seized one or other of them. 'Hey you filthy faggot! What were you up to yesterday? Were you stealing from so-and-so?' Beatings, bad goings on I tell you. I ate my daily dose of *manghia*[29] - by the ladleful!

After two months had passed of selling Zoula's newspapers and getting to know, close up, the ways and byways of the underworld, I too began to get the bug. It got into me, this rough seedy life. I saw I wouldn't be able to hold out and sooner or later this rebellious lifestyle would get into my bloodstream. Because of that I began looking for a chance to escape. Someone called Paramanis Stamatis had a fruiterer's in the central marketplace of Syros and he offered to take me on as assistant since I was smart and knew loads of people through my work hawking newspapers. I said yes at once, so as soon as we'd agreed on my pay I went home and told my mother. She was thrilled I was starting a decent job in a big shop right in the main square of Syros. So I started and it was going fine. I was very happy with my boss, even if he swore at me, because he not only paid me a good monthly wage but he also fed me and provided clothes. Above all I was pleased because I was close to home. Every evening as soon as we shut shop I went home and that made my mother so happy. The boss was very pleased with me too because I'd learnt my job well and spared him a whole lot of

---

29 *Manghia* the state of being a *mangas*. See Glossary.

running around. All this while I'd been growing and by now I was a strapping kid. The boss would go very early to market to buy the fruit, then I'd bring it back to the shop in a two-wheeled barrow. That was when the hard work began. We had a certain number of good households and whatever they bought from the shop I delivered in baskets.

Six or seven months went by. All well and good. I'd learnt to look after the shop on my own. I'd become a perfect shop assistant and because of that my pay began to seem less satisfactory. It wasn't enough for the talent and the effort I put in and really, I was getting very tired from the running around I did outside the shop. One day when Paramanis and I went together to market to do the buying, another greengrocer called Apostolakis, who had a good and a very big shop in the central square, seized the chance and said he wanted me to be his assistant. He offered double the amount I was getting from Paramanis. I said yes right away. It was a better job, not only because of the extra pay but also because now I didn't have to do deliveries - he had another boy to help with that. I set to with a will in the new shop, I was a great salesman, very enthusiastic on all fronts. In this shop I got to know the top people in Syros.

But Syros didn't only have good folks in it. Ermoupoli was a port, a great hub and it had all the shady business of ports which I'd got used to while I was working with the newspaper hawkers. That's how I got to know Gavalas. He was one hell of a *palikari*,[30] there was no one else like him anywhere; a crook, big time. Not a good sort. But you *could* say so what? As long as he was a *palikari* ... There wasn't a single state jail he hadn't served time in! He committed murder in every one of them. The guys he killed were other *palikaria* from all over the place. For example, he went to prison in Kalamata and there he killed the biggest

---

30 'Warrior', 'brave young man'. A word often used but difficult to translate, it evokes a flavour of old time chivalry and derring-do. See glossary.

Kalamatian big shot there was. He got hold of all the keys in there and soon he was running the show, boss cat of convicts and jailbirds. Whatever was going on he raked in the shekels and nobody squealed. He called the shots. He'd say to a man: 'Take this, take that!' Went to Patras, same deal. Bumped off the top dog and settled in. He played just the best *bouzoukaki*.[31] When they sentenced him to death, his mother went to the king to ask for a pardon so they wouldn't cut off his head. I don't remember which king it was, George or Otto, I just don't know. Here's what she sang to the queen to save him from the guillotine.

| | |
|---|---|
| *Through all the world* | *Εσύ'σαι μια βασίλισσα* |
| *Oh queen most high* | *π'όλο τον κόσμο ορίζεις,* |
| *You rule and choose* | *σαν θέλεις παίρνεις τις ψυχές* |
| *Who'll live or die.* | *σαν θέλεις τις χαρίζεις.* |

In the end they killed him over there in Syros. An army officer, a sub-lieutenant called Peltesis, took a squadron of forty guards with him. They cornered him, told him to surrender, which he didn't, so they killed him. He was a living breathing terror but they killed him. He was maybe about forty years old at the time. Later on I heard him talked of here in Piraeus; his exploits, all the guys he killed in this prison or that prison. A whole heap of stories. There were *koutsavakidhes*[32] there in Syros alright but I was just a boy and didn't know about these things. *koutsavakis* was a word I didn't hear till I got to Piraeus. All the hashish that went to 'Old Greece'[33] would have gone through Syros. How could

---

31 The ending - *aki* indicates a diminutive.
32 Gavalas was a perfect example of a legendary *koutsavakis*: a dare-devil, hashish smoking, sometimes *bouzouki*-playing tough guy. They tended to be at the more dangerous end of the *mangas* spectrum, carried knives, spoke a particular slang, wore colourful and eccentric clothes and often a jacket with the right sleeve empty. For further details see glossary.
33 'Palaia Helladha' refers to Greece before it acquired the 'new lands'. In the Balkan war in 1912 after the first Balkan War, Greece acquired Thessaloniki and most of northern Greece as well as Crete, which till then had been part of the Ottoman empire. Until the late 19th century Ermoupolis was the main hub, the biggest port in Greece and the centre of the shipping industry.

there not have been *koutsavakidhes* in Syra considering that's where the real deal was to be found? All this stuff came from Syros, obviously. After all, at one time there were forty cafés and about sixty *tekedhes*[34] registered over there.

I was too young to have gone to those *tekedhes*. They'd already died out. But I heard from older people later that there were various *manghes* who used to go there and smoke. The guys who dressed like *Zebeks* were pretty much the same as *manghes*, in so far as they danced, you know and did that sort of thing. They might have been *koutsavakidhes* too but it wasn't that they were real crooks. They worked. They had their jobs. They were okay. The *koutsavakidhes* who were around fifty years before I ever got to hear of them, dressed very well even then, with clothes in '*the black style*', as it was called, and 'jockey' trousers. I remember that because my uncles used to sew them. But I didn't wear them. I used to wear cheap cotton *drills*, because if my drills cost one and a half or two drachmas those 'jockey' things were five drachmas apiece. Back then the *manghes* had a code of honour, discretion. They kept an eye on each other and they dressed very well. Later on all those *manghes* from Syros came over here to Piraeus.

After I'd been seven or eight months in Apostolakis' shop someone suggested I go to the Athenian newspaper office. The director there was one Christos Kanistras. They knew I'd done this kind of work before and very successfully too. That's why they wanted me in their office. I agreed at once and to be honest, it wasn't because I liked this line of work, but I wanted more freedom of movement. At the shop I was always busy from eight in the morning until nine in the evening, which I didn't think was a whole load of fun. I went to the agency at once and started my new work the very next day. At that time it was one of the most lowgrade jobs there were. I had to set off for the newspaper office very

---

34 Hashish dens.

early at three or four in the morning as that was when the boats came in. The boatmen unloaded the papers and brought them into the office to share out between us. Then we went and sold them.

I used to take roughly five or six hundred papers plus magazines and lottery tickets. At that time there was *Hesperini, Hestia, Asteri, Patris, Embros, Nea Himera, Scrib, Ethnos, I Nea Helladha*[35] and various others. I set off all loaded up with this bundle and hawked my wares round Ermoupoli and Upper Chora. I got loads more money than I did in Apostolaki's shop, about fifteen to twenty drachmas a day. Like I said, I'd got to know a lot of people in Apostolakis' shop and that helped me a lot in my work as a paperboy. I had a lot of customers and I was the quickest at getting to the page they liked. Especially in Upper Chora, the village I was born in, they remembered me and felt sorry for me, bought my papers. Whenever I'd sold and got rid of my load, I'd go to some piece of waste ground, a stream, some place where no one could see me and I'd sit down, have a rest and flick through the papers. I used to read all the headlines and if I came upon something I wanted to read the whole of, I read it.

My mother, although she was against it to start with, began to come round to the idea, but on condition I'd come home to sleep every night, so that's what I did. Since I did this work from early morning until half past two, I used to take my kit box and work as a bootblack. I earned a fair amount from that too so all in all I did well considering how young I was. But then again, being so young wasn't without its dangers.

Third act now of the drama: the seamy life of the *mangas*, the street boy. Whatever sleaze was going on I saw it all close up: petty theft, dice, cards, houses of ill fame and so

---

35 'Evening', 'Hearth', 'Star', 'Fatherland', 'Forward', 'New Day', 'Scrib', 'Nation', and 'New Hellas'.

on. The loose women, the hookers, would see me selling my papers and magazines and they'd shout to me out of their windows 'Hey you, come on up here!' Up I'd go, they'd give me money, make me their little pet. I sure didn't object. The big guys, some vicious bastards among them, sent the bright eager lad to run their errands and he was all puffed up with the praises and friendship of these dudes. There were some as well who'd give me a kick or a slap, but I was a tough nut too and foul-mouthed with it. Up to that point I'd never been in trouble with the law. This was because all the good society of Syros, judges, lawyers, businessmen, everyone knew me from my 'profession'. I was doing fine. I loved my brothers and my sister and whatever money I made I gave to mama. We sent parcels to my father in the army.

*Markos, Jack of all Trades*[36]

*The many jobs that I have done,*
*Listen, I'll list them all.*
*I'll write them down, it makes me feel*
*Like crying when I recall.*

*Of all the jobs you've ever done*
*There's one you left undone.*
*Me who you loved you didn't wed*
*Or crown with a wedding crown.*

*I made up little packets*
*In the cotton factory*
*And little girls would bring along*
*The thread and reels to me.*

*Ah little girls would bring you*
*The reels and skeins of thread*
*And little thought you ever gave*
*To the bitter life I led.*

*Μάρκος Πολυτεχνίτης*

*Όλες τις τέχνες που'κανα*
*ακούστε που τις λέω,*
*τις γράφω και σαν θυμηθώ*
*μου'ρχεται για να κλαίω.*

*Όλες τις τέχνες που κανες*
*μα μια δεν έχεις κάνει,*
*εμένα που μ'αγάπησες*
*δε μου βαλες στεφάνι.*

*Μες το κλωστήριο μ'είχανε*
*κι έκανα πακετάκια,*
*νήμα και κούτσες φέρνανε*
*σε με τα κοριτσάκια.*

*Νήμα και κούτσες φέρνανε*
*σε σένα κοριτσάκια,*
*και μένα δε λογάριαζες*
*που έπινα φαρμάκια.*

---

36 *O Markos o Polytechnitis.*

| | |
|---|---|
| I didn't like this work at all, | Δε μ' άρεσε αυτή η δουλειά |
| I wanted something more | ζήλευα κάποια άλλη |
| And I became an errand boy | και ψυχογιός εγένηκα |
| In a wholesale grocer's store | σ' ένα χοντρομπακάλη. |
| | |
| And you became an errand boy | Και ψυχογιός εγένηκες |
| In a wholesale grocer's store. | σ' ένα χοντρομπακάλη |
| His daughter was a pretty thing, | γιατί είχε κόρη έμορφη |
| Her dowry even more! | κι η προίκα της μεγάλη. |
| | |
| Three days I stayed and then | Τρεις μέρες έκατσα εκεί |
| I wished to try another tack, | κι ήθελα για να στρίψω |
| To go about and hawk the news, | εφημερίδες να πουλώ |
| The paper-selling track. | στους δρόμους να γυρίζω. |
| | |
| You go about, you hawk the news, | Εφημερίδες κι αν πουλάς |
| The paper-selling track. | στους δρόμους κι αν γυρίζεις |
| You took the grocer's girl as well | επήρες τη μπακάλενα |
| And gave me loads of flak. | κι εμένα φοβερίζεις |
| | |
| At dusk with my two hands I grabbed | Το βράδυ το κασέλι μου |
| My blacking box to tout | το τσάκωνα στα χέρια, |
| Only St Georgy's sparrow-hawks | μόνο που δεν κουβάλησα |
| I didn't lug about, | τ' Άγιου Γιωργιού ξεφτέρια. |
| | |
| What if you are a shoe-shiner, | Λούστρος κι αν εγίνηκες |
| You useless down and out, | αλήτης κι αλανιάρης, |
| The thing you left behind is me. | πρέπει να το συλλογιστείς |
| That's one to think about. | εμέ δεν έχεις πάρει. |

Ah, what I've been through on the street! Being a bootblack, being just a lad and a good-looking one too, there were some vicious types. It's not all good folks in the world. There are bad guys too. When I was selling papers I used to go to a factory, Pousialos. It's still there in Syros. There was a mechanic in that place and he was a right scumbag. Whenever I went there he used to grab my cheeks and my bum. Now this was one of those things I'd seen and I knew about. It got to the point where I said to him one day, 'Hey you, what can I say! I'm going to serve you up such a feast you'll be shitting yourself!' I didn't mince my words. 'You think you can do me over you old sod! You won't know what hit you pal! I'll trash you, you old mother-fucker, and everybody round here'll be onto you! So many girls, so many chicks in here. What d'you want with *me*!'

I didn't want that sort of thing. I steered well clear. I set him up, this guy, he got thrashed. In the places where I hung about in the evening, selling papers, I was on good terms with the boys on the block. They all knew me. It was my patch. One day I was talking with one of them, a *koutsavakis* type, you know ... 'Look, he's bothering me,' says I, 'How can we fix things and give him a hiding?' Three guys turned up and they said 'Say you'll meet him at noon in such and such a place.' So that's what I did. What could he do, the poor bugger? The other guys set about him and gave him the mother of all beatings, smashed him to a pulp. Poor bastard didn't lodge a complaint. What could he say? Afterwards he was all swollen up. He didn't go to work. I started going to the factory again since there were other guys there who wanted newspapers. When he came back, 'Hell, *Frango*!' he says to me - he called me *Frango* because I was a Catholic and he was Orthodox. 'Hell, *Frango*, I'd never have believed it ...' 'There's plenty more where that came from,' says I to him, 'if you dare speak to me again. If I knew you had a son like me I'd go and fuck him.' I was twelve or thirteen years old then but very tough. And what *didn't* happen to me! It's a whole heap of things, my life story.

In 1915 the Allies' blockade was announced and we were cut off until 1917. No boats were allowed anywhere near us and Syros couldn't get by without imported goods. Everyone got very hungry. Only two boats managed to get through, the *Panhellenion* and the *Zatouna*. They brought just one newspaper *Le Progrès,* a French paper published in Athens. That's how everyone kept up with the news. Of course everyone in Syros knew French. The people in Upper Chora did because they were Catholics.

This was how I made my money. I might be lucky enough to sell this newspaper for ten or even fifteen drachmas. Any price, you name it, that's how much people thirsted after news. So once I was making money I started going to some villages round Syros. Since they knew my father and my family from the days when we were making baskets, and what with us being fellow Catholics too, the villagers did what they could to help. One would give me a barley loaf, someone else an *oke* of dried figs, or they might give me cabbages, cauliflowers, onions or potatoes. Thanks be to God, I managed to bring all sorts of things back home, and that was all through my sweat and being on the ball. I had what it took.

There was an orgy of smuggling going on at the time. My uncle the grocer was doing contraband sugar and cigarette papers. Even my mother was helping. She used to wind the sugar and cigarette papers round her waist like a bandage and carry them to the marketplace to Petsa the Grocer. But a sergeant of the Gendarmerie, Kiranis, caught her doing it once too often. They hauled us off to the lock-up, mama and us three, the youngest still a babe in arms. We were sentenced and we went to jail for fifteen days, us kids along with our mother.

In 1917 the blockade came to an end. I was a lad of thirteen by now and nobody could tell me I wasn't a fully-grown man. My father got back from the army. Not long after that I did a very dumb thing. One day, from high up on a slope I set a boulder rolling downhill, a boulder that weighed several tons. Just for larks. Down it rolls and falls on the roof of a house - luckily at a time of day when nobody was in. It smashes through the roof tiles and drops right *inside* the house. They'd go to the police. They'd be after me. What was I to do? Mama was crying, but I was scared they'd catch me so I stowed away on a boat and scrammed off to Piraeus. The high place from which I rolled the stone was Persinos and the place where it landed was Portara. They wrote to me ten days after I got to Piraeus to say that nobody was hunting me because the house belonged to my aunt, Mariyi! Here ends the drama of Syros. But my life is one long series of dramas.

# PART II: PIRAEUS

## CHAPTER 4

### COAL AND THE HARNESS

When I left Syros and came to Piraeus, I lived with an aunt of mine called Irini Altouva in Fotiou Street, Korytsas, down the far end of Tabouria. I met some fellow Frankosyrans and began to hang out with them in the evenings in the *kafeneion*. They were stevedores and because they knew my father I asked them to take me on as one of the team even though I was young. This was gruelling work for a boy of fifteen. I was carrying huge sacks of coal on my back. We worked by the ton and I started earning twenty to forty drachmas. Seemed like riches to me and now for the first time in my life I went and bought a pair of shoes. Till then the soles of my feet were always covered in cuts from going barefoot.

Every night, dog-tired, I slept with a couple of blankets on my aunt's floor. I felt like I was a burden even though I gave her sixty drachmas a week. She fed me and did my washing and from what was left I sent as much as I could to my mother. I hadn't yet learnt how to be a big spender. Letters were coming from home to me and to my aunt. My mother begged her to keep an eye on me and keep me from going any further down the wrong path. By now I'd begun to be quite a young blade and I'd taken up with all sorts of buddies, the boys of the neighbourhood. We're talking Piraeus here. A port, sleaze everywhere, gambling, whores and hashish dens. I was young but I managed to sneak into the *kafeneion* without being seen. I began to smoke too at Foukas' place. In those days everyone smoked hashish freely, without feeling it did them any harm. Nobody made it difficult for them. It was just three days in a cell for anyone caught smoking. The hashish was smuggled in from Turkey. There was stuff in Greece too but it was poorer quality. Whoever worked in the ports got into the habit and they passed it on to the haulers, the dockers, whoever was trying to forget their troubles.

Nine months after I got to Piraeus, my whole family arrived and we all lived together in Tabouria. My father got a job straight away carrying coal in the same place as me so we made ends meet. One day we went to load up one of those big old ships that had been sailing between Greece and America for years. They'd sent me down into the hold as trimmer to level out the coals with my shovel.[37] The others were emptying coal sacks from up top but I got lazy down there. What the hell, says I, let me just sit down and have a little kip and never mind, they won't pour in the coal. Well they *did* of course but *I* wasn't shovelling. They threw down ninety tons of coal and when they saw at last that I wasn't shoveling one of them says 'What's up with him? Something happened down there?' I was fast asleep. Flat out, eh? But when I woke up with ninety tons of coal on top of me I was terrified. What's this! How do I get all this off me? I struggled like crazy to get out from under. They pulled me out senseless, half suffocated. They only just managed to get me out by going in from the engine room. They tugged me out and shoveled up the coal so it fell in from above.

We used to wake up towards six in the morning. My father got up first, then he'd get me up too. 'Come on, let's go, time for work'. Up I'd get, still exhausted, only a kid after all, and scared too because it was crushingly hard work. Just imagine humping all those tons of coal around. But what could I do? I had to go with my father and he wasn't well. I was sorry for him.

---

[37] To distribute the weight evenly. This was dangerous work as that volume of coal in an enclosed space could cause a firedamp explosion.

We drank sage tea and a little bread. Milk never. Mama used to give us food to take with us so we could sit down there and eat. Towards nine or ten we stopped for a morning snack. In the morning it was a half hour walk to get from Tabouria to the coal bunkers of Vasiliadhis, in Kantharos. In those days just in front of the entrance to the port, there were the coal depots of the various shipping lines like Palios, or Embirikos. We used to fill up the lighters from the depots and put the coal on the ships. The coal came from England, Russia and a few other places. The freighters used to come and unload by the depots. We hauled the coal off the ships into the depots and then from the depots into the ships that were about to sail. That was our work.

Our group, ten or twelve men with the foreman in charge, gathered at Kantharos, just a little way up from the dry docks of Vasiliadhis where they put the hulls up and cleaned them - those would be the smaller boats, the ones that went to Syra, to Andros and the islands. In Stefanos' team there were ten of us, all from Syros and Catholics, nearly all relatives. Stefanos was Catholic too. There were about ten other work teams, Santorinians, Symians, I knew them all. They also stuck with family, more or less, ten or twelve men, Manoli's team, Yorghi's team and so on. These were contract jobs and there were other capos who supervised five or ten teams and gave out the work. They'd turn up and say, 'Here's a fifty ton lighter. You guys get to work on it, off you go and unload her.' Or they might shout 'Let the *Frankosyran* boys go do the job.' I worked hard and I got exhausted humping those great big sacks of coal on my shoulder. I used to say to myself, when's it time to stop? I was young and I had to do the heavy carrying. The old fellers did the shoveling. But they got tired too. This was my job day and night all the time for three or four years.

The capos were the middlemen between the various shipping line offices that owned the depots and the coal workers' union. All of us coal workers belonged to the union and we had a union boss, a guy named Yerasimos Galiatsatos. I think he was from Kefalonia this guy and in the end he turned out to be an embezzler. Every month we used to pay a *taliro*[38] to the union which took care of everything, like doctors if anybody needed one or went to hospital, not of course that you'd stay in there! We didn't have the money to stay even five days.

The foremen gave out the orders and organized things. It was the union who paid them from the money they got from the guys who owned the depots and the ships. They were union guys. They went to the offices and got paid. 'Today we loaded a hundred tons of coal onto this ship. Give us our money.' After we'd finished the day's work and set off home, Stefanos, our team foreman, would go to the union office: 'How much did we load and unload today? So much a ton.' He collected our pay. Our whole gang lived in Tabouria and in the evening we'd meet up again at a little *kafeneion* where people from Syros went. Stefanos would come and find us there and hand us our wages. If somebody wasn't there he'd pay him the next morning.

The work team foremen were all on a level with us but they didn't tire themselves as much as we others did who were just plain workers, like for instance, a guy would come along from the office and he'd go off again. We'd keep on working. Another would come along, fix things, see what was needed there and off he'd go again. The others though, the union capos who gave orders to the team foremen, *they* didn't work at all. This Stefanos was a good guy, a regular guy, one of us; not educated, didn't even know how to sign his own name. There'd be times when he might be working alongside of us. If he didn't have other work he couldn't just sit there giving orders, 'Move it, take it, shovel it!'. He went round, he carried stuff, but he was a bit freer than us workers

---

38 A note or coin worth 5 drachmas, roughly equivalent to a dollar.

who got in there and set to, right away, heads down. The foreman got the same pay as everyone else and we trusted him. He was a union man. Besides we knew what the coal we'd unloaded amounted to in money. We knew exactly. There was no question of his taking even one *taliro* over and above, I can tell you that for sure. Sometimes he even went short himself.

Summer. Terrible heat. The work was unbearable. In winter it might be a bit cold but you'd wrap up warm and by the time you got going you'd work better. As for what we looked like, forget it! In and out of coal bunkers, black as soot, with our drill trousers, shirt and boiler suit. Of course later, after we'd clocked off and gone home, we spruced up and looked like normal human beings. In the docks there was no place to wash. Everyone needed to go home to get soaped and scrubbed.

On our heads we wore a piece of cloth cut from a towel. We tied it round our hair to keep the coal dust from getting in but it still *did* get in. We tied a kerchief round the back of our necks as well, to stop the coal going down our backs. A towel was ideal for this, roughly a span and a half wide and a span and a half long. It soaked up the coal and the sweat. First thing we did soon as we got home was take it off and wash it or else we just left it there to dry. Next day same thing all over again.

When we got back home towards two in the afternoon, first, thorough washing - hair and everything, so as not to dirty the sheets. Next, some good solid food. Whatever there was in the house, beans, chickpeas, broad beans, pasta, dried salt cod, the daily fare. Then, naptime! I was just a kid and I'd be deadbeat. I'd fall on my bed and be out for the count till late afternoon, four or five. Later, we used to get up and go to the *kafeneion* but *I* didn't go there so much. I used to go to other places and find pals my own age. Some of them worked in the shipyards and others in the glass works, all kinds of places. We'd sit and chew the fat, talk about girlfriends, this that and the other. It was round this time, when I was working in the coal, that I began to get all lovey-dovey with the girl who became my first wife. I had *her* on my mind.

In Tabouria I used to turn up pretty often at the house of a cousin of mine, Koula Rigoustou. The girl I was in love with used to sit in the same courtyard. She was Orthodox, from the Peloponnese and she was called Zingoala. I went there a lot, just to see this tigress I wanted to marry later on. We tried hard to keep it secret, so her folks wouldn't see us. I wasn't worried about *my* family. They knew I was talking to her. Zingoala was always on the look out for a chance to talk to me on the sly. She'd go out to shop at the food store and I'd be waiting for her at the gate. Sometimes I'd meet her in the street and we'd have a chat. We said all the sweet nothings, 'Give us a kiss', 'I'll marry you, you'll be my wife', and 'When shall we tie the knot?' Maybe it's a true saying, 'Whoever loves you makes you cry'. We hadn't got to know each other more than ten days before Zingoala called me 'Frankish Dog!'

But still, for all the 'Frankish Dog', the love was pretty much like a thunderbolt. From the very first days it took hold of us and a year passed without the flame dying down. One day I grabbed her and we ran away. We stole off, ten o'clock at night, and later I took her home. She was a pretty, spirited girl, dark, lovely eyes and a beauty.

*I Married Young*                     Μικρός Αρραβωνιάστηκα

*Fool that I was I married young*     *Μικρός αρραβωνιάστηκα*
*A sultry babe with a saucy tongue.*  *κορόιδο που επιάστηκα*
                                      *και πήρα μια μπεμπέκα*
                                      *μαγκιώρα για γυναίκα.*

| | |
|---|---|
| The wedding had just every sort<br>Of swank, like waiting in a court | Στο γάμο μάγκα να 'σουνα<br>να δεις καλαμπαλίκι<br>σαν να 'μουνα υπόδικος<br>και περιμένω δίκη. |
| To hear the sentence, 'Married man,<br>Carry the load and carry the can'. | Και βγήκε η απόφαση<br>πως είμαι παντρεμένος<br>να κουβαλώ καθημερινώς<br>σαν γάιδαρος στρωμένος. |
| I took my wife, I paid the bill,<br>We took our stuff, went home to chill. | Επήρα τη γυναίκα μου<br>παίρνω το μπουγιουρντί μου<br>τα σέα μου τα μέα μου<br>και βουρ για το τσαρδί μου. |
| Woke next morning sweet and dozy,<br>Billing and cooing, very cosy. | Την άλλη μέρα ξύπνησα<br>τότε να δεις μεράκια<br>αφού δεν είχαμε ψιλή<br>αυτή 'θελε χαδάκια. |
| She didn't let me leave our home.<br>Chained by the nose I couldn't roam. | Να φύγω και να κουνηθώ δε μ'<br>άφηνε απ' το σπίτι<br>κι ένα χαλκά από σίδερο μου<br>κόλλησε στη μύτη. |
| I broke a cudgel on her nut<br>And I'm still running from that hut. | Παίρνω ένα ξύλο από οξυά<br>κι απάνω της το σπάω,<br>της ρίχνω ξύλο αλύπητο<br>φεύγω κι ακόμα πάω. |

After I'd worked four years on the coal I got lucky and went to Zea, to the customs house of Kyriakos Margioli where the pay was better. This guy was *capo* in the place where the depots were - the place where we unloaded the goods. He had about a hundred, maybe a hundred and fifty dockers working under him. Our lot was a twelve-man team, the toughest of the heavyweights. I had a harness on my back and I carried loads that weighed up to a hundred and thirty five *okes*. Other guys at the customs house who worked on the lighters, unloading sugar, rice and flour were getting eighty drachmas. But *we* were taking a hundred and twenty drachs. The heavy weight 'A' team had guys from Aouti, Mykonos, Santorini, Asini and me in there from Syros. Quite a kid hey? Then of course there were the refugees who'd begun to arrive around this time. We carried heavy loads with the *chamalika*. A *chamalika* is a thing like saddle-cloth which we put on our backs. It went under our armpits so the heavy stuff wouldn't dig into us. We worked from eight in the morning till two or three in the afternoon. Then we were off.

One day they loaded me up with something, maybe a table, not heavy so much as bulky you know; a tall unwieldy object maybe a hundred and fifty *okes*. I got it on my back and carried it from the wharf by the Zea Custom House all the way to the depots. That meant a ten minute walk all loaded up with four guys each holding onto a corner to keep the thing balanced. I got out into the road where the tramline was, straining under the loaded *chamalika,* and then I saw the tram coming! For some reason I got dizzy and I panicked. I shouted to the guys who were helping me 'Out from under! I've got to ditch! Can't hold on! Tram'll hit me!' They threw down the load and jumped free. It fetched up right up there on the snout of the tram, which ground to a halt and the gearbox flew open. I did some damage to the tram, but not a huge lot. In one place I'd broken the windows.

With huge difficulty and a lot of help I got the thing loaded up onto my back again and took it into the depot. The minute we put it down I didn't go back to the lighter we were unloading. I climbed to the top of a pile of sugar sacks to be alone and then I cried like a baby. I'd had a fright, I'd got tired out and I did some thinking. Mother of God! I said to myself, Jesus Christ! Is this going to be the work I do? Is it going to be all toil and sweat like this as long as I live? What can I do? My God, am I really going to live my life as a pack-mule? And what a mule, a mule and a half! I was begging the good Lord, 'Sweet Jesus, help me to leave, to get some other job so I'll be different somehow and make money and not be doing this. My foot had split open just under the arch and it was pouring blood. This was the first time I cracked under the strain. I had cried one other time when I was young, working on the coals, barefoot and with a cold. But this time I was grown up and I still cried.

By the time I was working at the Customs house I was already married to that mule I was talking about, my first wife. I stayed there some two or three years and after that her father took me on to work with him. What else could he do? I had his child and I was a first rate worker. He was a good guy, even if he hadn't in the least wanted to have me for his son in law, me being Catholic and all. A very good man though, an easy-going man. We unloaded grapes, molasses, or carobs, various cargoes they brought from Crete or the islands. It was there - you can still see it - at Zea's Customs in the harbor at Yannoulatos' at Tzelepi that the freighters unloaded and re-loaded cargoes. One time they put a box full of money on my back. It had come from England where they minted it. The crate wasn't that big but it was very heavy! You know how it is with money. Weighed a ton! While we were loading up, it fell off my back and flew open. I pocketed some of the coins. Two-drachma pieces, but they turned out not to be valid. I stayed there at Customs for eight or nine months altogether. After that I quit. No, I couldn't do this kind of work. It wasn't for me. 'I'm going to be a butcher' I said to myself. But along with these jobs I'm telling you about, I still had words and composing in my sights. I was thinking every day, when will I begin to write? For example, I'd written *Mia Cheimoniatiki Vradhia*. I'd written this in Syra when I was a child of thirteen or fourteen. Then I lost the piece of paper but I know it by heart. It's like my signature song this one.

*A Wintry Night*

A wintry night in darkness black
I wander on a lonely track.
The icy north wind feels so bleak
Eats my bones, and makes me weak.
Deep in my heart, my hidden soul
The pulse was beating like a toll

Hoping that round every bend
Of wilderness I'd find a friend
In the world, the universe.
But your heart's stony as a curse

And since you have no love for me
All the world's fickle treachery
And the bleak wind devour me.

*Μια Χειμωνιάτικη Βραδιά*

Μια χειμωνιάτικη βραδιά
Μέσα σε μαύρη σκοτεινιά
γυρίζω μοναχός μου.
Με τρώει ο έρημος βοριάς
από τα φύλλα της καρδιάς
χτυπούσε ο παλμός μου.

Πάντα για ένα σύντροφο,
γύριζα τον αγύριστο
τον κόσμο τον ντουνιά.

Κι αφού σκληρή δε μ'αγαπάς,
με τρώει ο έρημος βοριάς
κι'ο άστατος ντουνιάς.

Through all this time I wasn't writing. Too exhausted, and I was doing other kinds of work. Looking after that woman among other things. But this never left my mind, not that I ever thought I was going to earn money with this business. Never even heard of such a thing. But I still thought about it with longing and as I said, I liked reading the papers. Even with all this work, you can be sure I always had a newspaper at hand. I used to buy one and read it, and if I didn't have money to buy it I went to the *kafeneion* and read it there, not just one but ten if there *were* that many. I kept up with them all, every single one and I remember everything, the wars in Europe, first and second world war, everything. It wasn't even as if I had this thing going on, this composing work. No I wasn't counting on it. But I *was* playing *bouzouki* ... oh yes, I was playing alright.

## Chapter 5

## MANGHIA

So, like I said, there we are in that shit hole, otherwise known as *Zea*; a nest of thieves, cardsharpers, pickpockets, dope peddlers, hashish smokers, *manghes*, murderers and *koutsavakia*. I got to know a fair number of those types, good mixed with the bad, but later I spent more time in the company of the better ones. This bunch of friends brought with it the usual rackety behaviour of the time. At the age of nineteen I became the lover of a prostitute called Irini from Symi. Apartment number two at Vourla was where I first discovered sex. She was an older woman, twenty-seven or twenty-eight years old and she used to give me money and clothes. Then I fell in love with that girl from Mani, Zingoala so I left her. Even after my marriage, newlywed and all, we used to go with the floozies. There were so many everywhere at that time in Vourla. I was playing the *koutsavakis*; a ladies' man big time. Whatever I saw the others do I did as well. Little by little, step by step I went downhill, began to go to the hashish dens. I checked out all the *tekedhes* of Piraeus and Athens and the outlying areas and wherever there was a *tekes* I rolled in the filth along with everybody else. I was a proper *mangas* and a fully paid-up *chasiklis*. No one was a match for me.

**Drifter**

I'm a drifter,
I wander about.
I'm so stoned
My brain's fallen out.

**Αλανιάρης**[40]

Είμαι αλανιάρης
στους δρόμους τριγυρίζω
κι απ' την πολλή μαστούρα μου
το νού μου δεν ορίζω.

*Pitch in sister*
*Let's smoke us a chibouki*[39]
*Get stoned together,*
*You'll hear some bouzouki.*

*Make it crackle and whistle,*
*You dervish dude*
*Thyme scented flames*
*I'll smoke and brood.*

*Τσοντάρισ' αδερφούλα μου*
*να πιούμε τσιμπουκάκι,*
*μαζί να μαστουριάσουμε*
*ν'ακούσεις μπουζουκάκι.*

*Κάντονε ντερβισόμαγκα*
*τον αργιλέ να τρίζει*
*και με φωτιές του θυμαριού*
*να πιω και να σφυρίζει.*

The first time I found myself in the *tekes* was a life-changing experience. I was with a bunch of pals, Antonis the carter, Mitsos the boatswain and one-armed Vassilis the docker. They were hashish smokers these guys, about thirty-five years old, and they took me under their wing, took me to the *tekes* and gave me my first taste of the 'black'. Straight *arghile*. Made me very sick. My eyes blurred, I started puking and retching horribly, the world spun round and round and I couldn't budge from my chair. They poured water on my head to revive me and gave me sour lemon to eat. This happened at Athanata, Ayios Georgios, next to Anastasi, when I was seventeen or eighteen years old. Don't know why I didn't leave it alone after that. What made me go back? It was the dervish inside me.

What I mean by 'dervish' is that I was a *mangas* who could hold my head up high. I didn't make trouble. People respected me and I respected them. They loved me, I loved them. Whatever one guy said, the others backed him, up to the hilt. We were *manghes*, in a spirit of chivalry. *Manghes*. We made our money by the sweat of our brow. We had nothing to do with the *alaniaridhes*, the street boys, who stole and did all sorts of low down things.

---

39 A long stemmed Turkish tobacco pipe with a clay bowl.
40 *Alaniaris*, rec. 1934.

## Fix it Stavros

Fix it Stavros, fix it up[41]
Light the flame and cook it up.

Pass to Nikos Crazy guy
Make the carpenter fly high.

Smoke it Yannis, make it hiss,
You're the manghes' teketzis.

There to Nikolakis give some
So he'll stop us all being glum.

Let our Batis take a drag
our hellraiser, our old lag.

## Κάν' τονε Σταύρο

Κάν' τονε Σταύρο, κάν' τονε
βάλ' του φωτιά και κάφ' τονε.

Δώσε του Νίκου του τρελλού
του μάστορα του ξυλουργού.

Τράβα βρε Γιάννη αραμπατζή,
πού 'σαι μαγκιόρος τεκετζής.

Δώσε του Νικολάκη μας
να βγάλει το μεράκι μας.

Τζούρα δώσε του Μπάτη μας,
του μόρτη, του μπερμπάντη μας.

Time flew by when we were stoned and we'd all get home late at night even with work the next morning. When I got home late all stoned on hashish I used to creep in very quietly so as not to wake my father. I was ashamed and I didn't want to look him in the eye where I'd see all the pain he felt for me. He had the both of us on his hands too, me and my wife! He was eaten up with grief at my plunge into low life, and my mother, poor soul, who always wanted what was good for me, did a whole lot of complaining. I didn't listen at all. She was in trouble with my father. They had rows about me and whose fault it was. The two younger brothers followed my example. One, Leonardhos, went nuts at the age of seventeen from hashish. He lived on as a total head case and died of hunger in the war. The other, Frangiskos, drank wine and turned into a scary guy who pulled knives. He ended up murdering somebody and went to prison.

So, like I said, after I'd been swept off course into this seedy life, I began to go through the bad experiences that

---
41 *Kantone Stavro, Kantone*, rec. 1935.

went with it. One day they caught me in Sotirakis' *tekes* along with five others. They put the *arghile*, the straws and the hashish into my hands and brought me in handcuffs with the others, along the quayside of Piraeus and Zea to the police station in Retsina Street. Beatings, kickings and the next day off to the magistrates' court. Then two or three days in the clink and as many times as they caught us it was the same again. For me this adventure marked a turning point, the first night in a cell, fingerprints, magistrates' court and all that.

**In the Dark Last Night**[42]

*All in the dark two cops last night*
*Cornered me and held me tight,*
*To put me through interrogation*
*And take away my hashish ration.*

*I'd fixed a fine and secret hash*
*They trembled and they ran about.*
*Oh how they hunted for my stash*
*Mangas, now they'll dig it out.*

*The cops began to rage and swear*
*Next night they set me up a snare,*
*Och Aman! they stitched me up!*
*They lured me right into their trap.*

*Morning, it's the chief inspector,*
*By evening, the prison sector.*
*Sent down for being a mangas. Now*
*The cops relax and mop their brow.*

**Χθές Το Βράδυ Στο Σκοτάδι**

*Χτες το βράδυ στο σκοτάδι*
*με στριμώξανε δυο μαύροι,*
*έρευνα για να μου κάνουν*
*και το μαύρο να μου πάρουν.*

*Είχα κάνει φίνα ζούλα*
*που τους έπιασε τρεμούλα.*
*Ρε, ψάξανε να μου το βρούνε,*
*μάγκα τώρα θα το βρούνε.*

*Αγριέψανε οι μαύροι*
*μου τη στήνουν τ' άλλο βράδυ.*
*Βρε, και με κάνουνε πιαστό*
*βρε αμάν αμάν*
*με τραβούνε στο πλεχτό.*

*Το πρωί στο Διοικητή,*
*και το βράδυ φυλακή.*
*Βρέ, κι έτσι μάγκα με δικάζουν,*
*και οι μαύροι ησυχάζουν.*

As soon as we got out, first thing we did was run to find an *arghile*. Now the arrests began to be a regular part of my life. How could my father not be in despair?

---

42 *Chtes to Vradhi sto Skotadhi*.rec. 1935.

## Chapter 6

## REFUGEES

Musician - Composer Yiannis Etseiridis[43] and friends at Piraeus.

As a young man I didn't follow politics and political parties. But still I remember the clashes between the Venizelists and the royalists. I read about them at the time. I'm a royalist.[44] I liked the monarchy. Venizelos, to Hell with him, he's the reason why Greece came to grief and we got the whole population of Asia Minor on our backs. His fault! He was never a patriot. If he had been, he shouldn't have made that three-man government in Constantinople, him and Koudouriotis, instead of staying here and keeping an eye on the war front we had in Asia Minor. No. One of them should have gone to Constantinople and the other should have formed his three-man thing over here. Who did he think he was going to beat? *These* guys? Wherever the Turks

---
43 Born in Pontus in 1893, Yiannis Eitziridis (Yovan Tsaous) came to Greece as a refugee after the Smyrna Catastrophe and settled in Piraeus.
44 Markos' royalist views are typical of the 'Old Greece' where he grew up. The Asia Minor refugees and people in the 'new territories' that Venizelos secured after the Balkan wars and the First World War, were far more likely to be 'Venizelists'.

caught them they slaughtered them.[45] I was reading about those things. I didn't talk about it with anyone because I was young and my friends weren't interested. Still, I remember the Catastrophe[46] and the refugees.

How can I make you understand what it was like? Disaster! There wasn't any place you could get away from seeing what had happened. People lived in disused railway carriages and old shacks or they put up makeshift tents. A catastrophe, I'm telling you pal, a massive disaster! I hope our eyes will never see such sights again! What those poor people went through is beyond anything. They were brought low, absolute rock bottom! That was after they'd already been screwed over by the Turks who drove them out. And when they got here, the same! They did whatever they could. They were screwed. They did everything you could possibly imagine to make a crust of bread and put a roof over their heads. If a father had five kids, even girls, they'd be out pilfering all over the place. A disaster, my God! What were the authorities to do? Who to start chasing first? You think it was just one or two? No, there were too many!

And the locals didn't look kindly on them. They never stopped cursing them, 'Hey scram!' or 'Hey you, get lost!' They wouldn't look at them. They didn't have enough love to say 'Hold on, these guys are our family, they're actually Greeks. Let's embrace them.' This didn't happen, not as far as I could see. Maybe somewhere else ... Our local thieves just wanted to do them over, filch whatever they had and laugh at them. Swindlers. In the course of time, they all

---

45 Markos' seems to be running two episodes together: the events of 1916 when Venizelos, Koudouriotis, admiral of the Greek navy, and Danglis set up a triumvirate in Thessalonica, (definitely *not* Constantinople), in opposition to King Constantine's government. Venizelos wanted to bring Greece into the war on the side of the allies while the pro-German Royalists wanted to preserve neutrality; secondly, the debacle of 1922 when the Greek army was driven back out of Anatolia to the coast.

46 The Catastrophe, also known as the Asia Minor Disaster, precipitated the calamitous influx of an estimated 1,500,000 destitute refugees. Venizelos was out of power and in exile in Paris at the time of the Greek army's ill fated incursion into Anatolia so can't justly be blamed for the disaster. In 1923 he represented Greece at the treaty of Lausanne where the exchange of populations was agreed.

managed to get to the places where they belonged. Some went to Thasos, others to Tripoli, some to Thessaloniki, others to Serres, Kavala, the islands, or the Dodecanese. Year by year they went their way. Now of course, they've shot ahead. All these refugees that you see are top at everything. They're hard workers. Onassis, for example, there's a guy you take notice of.

The refugees did a lot for music, that's for sure. When they came over from Asia Minor the musicians came too. These people were brought up to work hard and play hard, all of them without exception. A guy might work like a dog all week but come the weekend he'd be partying. He'd be out and about, making sure the world saw him. Not alone. He'd take his wife and daughters, his whole family and go sit in a music dive - just as our folk have learnt to do from being around the refugees. To start with, we had our own musicians here who played almost only *dhimotiko*[47] songs. Sometimes the odd *amanes*.[48] But when these guys came they started doing *tsifteteli*,[49] *syrto*, loads of things, *manedhes, tzivaeria, aivaliotika* ... not so much *laiko*[50] song. No, not *laiko*. Like I said, *laiko* song was what I did, but these guys were playing old music.

Their coming didn't make any difference to me. My thing was *laiko* song, the *zebekika* and *chasapika* which the great *koutsavakidhes* used to dance in Syros. Not that I'm saying *only* the *koutsavakidhes* danced them. No, *laiko* music struck a chord, deep in my soul. It understood what made me tick. I loved it. The refugees sang other Turkish stuff as well. Great music. Later when I was playing on the platforms I learnt to sing one or two Turkish songs: *Tsakitzi* and *Tsanakale*. I played them on my *bouzouki* and sang them. *Tsakitzi* is a heavy Turkish *zebekiko*, beautiful,

---

47 Traditional folk music. See glossary.
48 Vocal improvisation. See glossary.
49 The Greek 'belly dance' in 4/4 metre.
50 What we now generally call *rebetiko*. See glossary.

beautiful! I don't remember who exactly I learnt it from, but there were so many from Asia Minor. Like for instance Karipis, who also sang Turkish, Dalgas and Tomboulis. All of this though belongs to a later time when I became a musician.

## Chapter 7

## SLAUGHTERHOUSE

Before going for my stint in the infantry I left off being a docker and went to work as a skinner in the Piraeus slaughterhouse. Some relatives of mine were working there, among them Joseph Daelis who'd pulled me out of the water when we were boys in Syros. It was round about 1922-3, after quitting the docks, that I started working in the market at the butcher's shop of Paraschos Kondhylis. He was from Syros, one of us. The guy took me on in his shop, as an assistant to begin with, and later I used to go and do the slaughtering too. My pay was four hundred drachmas a month, but then it wasn't such heavy work, even if I did go through some horrors there as well. I'd had no particular training for this work as a skinner. When I first went there I didn't know how to do anything. I did what I could, swept the shop, cleaned up and ran errands.

Later on they took me to the slaughterhouse to dilate the carcasses either by mouth or hand bellows. We'd make a hole in the leg, stick the bellows in there and pump up the hide ready for flaying. I worked there with a guy called Aristeidhis. This job I'm telling you about, I was just the new boy. I pumped up the carcasses, hung them on meat hooks and when they'd been seen to I took them down from the hooks ready for sending to the shop.

Big stench in the slaughterhouse. Worse than the meat market because there was the stink of pissing and crapping all over the place, the works! We got used to this filth. I was young then. It didn't get to me at first.

Markos, worker at the slaughterhouse.

But when I got wise to it and saw what went on, how shitty it all was, I understood I wasn't the right guy for this kind of work. I felt terrible, really terrible. I was sorry for the animals. I said to myself: Here we go again, am I going to do this work till I die? Slaughtering? What kind of a person am

I! I felt for the poor beasts. I was miserable and I prayed to God he'd find me some kind of work where I'd have some peace, get away from this horror.

But I worked for years at the flaying job, from the age of twenty-three to thirty in the slaughterhouse of Piraeus and from thirty to thirty-five in the slaughterhouse at Athens. At my boss Kondhilis' shop we used to slaughter about thirty goats a day, four or five cows and fifteen to twenty pigs. Since I was dogsbody, I had to leave at one or two in the morning to go from Ayios Dionysos to Paraskeva Kondhilis' place. Then with Aristeidhis who was a trained butcher, I'd get the cows and pigs moving to the slaughterhouse near Lipasmata. We had to light fires for branding them, first the pigs and then the cows, because at eight or nine the vet came for the inspection. Once the vet had been we slaughtered the goats. At two we had to have cleaned up and taken the new order for the next night's slaughtering.

I quickly became a pro at skinning. I took care to learn the job and before long I was an ace worker. The skill, you see, was to split the slaughtered animal with the knife, clean it, cut it into four quarters and send it down to the shop ready for retail cutting. Once I'd become a skilled worker I didn't slaughter the lambs. Another apprentice who did the dilating slaughtered them and my job was to cut them open, hang them up and skin them. Then I'd have to clean them, pull out their innards, get the muck out from inside, chuck it away and prepare the carcass for putting on the rack on the iron hooks above to drain for two or three hours till the vet came to inspect.

Here's how each animal is slaughtered. With a sheep you grab it, throw it down, hold it with your foot and cut its throat with a knife. It twitches for about ten minutes. As soon as the throat is cut you hold it down with your foot for three minutes till it blacks out. Then it twitches on the ground by itself. Next, you dilate it for skinning. That's done by the guy with the bellows who opens up the hind quarters so I can get hold of it and it's opened up for me to punch. With my hand in a fist like this I punch it and take the whole skin off. And here on the chest we stab it with a knife a few times, because otherwise it doesn't come off in one piece as it should. We put it on the hook till the other foreman, if he was there, came to disembowel it, pull out the messy stuff, the guts, the bile, the piss from the bladder and that was that. With the goats it was the same, identical.

As for the bullocks, we used to take them from the pen to the slaughterhouse. We tied them up to a ring till it was time to slaughter them. When the time came, I'd take the bullock, tether it to the slaughtering hook and strike from above the horns on the nape of the neck. Down it went. The knife goes in under the head where the spinal column meets the brain. The beast falls down dead. Some of them twitch. Then you turn it over on its back and cut its throat. Since the next thing is to cut it up, you have pulleys and ropes attached to its hind legs. You pass them through a large hook and hang it up high so you can open up the belly, pull out the tripe and all the filthy stuff, clean it and skin it. This animal has to be flayed with the knife - the pump isn't used. After that we split it into four with the hatchet. Two thighs, two flanks and then it's ready for the butcher's, for the guy at the counter to cut up in the *tezaki* to sell for retail. The *tezaki* is the place with the chopping block where they hang the pieces on the hooks.

The stuff draining out would fall to the ground where there was a hole and from there the blood drained into the sea. At that time I used to go and hunt for sailors' trousers to wear, oilcloth or some tough kind of material like that. I wore a shirt too of the same stuff. That was to keep the blood from running through onto my clothes. Of course they got stained inside but not much. After, I'd take the clothes off and hang them up in the *kanara*. *Kanara* is what they called the place where we stashed away our tools, the hooks and so on. Every shop had its *kanara*.

Now for the pigs: we used to drive them down from the pens around two or three in the morning, while there was nobody much about and get them into the slaughterhouse. Some we put in a pen and others we put in the *kanara* where we had a huge copper kettle for the blanching. As soon as the water was boiling we seized the pigs one by one and slaughtered them. We took them by the hind legs, gave them a whack and down they fell. We held them down with one foot and the knife went in from gullet to heart, a long knife. While one was dying we moved onto the next one. We'd slaughter five to ten. We'd leave them on one side till they stopped breathing. It sometimes happened that a wild sow got in with the other pigs when they brought in the herds from the mountains. I've had that happen to me. I slaughtered a sow and she turned out to be pregnant, a couple of days maybe from giving birth. I pulled out the piglets alive and trotting! But they didn't live long because I'd pulled them out of their mother's split belly. How could they live when they hadn't been properly born? No way they could live longer than five or ten minutes or half an hour at the most. I was so sorry for them! We put the slaughtered animals to blanch in the boiling water, then hauled them out again by the armpits. The skin would be ready for cleaning and the hair came off in tufts. The only skin that needed doing all in one was the wild boar, the male you know. That one we skinned with a knife.

After all this slaughtering you can imagine the craving I felt as I headed off to the *tekes*. One time I ran to the 'Cave of Koulos' on a stretch of the coast in Drapetsona - 'Forbidden' they call it, ever since the time when two or three guys got eaten by a shark there. At 'Forbidden' there was a cliff where we used to climb down and go for a smoke. Lots of us hashish smokers used to go there for more peace and quiet so the cops wouldn't be on our tails. There was spring water there, slightly brackish, just a trickle. We used it to clean the *toubeki*, the quality fresh tobacco leaf – or, failing that, the *tzoures*, the used tobacco leaves which we took from the *kafeneion*. We also needed water to put in the *arghile*. Getting down to the cave to smoke was a very steep climb. It wasn't just anybody who could get down there, only a few of us who could manage it.

One day, round about the time the refugees began to arrive, tired after work, I went there longing to have a smoke all by myself. In those days the hashish was very strong, Turkish stuff from Proussa. As soon as I had the *arghile* ready to smoke in my hands, I took a deep drag on the straw. Suddenly I felt sick as a dog and everything went dim. I keeled over thinking, How will I climb up the cliff and get away? The *arghile* has 'bitten' me. A 'bite' means that the *arghile* has chewed you up big time. I was legless, flat out. You'll scarcely believe what I'm telling you, I couldn't lift so much as a finger. Paralytic! At last I crossed myself and set off crawling on all fours. I climbed all the way up that steep cliff and all the while from down below the other guys were shouting 'Hey Markos, you'll kill yourself! Wait first till you've recovered!'

It was about half past eight or nine and when I'd climbed the cliff and got to the top, I still couldn't stand up. I set off again crawling on all fours across the bare mountain till I got to a hollow just behind the cemetery at Anastasi,[51] a distance of about a mile. Now I found myself in yet another den full of *chasiklidhes* having a smoke, refugees from Tabouria. They didn't come to the cave where we Piraeans used to go. They had their own place; kept themselves to themselves. I got near them, still on my hands and knees. Somehow I needed the comfort of human voices. As soon as they saw me they were scared in case I was a cop or some other alarming

---

51 'Resurrection'. A big cemetery.

thing. Then they understood I was high as a kite and I'd 'bought it'. That's what the *manghes* used to say if something like this had happened to you: 'He bought it'. And boy, hadn't I just! Like some cretin, just imagine crawling along, spitting and dribbling and could I lift my head? No, it was all the way down there. I was puking too, a pathetic spectacle!

Among these guys there were thieves and pickpockets, you know, riffraff from Smyrna. But one of them was this guy called Boudroumis and he was the biggest daredevil of all the refugees. He was a real *koutsavakis*, a *palikari* and a true *mangas* in every sense of the word. Didn't hurt a soul. And he had a girlfriend too, this Armenian girl Pakoui, a dancer. They had a child together. The Piraeus police killed him some time before the war in Chiotika. He killed and wounded some of them but then he fell.

As soon as I got near them I lay there close by and threw up. Then I got sleepy, but I was afraid to fall asleep as I didn't know what might happen. Meantime I hear one of them say to the others 'Why don't we strip him? His clothes and shoes are new'. I was wearing my new blue suit, a watch and a ring and I had no strength to resist if they stripped me. But I could still hear what they were saying. The guy who said those words was a low-down specimen, I got to know him later. At that moment up gets Boudroumis and this is what he says, word for word, 'Hey you faggot! you lousy scumbag, how would you like to be in his place and have 'em treat you like that? Anyone who does this, I'll have his eyes out!' Seems he was the kind of guy whose word is law and so it was 'Okay Nikolaki'. End of discussion.

After the others had finished smoking and gone away, I was left alone fast asleep on the ground. Sometime between midnight and one in the morning I woke up and headed for home in a pitiful state. That was the first time I had such a bad trip with an *arghile*. My mother cried, my wife grumbled. I didn't feel like she was sorry for me, at all.

Round about 1934-5 I left Piraeus and went to Athens as the pay was better there and I had more work. I was paid by the piece, earning 1,300 drachmas a week. Workers' wages in Piraeus: three to five drachs for lambs, rams and goats. In Athens eight drachs for pigs, fifteen for cattle, three and a half for lambs. I was a specialist in lambs but while they'd be slaughtering fifteen lambs in Piraeus I was killing two hundred in Athens. In Piraeus there was a union but it wasn't taken seriously and that's why it was easy to get a lot of work there, but now I'll tell you how it came about that I left.

When I was working in the slaughterhouse in Piraeus I worked for a butcher shop called Peppa, the biggest butcher's in Piraeus market. Me and this other guy Katsikas were the shop slaughterers and we did all kinds of animals, pigs, goats, lambs, sometimes cows. They all belonged to Peppa. Sometimes there was a shortage of meat when we didn't have enough animals to slaughter. In the pens there was a calf we'd reared from a newborn. We fed it and it grew to be about 240 *okes*. That's how we measured weight back in those days. So one day the boss says to me 'We'll take it for slaughtering.' Of course, he had it for slaughtering, that's what it was for, but when he said this to me I was furious, utterly miserable. This calf I'd raised up from when it was first born, am I supposed to take it and slaughter it now? No way, this thing's just not going to happen! The calf knew me and whenever it saw me, it came up and licked me. Well, to cut a long story short, it loved me and I took it off to be slaughtered. It was about half an hour's journey from the pens in Tabouria to the slaughterhouse in Lipasmata. As soon as I got to the slaughterhouse I tied the calf up to the ring where they tied the cattle, but he got the wind up and started bellowing and mooing. I felt so sorry for him; every step of the way I suffered with him. I tied him to the hook and stuck in the knife at the crown of the head, as you do when you kill those animals. Down it falls. What can I say! I mean it's the first time I ever saw such a thing in my life! The animal cried inconsolably, tears pouring out of its eyes. I threw down the knife and I said to the boy I had there 'You slaughter it. I'm not laying hands on that animal again!' So I went down and had a fight with the boss. He was a sick man, had TB, a complete wreck. 'Aren't you ashamed to slaughter a helpless animal in this cowardly way? What did the poor beast ever do to you? So what if you couldn't find meat to give everyone! Couldn't you just *not* give it them for one week! Did we have to slaughter it?' So we had a row and after that I stopped doing this job. I went to the slaughterhouse in Athens.

In Athens the union was better. They'd organized it so that we didn't have to run out to the pens to fetch the animals. There were some herdsmen who brought them to the slaughterhouse and shut them up in the *kanara* ready for the skinner and the butcher. Across the way from the slaughterhouse there were some cattle pens where they put the animals if they didn't all fit. I worked at the shop of Karkanias in the Athens Market with a guy called Pilaf Panayotis, - he was in charge and it was thanks to him, I guess, that I got up and left for the recording studios.

Sometimes, if there weren't many animals I didn't do skinning or flaying. I didn't lift a finger. Instead I had my *bouzouki*. The union had everything nicely set up. They had a shed where we put all the clothes, rags and knives. That was where we hid my *bouzouki* too. So I'd sit and play while the others did the skinning and whatever the group earned – it was usually three men and a boy – we divided into four. The boy didn't get the same as the men. He pumped up the skins and I guess he'd have got two or three *dekaras*[52] per

---

52 A silver ten-cent piece.

skin. I was loafing around in that place. Fact is, the other guys were all hashish smokers too. We'd put together an *arghile* in there and we'd smoke. *Bouzouki* and flaying. Fifty to a hundred animals. The boss, Pilaf Panayotis, would say to me: 'Markos, you play *bouzouki*, we'll do the work'. So that's what I did. Things were pretty good there. Everyday we started at about 6.30 am and clocked off about three in the afternoon. A good crowd of butchers, pretty much all of them *manghes*. I had other things going on there too, other bits of business, you know, going round the *tekedhes* playing music.

## Chapter 8

## THE ARMY

At the age of twenty, working as a skinner by then, I was called up for the military. Some people only start living when they get to the army, but by the time I'd reached the age of military service I already had an adventure-packed life behind me. I was assigned to the thirty-fourth infantry regiment, first battalion, third company, with Evstratios Kaloudhis for my company commander, brother of the bookseller on Filon Street. My battalion was above Korydhallo and the sergeant major of my company was Georgios Raitsis.

I went into the army with a good will but all the same I didn't forget my recent way of life. Old habits die hard. I went on smoking. I used to go down to Kokkinia. That's where the refugees were. Whatever you wanted you'd find it there, no problem. To start with they put me on manoeuvres. I had a strong tendency to absenteeism. Every evening I sneaked off home - from Korydhallo to Tabouria was walking distance. On the road I took to get to Tabouria there was a limekiln and that's where a whole lot of down at heel *chasiklidhes* used to gather. I'd smoke my *arghile* and then, stoned out of my mind, I'd head for home. I was newly married too. Present in the morning but absent at evening roll call.

At that time I loved a gypsy girl. A beauty, but they're filthy women. These gypsies were both very faithful *and* complete whores. She sure loved me: 'Markos, Oh Markos, my *bouzouki* boy' ... This gypsy was married and she even had four children. She did the rounds with her husband selling cloth or something like that. For some reason, I don't know what it was, she and her husband had quarrelled. I lived in the same neighbourhood, in Tabouria. She'd fixed up a tent to live in and my house was down the road from there. She wasn't a Greek gypsy, more like a Spanish one and her husband was a gypsy too.

So this broad, I don't know how it happened but she'd made up her mind to split from her husband. She headed for the hills. There was this place where we *chasiklidhes* used to go and smoke, far away from everyone. I happened to bump into her there. Some guy was trying to take her and set her up in a house. Lord rest him, he's dead now. As soon as he saw me he recognized me, he wouldn't leave me alone: 'Hey Markos, what kind of a broad is she?'

'She lives in my neighborhood, she's got four kids. Have you screwed her?'

'No way! She played real hard to get. She tells me she has a boyfriend.'

I was smoking and she came and sat next to me. I didn't know she was a hashish smoker too. I was about ready to get up and leave. I was a soldier after all. I was playing *bouzouki* too, because we had one hidden in the *tekes*. 'Get up', she said to me, 'Let's go up the mountain to some quiet spot.' So off we went and I fucked her there on the mountainside. But I was sorry for her. She had four kids. I used to say to her, 'Hey bitch, aren't you sorry for your husband and your kids?' For about a fortnight or three weeks that's where I kept heading, up the mountain. The *manghes* used to go as well. They wanted to screw her too, but she wouldn't go with any of them. Time came when she'd had enough. I couldn't give her anything extra. I kept telling her to go and settle down, go back with her man, but she didn't want to, not for anything! She went down to Piraeus, got on a boat and she was gone. God knows where she went to. I lost her. Never saw her again. A beautiful woman. So, after two or three weeks her husband comes to the *kafeneion*, lays hold of me and says 'Markos, maybe you know where Liza is?'

'I don't know' says I, 'where Liza is. Does Liza belong to me?'

'But some guys told me she hitched up with you.'

'I'm a soldier,' says I to him, 'Can't you see that? Why are you talking to me now about Liza?'

What was I to say to him? From then on she was never heard of again ... a great looking woman. I'd seen women aplenty but this one sure lingered in the mind. She used to dance on the mountain. Sultry Spaniard.

In the army we had thirty or forty days of exercises. I liked gymnastics. I was top of the class, though stoned more often than not. During this month I was sent for the first time for three days detention and they even sent me to jail. That sure was a dreamy place for me, a place to do whatever I felt like. First and most important thing was that I had my *baglama* with me. I smoked, I fixed things up, got hold of stuff. What with being stoned and all, I thought it was fun reading the army regulations in there. When the time came for the selection of corporals and sergeants, they wanted me to be a corporal and even told me to be a jail warden. I didn't like the sound of that so I started to play up. I got so uppity, I didn't take any notice of sergeant or captain or anything. My company, third company, became a platoon of corporals and I stayed on as a private.

In the corporals' exams I knew it all since I'd read the regulations but my behaviour was an obstacle to promotion. At one point, during the exams when they were testing these guys, my sub-lieutenant Evangelos Kouris says: 'If I get Vamvakaris up he'll make a laughing stock out of all of you.' Sure enough, he put me a question and I had it off pat. In front of four hundred corporals he comes up, shakes my hand. 'Well done Vamvakaris, that's the kind of soldier I want. My good fellow, what's to stop you being a good soldier? Now all these men will become corporals and you'll stay a private. What a shame they'll become sergeants and you'll just stay where you are!' I felt a tightness in my heart, but I had the idea and I still have it, that the cursed drug was filling my head with *bouzouki* and song writing. And it was impossible for me to put anything else ahead of the *bouzouki*.

Like I said, song-writing. That had already begun. It got started in the detention cell. I wrote my first songs in there, ones I later recorded: *Eprepe na'rchosouna Manga mes Ston Teke mas*[53] and *Charmanis Eimai ap'to Proi*[54] and five or ten others. I kept these songs at home as a memento but back then I hadn't yet put music to them. Like I said, I'd written my very first songs in Syra before I even learnt the instrument.

I was a regular in the detention cell. Whether it was for punishment or not I was happy to go there. I was peaceful in there. I didn't give a damn about anything: being let out or being a soldier; women, mother, father ... couldn't care less. Stoned. I loved being alone, I didn't want anybody else in there. Now and then they'd bring in some guy and I'd do what I could to put him straight, like a teacher - but not of my bad habits. No. I acted wise and sensible. The other kids were prepared to listen to me because of my smart brain and experience. They loved me.

I didn't encourage the other guys to be like me. If I felt someone showed a tendency that way, I used to say to him 'Look here, don't come back. If you do I'll have your eyes out! Don't you see what I've been through? Be good. Then you'll be let out.' But I used to hang out with people of my own sort, a cool bunch of dudes. They were mighty fond of me. The whole regiment loved me and lots of guys got hold of me on the side, to talk things over. The officers of the battalion and of the regiment, both of the higher and lower ranks, with just a few exceptions, loved me like a best buddy.

---

53 '*Mangas* You Should've Come to our *Teke*'.
54 'I've Been Dry Since Morning'.

I remember one incident that happened in the slaughterhouse of Piraeus with a vet called Pepa. He used to come there and he wanted me to stand to attention. He knew I was a soldier and that I was absent without leave, there in the slaughterhouse. He knew too from civilian life what a cheeky bastard I was. One morning, I don't remember exactly what he'd said to me, but I treated him to some choice epithets and as this guy had an uncle who was the garrison commander, he went and reported the whole thing to him. Next day the garrison commander sends ten guards to the slaughterhouse and they seal it off on all sides, Sergeant Nikolas Dalezios in command. But the boys knew me. They knew what a devil I was. Not only did they not catch me, they even covered up for me!

After five or ten days this business of mine had created quite a stir at the garrison. They kept coming for me and going away empty-handed. In the end I felt there was nothing for it but to turn myself in and put an end to the business. I headed off for the garrison under my own steam and arrived there one morning toward ten, at Tsamadhos Street. I was climbing up the steps when the sentry saw me. He completely lost it.

'Hell Vamvakaris!' he says to me, 'We've been shaking out heaven and hell to catch you and now you just breeze in all by yourself!' To which my reply was:

'Shush. Don't talk!'

The garrison commander was so furious he'd sent me a strict twenty-day detention, which I later heard in the regimental order of the day. But so what!

As soon as I got to the office, out came the adjutant:

'What do you want?' says he.

'You're looking for me.'

'What's your name?'

'Markos Vamvakaris.'

He was speechless. He seized me by the throat and laid into me. He was a good guy, as I soon understood. I didn't flinch through all the shouting and cursing. At last he simmered down.

'Hold on now, I'm handing you over to the Garrison Commander.'

The garrison commander was savage. I didn't say a word. They shut me in the lockup. At that time the garrison authorities were running around picking up deserters and draft dodgers, various flakey individuals. They kept bringing them to the prison. For most of the first night though, I was alone. There was a window in there but I didn't climb out of it. Round about three in the morning they brought in Michalos the *teketzis* from Piraeus.

'Hell, Markos!' he said, 'Dammit! They got me.'

'Hell, Yiannis what's the charge?'

'Draft dodger. How'm I going to get out of here? I've got to get out. I'm in deep shit.'

'See this little window … ? Don't look at me though, I'm staying put. I want to get clear.' After a while they brought in another draft dodger, Georgios Palakas, a right little number this one too. They both slipped out together and Michalos left me his hat, a new borsalino which I kept. Some others came too who I didn't know.

In the morning when they open up the prison, they find two are missing. The sergeant reports it and they come badgering me: 'How did they get away? When?'

'If I'd seen them I'd have gone too.'

They started ranting and raving. I asked them to send me back to my regiment. They started on at me:

'Damn it, Vamvakaris! Aren't you ashamed they gave you the slip?' I had quite a name for myself even there. Since I was driving them nuts telling them to pack me off back to my battalion, the day came at last, after about ten days, when they sent me back. I got there and started doing my usual thing.

I remember a captain by the name of Ioannis Zacharakis who advised me to sit tight and behave so I could get my discharge. In fact I liked the army, quite wished I could stay for good! I didn't pay much attention to what he said. He could see I wasn't shaping up, that was for sure. Then he gave up on me, like I didn't exist. I forgot to say that when they called me up they provided me with the usual kit, including my own weapon, a new *Mannlicher Schonauer*. I saw it and thought it was a shame such a useless individual as me should own such a thing. After two or three months had passed they had an inspection and found my rifle exactly as it was when it came out of the depot.

As soon as the lieutenant saw the rifle with all that grease still on it he clapped hands on me and yelled, 'What's this shambles! Why don't you clean your rifle?' I had absolutely no idea of saving my own skin! I said to him: 'Mr lieutenant, however many inspections you do, you'll find it the same and even worse. Please let me put it back into storage.' That wasn't going to happen though, and since I felt sad about it and didn't want to be called a disgrace, I started giving two or three spliffs to one of my fellow soldiers on the understanding he'd clean the rifle for me. I gave him very strict instructions: 'You're going to make it shine like Ayios Charalambis!'[55]

After the garrison commander returned me to my battalion I soon found myself back in the cell. Since I was a hardened and hopeless case, I didn't bother with anybody except those who treated me nicely. They brought in a prison guard called Kotsakos from Corinth. He came along one evening and played lion. He wanted to tame me. He

---

[55] St Charalambos, one of the earliest Christian martyrs, whose name is a compound of 'Joy' and 'Shining light'.

said a thing or two and I gave it him back even worse. 'We'll see about that tomorrow,' says he.

'Fuck you and your prison!' I replied.

So along he comes next day to give me a 'haircut'. If I'd let that happen to me I'd have lost my untamable badass reputation. I'd have had to take a beating. The barber knew me. He wasn't setting foot in the cell.

'Go on' says Kotsakis, 'or I'll report you to the battalion.'

Then I swung round and said to Kotsakis:

'Pah! Why give orders to that poor devil! If they made you a prison guard that ought to mean you're a man. But you're a *woman*! How about you take the razor yourself and give me a haircut, hey?'

Divine inspiration. Kotsakis backed down. Nothing happened. I'd made up my mind, no matter what, to hit him if he came anywhere near me.

By now we were getting to the point where it was time to get discharged. I'd served a fourteen-month term, I'd brought nothing to the army and been one hell of a bum, not interested in anything except my *bouzouki* and my hash. I had a complete lack of respect for anyone after so many lock-ups, detentions, visits to the garrison commander's office and what not, but I still had the cheek to want my discharge papers.

Like I said, there were some officers in the regiment who hated me and others who had a soft spot for me. In the ranks I was very fair and totally okay with the other guys. I'd won the affection of my fellow soldiers. At that time up at Profitis Elias we had some fountains with running water. Everyone round there suffered from the lack of water and every morning outside the gate of the battalion headquarters a gang of little boys and girls gathered with their pitchers to fetch a bit of water. As I was hanging about there one day, lying on the ground, I saw a pitiful sight. The soldier who was guarding the fountain let the kids come up for water.

But when they got to the tap he took out a whip and lashed them on the legs. Across the courtyard was the battalion headquarters. A major in charge of accounts saw the whole scene from the window and before he'd had time to shout, I'd already leapt up with a shovel. It was aimed at the guard's head. 'Hey you!' says I to him, 'drop that whip and leave the kids alone!' So the guy drops it. I put down the shovel, pick up the whip and thrash him with it. 'How do you like that eh?' The major who was watching shouted down from up there: 'Good for you Vamvakaris!' From then on I had the greatest respect for him even if I had no dealings with the man. Because of this thing I did, my name was on everybody's lips. I'd done it without a second thought. Never paused to think whether I'd be punished.

Three days later the regimental adjutant instructed his bugler to summon my sergeant major. He told him to bring me over. I'd never met the adjutant before, so off I go to his office. I salute like a proper soldier and stand to attention. 'At ease' says he, 'Take a seat'. He rings a bell, tells a soldier to bring a couple of coffees.

'I've often heard that you play a little tiny *bouzouki*. What do they call that?'

'*Baglamadhaki.*'

'Ah, so that's the *baglama* they talk about. It sounds so sweet eh? Will you come one day, bring it with you and we'll shut ourselves up in my office. We'll invite the deputy governor so you can play a little.'

'At your service, adjutant, sir.'

'Vamvakaris, I gather you also smoke a bit of 'black'. That's what I've heard.'

I answered on the level.

'Yes, adjutant, sir.'

He pulls out of his pocket a nickel twenty-drachma piece.

'How much is it for a dram?'

'Fifteen drachmas.'

'Keep the extra *taliro* and drink a coffee. It's on me.'

I saluted and left. About a week later I was feeling down in the mouth. I went and asked him 'Is there some way I can go home and then come back at whatever time you tell me to in the morning?' He says to me 'Be here at roll call.' So that's what happened. He called me to the office a few days later. Little by little the adjutant and I became friends and I let him know that I was married and had children - not that I did of course, not even one! - I was suffering and so on and so forth. Now we started thinking how to arrange my discharge from the army, even though I had two year's worth of detentions and imprisonments stacked up. Later on, having reached a confidential agreement with the regimental deputy commander, the adjutant says to me:

'Will you do whatever we tell you to get your discharge?'

'Yes.'

'Some day soon the garrison commander's fiancée is going to come here. Since you're such a headstrong type, barge your way into his office. When he sees you he'll be dumbstruck.'

I did as he advised me. I burst in and saluted him in faultless military style. As soon as he saw me the garrison commander got into a state, his head began to twitch. His fiancée turned to him and said:

'Christos, who is this?'

'You see this man, he's the most lamentable soldier in my regiment.'

'Is he a thief?'

'No.'

'What is he Christos?'

'He doesn't stay even for one day, in his company. He's a regular absconder and he's ruined my regiment.'

'As long as he's not a thief' says the girl, 'he'll be fine. Everything can be forgiven.'

Then I got started on my rules and regs.

'The honourable garrison commander finds fault with me for being absent but I've read my soldier's handbook. I happen to be married. One article says that when a regiment is stationed in the same area as a soldier's home, the soldier is allowed leave to go sleep at his own place. And I've got two children.' I didn't even have cats! Says the garrison commander, 'Oh yeah, so you're the kind of guy we can allow to go home and you'll be back next day? You'll go to work in the slaughterhouse and start a rumpus! Didn't I tell you to sit tight and behave yourself if you wanted your discharge? I've reached the point where I've a good mind to send you on detachment to Samos to sort out the Yiayias brothers.'[56]

Then his fiancée said to him again:

'Christos, all that belongs in the past. He's got guts this soldier. Seems good-hearted too. I like his style. You simply *must* let him go, Christos, you can manage it somehow.'

Says I: 'Sir, garrison commander, the only way you can discharge me is by commuting incarceration to custody. Do it and I can't thank you enough. Happy Wedding!' I made my exit. Outside the door was my friend the adjutant and the major, the deputy administrator. I told them what happened. The major said: 'Hey Markos we love you, but once you've got your discharge are you still going to come and see us or are you a friend only till you get away?'

At last the time came for my discharge. They called me to the administrator's office and gave me my papers on which it said I'd done fourteen months service. I went home in civvies and began to fix up a house so I could settle down.

---

56 Refers to the 'kinima ton Yiayiadhon' i.e. 'the Yiayias brothers' Movement' 6th June 1925 when the Yiayias brothers, described by the Greek government as a bunch of brigands, tried to set up Samos as an independent state. They are celebrated by the *rebetiko* composer Kostas Roukounas in his song of 1936, a tsamiko: *Stis Samou ta Perichora* – 'In the Outskirts of Samos'.

# Chapter 9

## WRECKAGE

I hadn't had any children so far and that was my wife's fault. Not being able to hand on my father's name was a great sadness for me. Caused a lot of heartache.

| Wreckage[57] | Καραβοτσακίσματα |
|---|---|
| Bitterness and torture, | Βάσανα πίκρες φαρμάκια |
| Broken up with misery | καραβοτσακίσματα ω! |
| Like a rock lashed | Σαν το βράχο που τον δέρνουν |
| By the waves of the sea, | της θάλασσας τα κύματα. |
| | |
| Am I to blame you make me sore? | Τι φταίω και με παιδεύεις |
| Oh what is it you're looking for? | αχ τι γυρεύεις |
| There's someone else | κι αλλον λατρεύεις; |
| That you adore. | Δε μ'αγαπάς αχ πές μου το |
| You don't love me, go on say it! | γιατ' είμαι μόρτης φουκαράς. |
| I'm the riff raff, a poor sod. | Θα σβήσω πια δε θα ζήσω |
| I'll switch my lights out, go and die. | δε θ'αγαπήσω, θα λησμονήσω |
| I won't love you and I'll try | στα καραβοτσακίσματά μου |
| To forget. No don't laugh yet, | μη γελάς. |
| At such a poor old broken rod. | |
| | |
| At home they scold me cos of you, | Μες στο σπίτι μου για σένα |
| And say harsh words, a bitter brew. | όλοι με μαλώνουνέ ω! |
| | λένε ζόρικες κουβέντες |
| | που με φαρμακώνουνε. |

Little by little I started not going to work. My *bouzouki* came before everything. It was my great passion. For the *bouzouki* I pushed aside all other kinds of work. Like I said, I started not going anywhere and not earning money. It was my poor wretched father who took the brunt of it all. He put food on the table for me and my wife. The trouble he

---

57 *Karavotsakismata, chasapiko*, rec. 1935.

had with me, don't even ask! I was the oldest son after all, the one he might have expected a helping hand from, like every parent expects to get some kind of comfort from his children. As if that weren't enough I was doing the other stuff too. I was hooked on hashish. There was never a time when I didn't have the shakes, as I later wrote in my song *Charmanis Eimai ap'to Proi*.[58] I was always stoned. I didn't take any kind of liquor, just the 'black'. I mean I was a *chasiklis* through and through. I made the rounds of all the *tekedhes*, both in Athens and Piraeus, that's how I passed my time. Seems like it was written on my cards, the hand I was dealt in this crazy world. Talk about misery! We'd hit rock bottom and it was all down to *bouzouki* and hashish. But with the *bouzouki* I was a big hit. Wherever I went they gathered round and listened and I always held on to the hope of seeing better times, me and my *bouzouki*.

*If God is Kind to Me*[59]

One day if God is kind to me
I'm going to make some dough
I'll build a fancy music hall
And set up quite a show,

To lure the loaded customers,
The ditsy girls, the glitz,
With frothy arghiledhes
All prepared by Billy Fritz.

And Greta Garbo, trust me pal,
Will light up the tsibouki,
And in the corner Jean Kepouras
Playing on bouzouki,

*Αν μ' Αξιώσει ο Θεός*

Αν μ' αξιώσει ο Θεός
λεφτά και αποχτήσω
θα χτίσω ένα μέγαρο
τους πλούσιους να ελκύσω.

Θα 'ρχόντουσαν πελάτες μου
κορίτσια να 'χουν τρέλες
κι ο Βίλλυ Φριτς θα σκάρωνε
αφράτους αργιλέδες.

Κ'η Γκρέτα Γκάρμπο μάγκα μου
θ' ανάβει το τσιμπούκι
κι ο Ζακ Κεπούρας στη γωνιά
θα παίζει το μπουζούκι.

---

58 'I've Been Dry Since Morning'.
59 *An m'Axiosei o Theos*, rec. 1935.

*For look-out, Jimmy Londos,*
*Champion muscle man, the tops!*
*Lilian Harvey will be there as well*
*To chuck out women cops.*

*Κι ο Τζίμι Λόντος για νταής*
*θα κάθεται στις τσίλιες*
*κι η Λίλιαν η Χάρβεϊ*
*θα διώχνει τις μπασκίνες.*

*A mosque I'll build for dervishes*
*To pass the time of day,*
*And chicks'll roll up in their swanky*
*Open top coupé.*

*Πρέπει να χτίσω ένα τζαμί*
*για όλα τα δερβίσια*
*και με κουμπέ πολίτικο*
*να 'ρχονται τα κορίτσα.*

Around that time people kept buttonholing my father: 'How did your son turn into such a lousy good for nothing?' The pain he must have felt, God rest his poor old bones, doesn't bear thinking about! Before he died people went and said to him: 'Your son Markos plays good *bouzouki*. Have you heard him?' And my father would say: 'No I haven't heard him.' I had so much respect for him. I didn't want to break his heart because I knew how worried he was about us and about me having taken a wrong turn. From time to time he had a word with me and then I'd say to him 'Don't worry, Papa. I'll get back on track. I'll get back to how I was before. The day will come I'll have three hundred drachma notes under my pillow. That's what I'll get every day and I won't be working. I'll be sitting around with my *bouzouki*'.

'That's what they all tell me. That you're playing *bouzouki*.'

'The *bouzouki*'s what brought me to this.'

Of course he was my parent and I spoke nicely to him. You can't imagine how respectfully I spoke to my father. Oh boy! I don't see this sort of thing now. Yes of course, my kids now, they love me and all that, but still, what I felt for my father and how I spoke to him, I've not seen anything like that so far in my children. I wanted to make him happy and not have any worries because of me, because he wasn't a well man. He died young at the age of only forty-four. Boy did he love us! He ran around day and night, into the hills, into the valleys to make money, to provide for us when we were little. A good father. And as for my mother? I can't begin to tell you how good she was, how clever ... everything about her. My mother loved me too. I was the first you know, and I'd turned out unlucky with my marriage, being married to that dreadful woman. Mama was eaten up with the misery of it. She was the only woman who took my wife to task. My wife said to her, 'If you just turned a blind eye you'd be fine.' Then my mother would say: 'When it's my son we're talking about, how am I going to turn a blind eye?' Mama ... Lord rest her soul. She suffered. What with me being a lay-about, and then there was Frangiskos, who was in and out of prison every other minute. Like I said, he drank too much and got himself a scary reputation. A hell-raiser. He pulled knives, got into fights. Hard as nails. Didn't listen to anyone, neither his father nor his mother. He came and went as it suited him with never a word to anybody. I mean sometimes he'd just disappear, maybe a month at a time, come back empty-handed with not even one drachma to help his family. He didn't give a damn - rotten apple through and through. He used to get changed, put on clean clothes that his mother washed for him, then off again!

Imagine what my poor father went through, still supporting his oldest son, a married man too, and with another son who didn't give a damn about anything. The sadness and trouble ate into his vitals every day. Two strapping lads and both, good for nothing. Our mother had to bear it too, had to hear a whole load of filthy language from her two older boys, the ones she expected to see some help from. It was trouble on top of trouble, a miserable life.

An even worse blow was the second son Leonardhos who'd gone crazy and we couldn't keep him off the streets. Everyone made fun of him. My parents suffered so much as he'd got into this terrible state at the age of only seventeen. What doctors didn't they take him to? Clinics, psychiatrists, just everywhere, even to some bogus old witches who said they could make him better. There was the girl too, Grazia, seventeen years old who worked at the factory and brought something home but not much, no help at all really - a good girl though and very decent. Plus another little girl, Rosa aged six, who needed looking after. They lived a life of poverty and every day brought more worries.

Like I said, I didn't mind about anything except my *bouzouki.* I kind of knew it would do me proud one day. But I couldn't face my father because he was a very upright sort of man. When I saw him, no matter what he said to me I couldn't get a word out in reply. I loved him like no one else ever loved their father, with tenderness and respect. My heart bled for him. They told him my wife was going to the bad and he could see she wasn't much of a wife to me. We boys just about worried him to death and sure enough he went to an early grave.

He died one day in 1930 at the age of only forty-four. He loved us and everybody loved him, all the folks who'd ever had anything to do with him. The shopkeepers of Athens and Piraeus loved him because he made them baskets - he still did that work over here. They knew what a thoroughly good guy he was, a man who looked after his family. Rich people knew him, guys with money. His three bosses here sent a coffin each! 'Dhomenikos Rokos has died' they said, 'Let's send him a casket.' So one arrived and then another, then another again! You can figure out from that what kind of a man he was. God rest his dear soul. We buried him at Anastasi in Piraeus, the place where I started playing later on. The poor guy left behind two orphaned daughters and a boy, Argyris, six months old in his mother's arms. He got some peace at last. It was written on his cards, I guess. He didn't live long enough to see me playing on the gramophones and making money, like, you know, I'd always said to him: 'Papa, you'll see, the time will come I'll free you up from all the work you do. You'll sit around and I'll look after you.'

My poor mother worked in the factory and so did the girl. From time to time I gave them some money if I had it. My mother too was up there with my father, a model and an example. She loved all her children, a very good mother, the soul of honour. She wouldn't put up with any tittle-tattle about me; wouldn't hear it. When the time came for the older girl to get married they found a decent guy and so she set Grazia on the right path. That was a weight off her shoulders. I always did right by my brother-in-law and sister as much as I could - I mean I helped because her husband was hard up but a good guy. So the girl had a family and lived a very decent life.

The thing that got *me* down was this broad I'd married, the slut. I loved my wife like crazy. I was devoted to her and I wouldn't hear anything from anybody. Filthy bitch. I never expected such a thing from this woman. I'd run off with her, it was for love I married her. Here's what happened. I was out of work and everyone at home was suffering badly. I went to a friend of mine and told him my troubles. He was a fellow Syran, a distant relative. He helped me all right but he had something else in mind. He wasn't a man of honour. He was a thorough scumbag. That became clear from what happened later. My wife, cheap little number, took a shine to him. Less said the better! No need to spell out the obvious. First time a friend took advantage of my bad luck. He handed me a glass of water. Turned out to be poison.

*Self Interest*[60]

*If your pocket is empty*
*Don't look to another*
*No one will care for you,*
*Even your mother.*

*Το Συμφέρον*

*Όταν δεν έχει η τσέπη σου,*
*κανείς δε σε κοιτάζει,*
*ούτε η μάνα σε πονεί*
*ούτε σε λογαριάζει.*

---

60 *To Symferon*, rec. 1954.

*Oh pocket, stay full*
*And you'll have no fear.*
*No one can give you*
*What isn't there.*

*And if, when you're poor,*
*Some guy offers to lend*
*He'll stick in the knife,*
*Not act as a friend.*

*Self interest*
*And a well stuffed purse*
*Have always governed*
*The universe.*

*Τσέπη μου γεμάτη να 'σαι*
*και κανέναν μη φοβάσαι,*
*τσέπη μου γεμάτη να 'σαι*
*και κανένα μη φοβάσαι.*

*Άμα δεν τα 'χεις δεν μπορεί*
*κανένας να στα δώσει,*
*κι αν θα σου δώσει μια φορά,*
*βαθειά θα σε πληγώσει.*

*Στον κόσμο το συμφέρον πια*
*τα κανονίζει όλα,*
*παντού τα πάντα κυβερνά*
*αυτό κι η πορτοφόλα*

My wife was a slut and I didn't say a word to anyone. Poor devil, I didn't want to lose face in the neighbourhood. If anybody wanted to speak to me he was wasting his time. I'd gone to the dogs as well. Meanwhile I'd tell her 'You're heading for the gutter' Every day I had scenes with the bitch. Things went from bad to worse.

## Chapter 10

## BOUZOUKI AND THE TEKES

In Tabouria I was broken in to the hard life of the Piraeus docker, I fell in love, got married for the first time and got hooked on hashish. But the most important thing by far was that I went crazy over this instrument, the *bouzouki*. Just before my stint in the army late in 1924, I happened to hear *barba* Nikos from Aivali playing his *bouzouki*. I loved it so much I made a vow, if I didn't learn *bouzouki* I'd chop my hand off with a meat cleaver, the bone chopper they use in the shop. I considered my oath sacred and binding. It's such a great thing, such a great instrument this *bouzouki*, I said to myself, and that was the beginning of misery for my family, my father and mother. I stopped work altogether after that. I had a job as a skinner in the Piraeus slaughterhouse but I didn't work. No. My work was only *bouzouki* and hashish. From then on this instrument held me in chains. There was nothing else for me in the world.

But it wasn't the first time I'd heard it. Apart from the *gaida* my dad used to play a bit of *bouzouki*, just a little. Even in Syros as a boy, I heard many old *bouzouki* players. Manolakis, Trisimisis from Upper Hora, Stravogiorgis the blind man, Maoutsos, Andrikakis, the barbers Vafeas and Karayiannis and Pankalakis who played excellent *tzoura*.[61] I heard all these guys playing there when I was too young to have any idea about this sort of thing, and others I heard here in the *Tekedhes*. The one called Vafeas was one of my clan, a Frankosyran from Upper Chora. He was a barber and I used to go to his shop. I mean, even then it was clear that I liked the instrument. I used to walk from Skali, where we lived, to Gourna twenty minutes away just to hear this guy when it was his usual time to play in the *kafeneion*. He

---

61 An instrument resembling *bouzouki* but smaller - though not as small as a *baglama*.

played *taximia*.⁶² There wasn't much in the way of folk songs in Syros, just the odd *syrto*, the odd *kalamatianos* handed down from father to son.

I'd seen and heard all this stuff in Syra, but when I heard *barba* Nikolas Aivaliotis, the instrument took me over. In Syra when I was young, about ten or twelve years old, my father had made friends with this guy Nikos Aivaliotis who played *bouzouki*. He used to play *taximia*, heavy Turkish *zebekika* and *manedhes*, that sort of thing. He used to sing too but I don't remember the songs. Round about that time Aivaliotis killed a guy and went to prison for ten years at Anapli. After he got out he lived in Piraeus and came to find us. One evening my father said to him 'Nikos, why don't you bring your *bouzouki* and we'll sit and have a glass of wine?' He wasn't much of a wine drinker but he was the man for a party and he loved *bouzouki*. So Nikos came one evening and I happened to be at home. From the moment I heard the first *penies*⁶³ of Aivaliotis, who's still alive by the way, a fisherman in the Piraeus Fish Market, I was struck dumb!

Six months after my father brought him to our house, me and Aivaliotis, this guy who'd inspired me with such a passion, ran into each other one evening at Michalis' *teke* in Chiotika. Being an old jailbird he used to hang out in the *tekedhes* like me. By then I'd already learnt to play so well that when he came in and heard me he was astonished. In just six months I'd become the best, a proper wild beast on the instrument. Being the younger man I was very respectful in his presence. The minute he sat down I gave him the *bouzouki* and I said to him 'Take it *barba* Nikolas, you play.' But before coming in he'd been sitting there outside for about five minutes listening. He liked my playing so much

---
62 Instrumental improvisations usually in the mode of the song that is to follow, but also played on their own.
63 *Penia* meant the action of striking the strings with your *penna* i.e. plectrum. In old recordings the singer can sometimes be heard shouting 'bravo' to someone's 'lovely *penia*' (*penies* is the plural).

and he didn't even know it was the son of his friend who was playing. 'My boy, what am I supposed to play? *You* play. Let me hear you, you play so well. Play us a *taximaki* or a neat *zebekiko*, because I sure do like your style.'

In these six months I'd learnt to play so well but meantime I hadn't even figured out how to tune my *bouzouki*. Aivaliotis used to come sometimes to the *teke* I went to and so did a guy called Mimikos Boyatzis who also played and if they came along then I got it tuned. At that time various old *bouzouki* players used to come, Yannis Yalias,[64] who's still alive and lives in Chatzikyriakeio, a guy called Alekaki, the best *bouzouki* at that time, but not up to my standard. There was another guy from Athens called Manetas and a printer called Georghios Skourtis. All of these were good *bouzouki* players at that time. There were lots of them but especially one Apostolis Zoumaritis. Very good *bouzouki* but a very bad man. I used to study his playing because he played very well, for all he was a vicious drunk. One day, just outside Syngrou Prison in some ramshackle taverna, we ran into each other. He was playing and since he'd heard there was a certain Markos from Syros playing very good *bouzouki* in Piraeus, and he happened to hear me, he got jealous and he says 'Hey you piece of baggage, didn't I tell you, when I'm playing, get lost!' Being a pig-headed sort of kid I didn't take any notice of what he said and I didn't leave either, even if that meant we had a bit of a scuffle and people had to pull us apart. In the end it was he who left. This was the first time I realized there's a lot of envy in this business.

Like I said, I learnt the instrument in six months. Nobody gave me lessons on *bouzouki*. Now I had music to calm me down but the hashish, the *arghiledhes*, all that back and forth, it never stopped.

---

64 A nickname. *Yalias* = 'spectacles'.

## Sometimes the Loulas Feeds me

Sometimes the loulas[65] feeds me,
Sometimes I lose control
For hours it puts me in a dream
I don't speak to a soul.

Nature set me up at birth
With misery and pain
Which passes only with hashish.
Then all is right again.

## Ώρες με Θρέφει ο Λουλάς

Ώρες με Θρέφει ο λουλάς,
ώρες αδυνατάω,
ώρες με ρίχνει σε νταλκά
κι ανθρώπου δε μιλάω.

Με πίκρες και με βάσανα
με προίκισε η φύση
κι όλα περνούν και χάνονται
μόνον με το χασίσι.

For me the only school was the *tekes*. I listened to the old guys and I played, on my father's instrument to start with, but later I made huge efforts to get my own. Piraeus back then was full of *tekedhes*. The first *tekes*, so I've heard, was that of Zouanos Kalokairinos, by the public baths. He played *bouzouki* and danced good *zebekiko*.

'In the yard at Zouanos' place
They killed a chasiklis ...'

Μες του Ζουάνου την αυλή
σκοτώσαν ένα χασικλή...

That was before my time. He died, that guy. I used to hang out in lots of *tekedhes*, Kolobotsis, Michalos', Salonas', Aviglis' and so on. Lykadhiotis had a little joint like a *kafeneion*. Then there was Yerasimos', also at Gazochori, where the *tekes* was a little side room where we smoked before coming out to sit in the *kafeneion*. There were loads of others, all more or less the same. The *tekes* would be just a shack or a hut, just one clean good-sized room. That was all.

The *arghile* was sometimes made of coconut or sometimes from a small clay beaker like the ones children buy at the *paniyiria*. Or possibly a milk can. The *teketzis* would go to the greengrocer and buy a nice looking coconut specially for the purpose. It was tough and lasted a long

---

[65] *Ores me Threfei o Loulas*, rec. 1933. The verse Markos gives here is different from the recorded version. The *loulas* is the hollow bowl of the *arghile* where the charcoal is placed.

time, unless you dropped it. They scooped out the insides and inserted the air-valve on one side and a straw on the other. We all smoked from one *straw* however many of us there were and we sat close up. The *tekes* didn't have many chairs, maybe two or three, but it had little sofas, small round tables and low stools, makeshift things. The minute the *chasiklidhes* started smoking, they didn't care whether they were alive or dead. They were totally chilled; didn't bother anybody. They just wanted to eat when they were hungry and nothing else. To sleep and dream. They didn't mind if the *tekes* was a crummy old shack.

Salonas' *tekes* was a couple of wooden huts over there in Kastraki where the refugees were. Salonas was always very dapper, with his rings and his suit, dressed like a lord. I think he was from Salonica, from good family, father in the diving business, but Salonas had left all that. Fine, he'd go visit them but he didn't have that much to do with his family. He was a loner. A good guy, pretty laid back and fond of me. Really a great friend. The more down at heel types went to Salonas' while the finest *manghes*, the top dervishes, went to Michalos'. That's where you'd see the top-notch *chasiklidhes,* by which I mean the more serious, dapper, more *koutsavakis* types, the laid back, really cool guys - workers with proper jobs. Decent guys.

| | |
|---|---|
| *I've had the shakes since morning* | *Χαρμάνης είμαι απ'το πρωί* |
| *And I go for a puff* | *και πάω να φουμάρω,* |
| *At Michalos' tekes,* | *μες τον τεκέ του Μίχαλου* |
| *He's got the fine 'black' stuff.*[66] | *πόχει το φίνο μαύρο.* |

Michalos had some shacks where he lived with his wife, but the smoking hut was somehow different, a bit smarter. We used to go to his place in Chiotika at any time. You think he was ever shut? The *manghes* would go at all hours of the night, knock at his door and he'd open up for us.

---
66 *O Charmanis*, rec. 1933.

Same with this guy, Aviglis, over at Chiotika. He had the most civilized joint and he was the best *teketzis*. They say - I heard this later on - that Salonas would grass to the police and the same with Michalos, but this guy never. The police beat him black and blue, left him legless. He got prison and exile to various islands because he wasn't telling them anything, while the others *did* supply information. Aviglis was squinty in both eyes, an old diver. He had a big family, girls and boys and his own little half-built house near Lipasmata.

Some of these places had dirt floors and others had planks, but it was mostly dirt since from time to time we used to let fly a gob of oily phlegm or a 'sapphire' as we called it. The minute you took a drag you might get seized with a coughing fit so we had a tin can of water for spitting in. The thing you *had* to have in a *tekes* was the brazier. In front of the *loulas*, we had the brazier burning with different kinds of charcoal, walnut, almond or mountain thyme. The best fire, as far as the *manghes* were concerned, was from mountain thyme. The brazier pretty much always had charcoal. But if it was a *Tekes* like the one Stavrakas had over by the railway lines, we used to go and gather thyme and then leave it to dry in his yard. When we were about to fix an *arghile*, he didn't put on charcoal. We'd light up the thyme and the fire from that was something else! When there wasn't any thyme, cotton did the trick. They wound it round and round and roasted it for the *arghile* and they called it *roufiana*.[67]

One time Stavrakas' son gave us a fright. The whole family lived there where the *tekes* was. You know how it is when a guy has three girls and only one boy? Well this little boy could do no wrong. Whatever he broke, whatever he did, never a harsh word. So one day we were lighting up a

---

67 From the same Germanic root as the English word ruffian. Hruf = scab or scurf, hence anything of low or brutal character. *Roufianos/a* in Greek usually means pimp or informer.

fire with bunches of thyme for the *arghiledhes* and he fell in and got burnt! We saved him but it was tears and wailing; he sure got burnt. Dreadful! That's what it took to make him calm down. From then on whenever he was naughty they used to shout at him 'Be good Nikos! Hey! Sit tight and behave or you'll fall in the fire!' They were shitting themselves, mama mia! Stavrakas ... God rest his soul, the Germans killed him. He was going into the blockade to steal insulating tape from the electrics. They caught him and shot him.

What the *manghes* were always after was good stuff to smoke and to be left in peace by everybody, especially the cops. That's why they often took to the hills. To smoke a slow *arghile,* nice and peaceful, not light up one minute and put it out the next. They'd go sit in a cave on the mountain. There was no *teketzis* there. Each guy took some hash and a straw. They took a pitcher of water as well if there wasn't a spring. The *arghile* was hidden up there and the *manghes* knew where to find it. After they'd been and smoked they cleaned it and put it back in the same place. These things went on in various caves, and hideouts. Sometimes they stowed the *arghile* up a tree so the cops wouldn't find it.

One real regular *tekes* was Gravaras' up in Athens in Anaryiron Street just where you head off to Menidhi. He'd built that place and made it very decent. It sure was a neat dive. Spotless. A fine big room with everything you could possibly wish for. It had an inner room where we smoked and then we'd come out afterwards and sit in the main saloon. After getting stoned something sweet was just what you wanted, a little baklava, a little kadaifi, to sweeten up your mouth. The whole of Athens used to pass through, all the smart folk in Athens. There was an orchestra there, and you could drink whatever you fancied. To start with it was only a piano: Manolis Tourkos, the idol of the *mangas* fraternity. He played heavy Turkish *zebekika* and some *chasapika*. The manghes just adored this guy because he played all the Turkish love songs. It was always 'Hey let's go hear the Turk and have a good time.' Just piano. He didn't sing but he played well. Dead now. He was a great hashish smoker too. As for Gravaras, it's about five or six years since he died. He was a *palikari* though, a *palikari* no question. From Mykonos, an island in the Cyclades. Like I said there were many *tekedhes*, but the crown of all the *tekedhes* was Gravaras'. This guy Gravaras was a housebreaker like no other, one of the best. Top of the game. We did time together in the lock-up, me and Gravaras at Palia Stratona.[68] I knew him well. A very quiet man, very talented. When he got out again, he went back to burgling. He really was one of the greats when it came to house breaking. Those guys are thin on the ground but Alekos Schizas was another.

All these things we're talking about are from the thirties to the forties. They were still around during the 'Hunger'.[69] Under the occupation you could still get hashish and in fact it was sold more openly. One time the Germans caught me in a *tekes* and let me go. But the minute they'd gone, just as everyone had calmed down, our own police swooped in and boy did they clean us up! 'Light it up and put it out', that's how things were done in the *tekes*. Quickly, because we were scared of being nabbed by the cops. We wanted to have our smoke and then get out so that if they came they wouldn't catch us in there. Even if they sectioned off the area, they might not find the *arghile*. If we were sitting outside and saw the cops we scarpered. But if they caught us red-handed they seized the *arghiledhes* and marched us to police headquarters, handcuffed in single file. Then everyone would point and say '*chasiklidhes*'. I didn't care. Because for me the *bouzouki* was the only thing and that was that.

---

68 The Old Barracks.
69 The famine of 1941-2 under the Occupation in which, according to a Red Cross estimate, at least 250,000 people died, the worst hit areas being working class districts of Athens and Piraeus. It was generally referred to by Greeks as *I Megali Peina*, i.e. 'The Great Hunger'.

For the *bouzouki* I lost everything, as I told you. But I also gained everything.

Markos, 1929.

## Chapter 11

## ALL THE REBETES OF THE WORLD

The world said bad things about the people of the *tekes* but for me these people were both good and bad, just like everywhere.

Lemonadhika. Markos is fifth from the right in the top row.

Probably more good than bad though - especially when they were getting stoned. Even the nasty guys used to become placid and easy going without a mean thought in their heads. That's why we longed for hashish and went all out for it. From the moment we were smoking, we didn't do a thing. We just sat there stoned up to the eyeballs. We'd stare into space and dream. We enjoyed seeing, we enjoyed hearing. The way they put it was 'I'm going to hark up and listen.' Just that, nothing else. I could have gone and drunk ouzo, or wine and got smashed and looked a fool, so that tomorrow or the day after my heart would seize up and I'd die. I could have done all kinds of things. When you're drunk you do loads of crazy stuff. But with this you just sit, you're at peace and your nerves calm down. If you're upset, hey, it calms you down, you sit quiet and everything seems good. This life that you lead is what it is and you're okay with it. You can see and enjoy the beauty of things. The guy that gets stoned sits and sees. That's why I sat playing *bouzouki* in the hash dens and everyone around me was doped up too. They sat and nobody spoke a word, just listened to the *instrument*, the *bouzouki*. And for me, as long as I played, the whole world was mine. Nothing else mattered, nothing at all.

I didn't spend money on hashish. Never had to pay. In those days I'd go into the *tekes* with my *bouzouki* and it was on the house; sky was the limit, same both with the *teketzis* and everyone else. The *teketzis* used to take ten or twenty *talara* and put them in my pocket. No matter what *tekes* I went to I never paid. I often ran into people who recognized me from Syros. They saw it was me, Markos, from back then. But now they loved me even more because I was playing *bouzouki*. 'Markos!' I mean they gave me respect. In my gang of *manghes* along with me there was Stratos, Anestos and Batis. They looked after us, paid for our drinks or hashish, made much of us and especially me. Which is why I wrote *Oloi oi Rebetes tou Dounia* (rec. 1937).

| *All the Rebetes of the World* | *Όλοι οι Ρεμπέτες του Ντουνιά* |
|---|---|
| *All the Rebetes of the world*<br>*Love me so!*<br>*They kill the fatted calf for me*<br>*And grieve when I go.* | *Όλοι οι ρεμπέτες του ντουνιά*<br>*εμένα μ'αγαπούνε.*<br>*μόλις θα μ'αντικρύσουνε*<br>*θυσία θα γενούνε.* |
| *Those who don't know me*<br>*Already soon will,*<br>*I take my stroll,*<br>*Let'em laugh their fill.* | *Κι όσοι δε με γνωρίζουνε*<br>*τώρα θα με γνωρίσουν,*<br>*εγώ κάνω την τσάρκα μου*<br>*κι ας με καλαμπουρίσουν.* |

| | |
|---|---|
| I was born poor | Εγώ φτωχός γεννήθηκα |
| And I've been through the mill. | στον κόσμο έχω γυρίσει, |
| Deep in my heart | μέσα απ'τα φύλλα της καρδιάς |
| I'm suffering still. | εγώ'χω μαρτυρήσει. |
| | |
| Here on the street | Όλοι οι κουτσαβάκηδες |
| The hardcore guys | που ζούνε στο κουρμπέτι |
| They too hide pain | κι αυτοί μες την καρδούλα τους |
| Behind their eyes. | έχουν μεγάλο ντέρτι. |

I didn't see visions and dreams. Other guys thought they were flying or swimming. I didn't see that sort of thing. But when I was with my first wife I had a dream. Like I said, I didn't have children with her but one night, stoned as usual, I dreamed I was on a huge endless railway line and I was walking on the wooden bits between the rails. Seemed like a little old man appeared to me with a knapsack on his back and a stick. 'Now listen and behold!' he said, 'It is Saint Antony who speaks to you.' I woke up next morning and bam! Someone had dumped a baby in front of our house. I didn't keep it. We took it to a baby hospital.

When I was stoned I was happy simply to relax and sit around. I didn't need to be in the *tekes*. I'd sit in a *kafeneion* with regular folk. People might recognize me but they didn't bother me. They wouldn't say there goes a *chasiklis*. Hell no! Just me sitting in my *kafeneion* having a good time. Sure, I might not be planning a night at the movies. No. That's not what these guys did. They were more likely to go to the bordellos, stoned as they were. With the girls there, one guy would get in a fight about his 'sweetheart', another just wanted a chick for the night and so on. I didn't get into all that. You see, hashish brings on an appetite. Being stoned can make you very hot. You could *eat* a woman alive. You have such desires and such dreams.

From time to time of course, if the hashish happened to be particularly strong, like that time I mentioned when I 'bought it' down by the cave of Koulos, I'd suffer some kind of bad trip. I remember another time I'd just come out of a *tekes*, Kyriakos', and once again, right near Anastasi, 'I bought it', as we say. There were fields of fresh hay over there. Five or six hours I was out for the count. Crashed out on the hay till I recovered. But the state I was in ... helpless! Touch and go whether I'd pull through or not. Couldn't budge from the place I fell. In all my life it happened to me five or six times that I got so stoned I collapsed. Then I always said I'll never smoke again, eh? It was damn frightening. I said, what if my heart stops and I die or what if I go nuts? Because lots of people did go off their heads. Take my brother Leonardhos. When he turned seventeen he smoked a lot and he went insane. I tell you, he wasn't even just nuts. I mean, a mad guy is one who still treads on his own shit. This one was a basket case. He had hallucinations and used to run around shouting 'Get rid of them! Make them go away! They'll eat me, they'll kill me!' There were certain streets he refused to cross. My favourite brother that was. Just as well he died in 1941. What a terrible life! He died from getting stoned.

People say a *mangas* is someone you shouldn't go anywhere near. But I can assure you that a *mangas* is a laid back, very placid kind of guy. He doesn't do anyone any harm. Not if he's a decent sort. If he's a rogue of course, he'll still be a rogue. The *manghes* were serious individuals. I was a *mangas*. I didn't bother anyone. I wasn't looking for trouble. Each to his own. Of course the folks at home didn't want me to go down this path, but for me, sadly, it was the *instrument* that did it. Lots of us *manghes* worked hard and earned our bread with the sweat of our brow. We did as we pleased. Everybody knew from our clothes, I guess, that we were *manghes*. Sometimes we'd go to some neighborhood, two or three of us; sit and drink a coffee. People didn't know us there but they'd say: 'Who are these guys? They're not from round here. They're different.' Who knows how they picked us out? We were always dapper. I loved having my clothes clean and pressed, everything just dandy. I was in time to wear, though not for long, the fashionable black suits of cheviot wool. Top quality. The 'jockey' trousers were very chic too, a little narrower down below and wider up top. If I wore some drill trousers, made in the factories here, we'd cut them and stitch them in the 'jockey' style.

Like all of them, I liked to dress well. I dressed in the *mangas* style, like a free spirit, you know, not flashy with a tie and a *republica* and all that. No. Sometimes I even wore a workingman's cap. What I mean is I always dressed *stylishly*, especially later when I had money. English suits, yes, but I always looked a tad raffish. I mean, I might be wearing the finest suit that cost a thousand, maybe two thousand drachmas, but I'd still be wearing a flannel undershirt, while somebody else with this outfit might be wearing a bow tie. These days, since I got ill they take me to all sorts of fancy places and then I wear ties. I swear to God, I wear ties because my wife yells at me and my kids yell at me, but what I really like is good flannels. I may have dressed with a touch of the raffish but also like an upstanding citizen. I remember some rich old guys in Syros, shipping line tycoons with loads of money, and I used to watch how they dressed. After all wasn't I the guy that wrote the song: *Imouna Mangas mia Fora me Fleva Aristokrati?*[70] It's not like I was trying seriously to look like aristocracy. No. Just simple and decent. My shoes, regular flat boots, no laces. I like to be well turned out. As I said: flowers, letters and music are what I like. And add to that fine clothes. Of course I love all that, but not in a spivvy kind of way. Just to be dressed in the way that's right for me.

The *koutsavakidhes* were well dressed with rings, watches, shiny shoes, moustaches eh? Beautiful wide twirling

---

70 'I was a *mangas* once, with blue blood in my veins'.

moustachios which they didn't trim. The hair was parted, a smart cut with the back of the neck shaved, and a fine *republica* hat, because at that time they made Borsalino *republicas*. I wore those too and in fact I'm on the point of writing to my son when he goes to Italy to ask him to bring me one, a brown one and a black one. Still, I don't like the borsalino as much as I like the workingman's cap.

For us, if someone said so and so was a 'dervish' that really meant something. What we meant by it was that someone was a very cool guy indeed, clever and quiet. All his dealings sensible and good, whatever he did. A 'dervish'. This kind of talk is Turkish and it means probably that he's like a priest or a monk. Do you see what kind of things we had in our heads? Either *koutsavakis*, or *mangas* or 'dervish', it's all the same except that the dervish is tops, and of course everyone thinks of the *koutsavakis* as a bad person. But the *koutsavakis* didn't bother anybody. He didn't want anyone to bother him either, that's for sure, but generally he kept a low profile. There *were* aggravations that sometimes ended in bloodshed. For instance, you might annoy a *koutsavakis* without realizing. If you insulted him that didn't go down well at all. He'd jump you, stab you with his knife. He'd as soon kill you as not, it wasn't unlikely. They always carried knives; a small knife worn at the waist like a penknife, razor or screwdriver. I mean, they weren't the sort to pick a quarrel. They did quarrel but only when you provoked them. They were generally skilled workers, tailors, metal workers, or mechanics. They might also be fishermen, grocers, shop assistants, butchers, all sorts. Some had lots of money and some didn't. They loved the *laika*, by which I mean *our* music. They danced too, *chasapika, zebekika, servika*, but not *tsifteteli*.

Of course in the *tekedhes* where I used to hang out with the *manghes*, we'd hear a lot about various *koutsavakis* personalities, for instance, that Scrivanos was a great *palikari* and whatever prison he went to the prisoners held him in awe. He got into fights, he killed, he let nothing drop. But still, like I said, he was a serene kind of guy. It's like a well, if you don't drop a boulder in it you don't get splashed, isn't that so? I heard these things from all sorts of people, not just in Syra but here as well. Scrivanos, Gavalas my fellow Syran, others were the Bertonomoi boys, Cretans. They were in the prisons too. I heard a lot about this sort of thing but I wasn't that interested because my mind was always on the *bouzouki*. From time to time if we happened to be talking, I'd pay attention and listen.

Of course there were *manghes* and *koutsavakidhes* who weren't workers. They didn't earn their bread with their own sweat but by theft for instance. Like one guy I knew, the one and only Alekos Schizas, prince of thieves. He only had to take one look at the padlocks and they unlocked themselves! I got to know him and every day I used to go to his house in Kremydharou at Kastraki. We smoked hashish together. He had money this guy and I used to teach him *bouzouki*. The Athens Police were after him on account of some recent burglaries. They knew it couldn't be anybody else but it took them a while to track him down. A whole bunch of us used to go to his house, me, a guy called Dhaskaleos, Constantinidhis, and Gatos, an old thief, a big time thief. One day we were all there together and they swooped in on us. Put us in Palia Stratona[71] as a 'gang'. The newspapers published the story: 'We caught a gang led by Alekos Schizas'.

The night before I'd had a dream. I was stoned. Well, you know, there was never a time I was cold sober. I saw a big red fish in a frying pan. Very next day they clapped us in handcuffs and I went to prison with an eight-month sentence. I'd been to prison at other times too but never for so long, two or three days, nothing much. It was just at the

---

71 The old Barracks', a prison.

time I was beginning to bring out records and every evening this guy from Monastiraki, used to come and sit outside the window singing songs from the records I'd made. Holy Mother of God! What a horrible thing had happened to me! I was going nuts. I said to myself I'm losing it, I've forgotten it all, I'll never play again. What misery day and night! I didn't have my *bouzouki*.

Alekos Schizas was from a big Athenian family. There are Schizas in Athens with big shops, his uncles, his siblings, his cousins. From a good family but they disowned him because of this business. But with all the dough he made, what did he do? He shared it out among the poor, whoever was hungry. He'd get to know for instance that a family was starving. He'd go there and give them money or he'd send it to them. His generosity was beyond anything. Fine, he was stealing stuff, but he gave it all away! Alekos did so many kind things of this sort. He was sorry for poor people. The Germans killed him and he left this world in '43. He was my *koubaros*,[72] and a great guy even if he *was* a thief. I tell you, he used to steal the money, keep it safe, then give it away to the poor. Not just to one or two families but to lots, thirty or forty families. He didn't take a soul with him when he went to steal. No accomplices. A lone wolf. The police used to beat him up. 'Confess, out with it!' Not a chance. Ten years in jail. He'd go and do his ten years. Out he'd come. The same all over again. As long as he lived he had the cops breathing down his neck. He smoked and he played *bouzouki*. He was a great guy, I tell you.

I got to know all sorts of people there in Palia Stratona. I got to know Panayotakas Gravaras, the greatest *teketzis*, a thief and a *palikari*. A killer. Any guys who gave him aggravation, he wiped them out. Killing, back in those days, was something people did just because they felt like it. 'I'll kill, I'll do time for ten years, then I'll be out.' They were

---

72 'Best man', sponsor or godfather.

hard core. Like I said, there was this *tekes* that Gravaras had at Ayoi Argyroi on the way towards Menidhi. One evening the Kaklanoi boys, three or four brothers, came down there to play heavy. He clobbered one of them with his pistol, lays him out flat. The rest of these guys are still alive. I was in the slaughterhouse in Athens same time as them. They were butchers.

It was also there, when that bad thing happened to me with Schizas, that I came face to face with the famous detective Maroudhas. One day they called me to the visiting room, 'Markos Vamvakaris!'

Off I go thinking it must be one of my folks. The minute I get to the grill a voice says to me:

'How do you do? What's new?'

'Doing fine', says I. 'Who are you?'

'Maroudhas' he replies. Maroudhas!

'What do you want?'

'Hey, I want you to tell me what you know,' he says, 'give evidence.'

'You! When you've got the whole prison. Pah to hell with you!' says I to him, scowling, 'Bastard!' Back then he wasn't an inspector, just a plain policeman. He hadn't yet turned into quite such a big cheese. He'd come to interrogate me, get me to squeal. But I didn't know anything, hadn't seen anything. Was I supposed to tell him lies? I made his personal acquaintance through the bars of that prison! I'd heard of him from other guys, some great stories, like I'd heard of Barachtari and Gali Gali, but those last two were before my time. In those years they came down heavy on thieves. They used to come to the bars down here and keep an eye out for pickpockets and all those sorts of people. Barachtari was a scourge of hashish smokers, and *koutsavakidhes*. At that time their special way of dressing was to throw a jacket over their shoulders, put an arm into one sleeve and leave the other dangling empty. Barachtari clamped down on this fashion by cutting their jacket sleeves off whenever he caught them. Mitsakis sings about that in one of his songs, a *chasapiko*: *Stin epochi tou Barachtari*.⁷³ There was a song too about the other one, Gali Gali, another fiendish cop who tormented *manghes* and *koutsavakidhes*. A right devil, a terror!

While I was still there in the prison I had another dream. I seemed to see a Turkish girl dressed in red. When I woke up and told my fellow inmates one of them says: 'You'll be getting out of here.' Sure enough, half past ten the next morning they shout 'Markos Vamvakaris, take your clothes and leave.' Without a trial, without anything. Same with the others, while this guy Schizas, they sentenced him, gave him two and a half years or three.

The only crimes the police chased me for were hashish, women and *bouzouki*. Those weren't crimes. There were *manghes* who had blood on their hands. Like for instance Mathesis⁷⁴ and Scrivanos. Don't even talk to me about that Mathesis! Thug! Less said the better! I can't stand the sight of him. He was *not* a good guy in my book. I found out later on he had a big crush on a girl in Vourla, down there in the bordellos. A Cretan girl, she was crazy about me. It was me she wanted not him. I wrote this song for her:

| Black Eyes, Black Brows⁷⁵ | Μαύρα Μάτια Μαύρα Φρύδια |
|---|---|
| Black eyes, black brows,<br>Black frizzy hair,<br>Face pale as lilies,<br>Beauty spot just there. | Μαύρα μάτια, μαύρα φρύδια,<br>κατσαρά μαύρα μαλλιά<br>άσπρο πρόσωπο σαν κρίνος<br>και στο μάγουλο ελιά. |

---

73 'In Barachtari's time'.
74 Also referred to in songs as *O Nikos o Trellakias,* 'Nikos the crazy guy'. Mathesis told the story differently in his brief memoir after Markos' death in 1972. In his version he claims to have stabbed Markos in the buttocks with a fork to pay him out for blowing his cover during a police raid. Clearly no love lost between the two of them but they must, at one time, have been good friends.
75 *Mavra Matia, Mavra Frydhia* rec. 1936.

Such prettiness my flirty chick,
I never yet have seen
In all the whole wide world,
My sweet, or any place I've been.

Black eyes, I fear because of you
My brains have gone astray,
I'm going to die, I can't hold out,
I'm wasting all away.

Bewitching eyes with a sweet glance
The pain begins to gnaw
The secret folds inside my heart
Where misery is raw.

Τέτοια ομορφιά ποτές μου
αχ! τσαχπίνα μου γλυκιά
δεν την έχω απαντήσει
μες σε τούτο το ντουνιά.

Μαυρομάτα μου για `σένα
εκατάντησα τρελός
Θα πεθάνω δεν αντέχω
έχω γίνει φθισικός.

Πόνους έχω εγώ κρυμμένους
μες στα φύλλα της καρδιάς
με τα μαγικά σου μάτια
όταν φως μου με κοιτάς.

He was jealous and hated me because of this business, thought I'd steal his broad. One evening he caught me unawares and whacked me with a stick, dislocated my arm in the Piraeus marketplace, in full view of everyone. I went through agony for ten days before I got better.

A nasty piece of work, this guy Mathesis. He also killed Stringlas, a *palikari*, one of the greats. He'd slipped and fallen in the marketplace. He shot him with a pistol when he was down. For sure he couldn't have killed him if he'd been on his feet! No matter what Stringlas was like, the guy who killed him was ten times worse. Mathesis was a Koulouriot from Salamina and his father was such a great guy, you can't imagine! Had two boys and a fish stall in the Piraeus market. One of them, Mitsos, was generally a good sort but this one, Nikos was something else. Mathesis is still alive, also married with grown up boys too. They're away at sea, first mates, captains, I don't know what. Mitsos died.

Apart from the killers, the *manghes* back then, even the thieves, were great guys. They minded their own business and they knew what they liked: hashish and *bouzouki*. They weren't moneygrubbers. Not like these famous guys we have now, the new *bouzoukia*, up to their eyeballs in money.

They've gone crazy for it. Nothing else interests them. They've raked it in and they've made it big. Really they do any kind of shit, even get buggered just to get a taste of the sweet stuff. I'm not saying *everyone* does this kind of thing, but broadly speaking, I mean, they're degenerates. That's not how it should be. The *bouzouki*, like I told you, is what the hardened criminals laid hold of. Killers with life sentences, the guys on death row, those sorts of people. Same with both *bouzoukia* and *baglamadhes*. Nowadays, as you see, just anybody picks it up. A guy's not even likely to think what he's got his hands or to say 'I've got a *bouzouki* and it's a sacred thing, because it's come out of that world.'

Like we said, that's why the police were hounding it and that's why the police were chasing *me*. They didn't want the *bouzouki* to spread. But still, it *did* spread.

**Bouzouki Joy of All Creation**[76]

*Bouzouki, joy of all creation,*
*Who filled the manghes with elation,*

*The filthy tricks the rich once played*
*On you, bouzouki, now are laid*

*Aside. On rugs you sit and schmooze*
*In high rise lounges where they booze,*

*And even, oh bouzouki mine,*
*You're higher than the violin.*

*The elevator takes you high*
*Up to the penthouse in the sky*

*Where pampered ladies wrapped in fur.*
*Sit and clap and sweetly purr.*

**Μπουζούκι Γλέντι του Ντουνιά**

*Μπουζούκι γλέντι του ντουνιά*
*που γλένταγες τους μάγκες*
*κι οι πλούσιοι σου κάνανε,*
*μπουζούκι μου*
*μεγάλες ματσαράγκες.*

*Τώρα σε βάλαν σε χαλιά*
*και σε σαλόνια επάνω*
*ακόμα κι από το βιολί,*
*μπουζούκι μου*
*δυο σκάλες παραπάνω.*

*Με ασανσέρ ανέβηκες*
*σε πολυκατοικίες*
*κι έπαιξες και γουστάρανε,*
*μπουζούκι μου*
*ανφάν γκατέ κυρίες.*

---

76 *Bouzouki Gledi tou Dounia*, rec. 1947.

| | |
|---|---|
| *Higher yet You will go far,* | *Τώρα θ' ανέβεις πιο ψηλά* |
| *As far as Ares god of war.* | *θα φτάσεις και στον Άρη* |
| | *κι ο Απόλλων ο Θεός,* |
| *Apollo too, bouzouki dear* | *μπουζούκι μου* |
| *Hearing you will raise a cheer.* | *κι αυτός θα σε γουστάρει.* |

You just can't imagine what a bad rep the *bouzouki* had here for fifty years. With those pieces I played and sang they were afraid people would turn into the sort of folk I've been telling you about, thieves and murderers. The *bouzouki* has such power. It *had*. Now it doesn't any more. Now you might see a European style band say, and they'll have a *bouzouki* in it! The *bouzouki* now, well ...

I've written a song:

| | |
|---|---|
| *My bouzouki, you are heard*[77] | *Μπούζουκι μου π'ακούγεσαι* |
| *In USA and Europe,* | *Αμερική κι Ευρώπη* |
| *And people all around the world* | *και σ'έχουνε για ίνδαλμα* |
| *Make you their special pin up.* | *στον κόσμο οι ανθρώποι.* |

Yes, it's idolized by everyone everywhere. That's what's happened. Here's another one I sing:

| | |
|---|---|
| *My bouzouki in the world*[78] | *Μπουζούκι μου μες το ντουνιά* |
| *You have outstanding grace* | *έχεις περίσια χάρη* |
| *All over earth you now are heard,* | *από τη γή ακούγεσαι* |
| *From here to outer space.* | *επάνω στο φεγγάρι.* |

It won't be long now before they take *bouzouki* to the moon. You think they won't take it there? You bet they will! It's *bouzouki*. A sacred thing.

---

[77] *Bouzouki mou p'Akouyesai.*
[78] *Bouzouki mou, Mes ston Dounia.*

# PART III: GOLDEN YEARS

## CHAPTER 12

## THE FAMOUS QUARTET

The Famous Quartet: Stratos, Markos, Batis and Delias.

When I went off to be a soldier I was playing the *baglama*, but then of course I stopped. It would have been very cheeky to carry that around. You couldn't be seen playing the *baglama* without having hashish-smoker written all over you. This was an instrument you had to hide under your jacket or in your back pocket, like my poor old pal Yiorgos Batis used to do for instance. He was a guy I did a lot of work with. It was only after I was discharged from the army that I properly got going with the *bouzouki*; like I told you, after Nikos Aivaliotis came to our house.

Me, Stratos, Batis and the other guy Anestos, used to go round the *tekedhes*. That's where we got to know each other. Stratos was singing and I was playing *bouzouki*. Stratos at that time worked in the Port of Piraeus at ELPA.[79] He was a boatman of some sort - don't remember exactly what his job was. He was a great guy, very laid-back. We used to meet up every evening at about the same time and we'd say 'What's the plan for tonight?' Usually ended up with us heading for the hills. We didn't want to have people looking at us and saying mean things. Not that anybody made fun of *me*. I was a serious kind of guy. Eh ... fine, they could say whatever they liked but no one made fun of me, because I was playing the instrument. They all loved me, but Stratos was a bit of a loser. They pushed him away. They called him a 'dope' because he was up to his eyeballs in hashish. They used to tell him to get lost, you know, but I stuck by him. We used to go sit on a hill here at Perama and practise together, sometimes with the *baglama*, sometimes with *bouzouki*, nice and peaceful, nobody watching. I wasn't working at that time even though I was a skinner in the Piraeus slaughterhouse. This *bouzouki* thing had taken me over completely. I lived and breathed *bouzouki* - couldn't do anything else. I belonged to the instrument, body and soul.

Poor old Stratos used to do the shopping, brought along food for us to eat. Thing was, I knew he was going to make it big one day. We came up together, side by side, each of us in a different place doing our thing. He went to Columbia and I went to Odeon. When it came to making records, Stratos was the first and then it was me. I mean our first recordings came out in the same month. To start with I was giving him songs and he recorded them, like for instance:

---

79 *Elliniki Leschi Autokinitou kai Periigiseon.* 'Greek Motoring and Tourism Club.'

*Mia Xanthia Treli Galanomata*,[80] a nice *chasapiko*. Stratos sang that one and a whole lot of other ones that I don't remember. They teased Stratos because whatever place he was in, no matter what he was doing, on his feet or sitting down, he was always singing a song, 'Ooh wah wah' like that, mouth wide open singing his head off. Me though, nobody could take the piss. I was different, more serious, not like Stratos. Stratos was a great guy, but he let it all hang out, as he still does even now. I was more of a heavyweight, more serious. A man of few words, it might take you an hour to get a word out of me.

This guy Stratos, his background was Asia Minor, Aivali. Those people came over and settled here a bit before the destruction of Smyrna, you know, the Catastrophe. Some settled here in Athens, others in Volos. He's got family in Volos. We've been there playing together twice in recent years and he took me to see his folks. We hung out with them, very good folk, but poor; fishermen and dockers in the port of Volos; great people.

Back then, when we were going about together doing voice and *bouzouki*, he went off one fine day for a smoke with some random guys. I wasn't there. The cops set them up, caught them red-handed and sent them to exile in Sifnos. In fact I used to sing him a little song in those days.

Whenever he said to me 'Come on Markos, let's head for the hills,' I'd reply:

| | |
|---|---|
| *Wherever you want to go just go!* | Αντε να πας αυτού να πας |
| *But leave me, let me be.* | και μένα να μ'αφήσεις, |
| *And when you've had your punishment* | κι όταν θα πάθεις τη ζημιά |
| *Then come and talk to me.* | να'ρθεις να μου μιλήσεις. |

Which is exactly what happened to him. But he sure did have a fine time in Sifnos, don't even ask! What he told me

---

80 *A Mad Blonde Blue-eyed Girl*, rec 1939.

about those people! They're great the Sifniots! He's got a history this guy! But it can't be anything like mine.

Yiorgos Batis, God rest him - he's dead now, since five or six years ago - I had some great times with this guy. He used to lend us money and when we had work we paid him back. We took him with us to play gigs and whatever I owed him or whatever Stratos owed him or anyone else, we paid him. I don't know where he found it but he always had money. He was 'the one and only Batis'. He sold all kinds of old things in the fleamarkets of Piraeus, *bouzoukia*, guitars, bric-a-brac, worry beads, rings and whatnot. He had a secondhand shop in Karaiskaki where he bought and sold these things, pawned various items, nothing special. Batis had a number of *bouzoukia* and he gave them all names. I saw a *baglama* of his, which he called *Mangas* and another called Dervish. There was a *bouzouki* called *Markos* and another called *Tsiftis*.[81] He was ... how can I put it? There was only ever one Batis!

He had one or two little shops which he rented out. He was good with money, a clever guy, very smart. He used to sing and play *baglama* in the *tekedhes*. We were joined at the hip, me and this guy. It was Batis who brought out Anestis Delias, the Smyrnian, 'Artemis' as he was called, but Batis christened him '*Artzi-Bourtzis*'.[82] Batis was a laugh-a minute sort of guy but he didn't even know how to play anything at all. And if he recorded a song on the radio, Stratos used to sing it for him; like for instance: *Zoula se Mia Varka Bika*.[83] He put in the music for this song on the *baglama* just any old how. The verses were given him by a fellow Syran who was going to give them to me, but I said I didn't want them. He was a gas, Batis was. A comedian, the life and soul of the party - right up to his final breath he made us laugh.

---

81 Literally a type of eagle, but slang for a 'smart dude', impeccable in both appearance and behaviour.
82 'Harum Scarum'.
83 'Secretly I got in a boat', Batis, *zebekiko*, rec. 1934.

Batis was the oldest of us, then Stratos, then me and then Delias. He was a native of Piraeus but he always said his father was from Syros and his mother was from Vilia. Batis and I had loads of adventures. They caught us with hashish one time and put us in the clink; two or three days inside, then we paid up and left. Together with Batis I got to see the whole of Greece, Saloniki, Serra, Drama, Kavala, Komotini, the islands, Syros, Paros and Andros. I went to lots of places with Batis and the band. But Stratos sometimes played with other people and not with us. I went to Saloniki once with Stratos and twice with Batis. I went to Patras too, Preveza, Lefkadha, Arta and Messolonghi; also to Gytheion, Nafplio, and Argos.

Delias was just a kid and he lived in Kastraki where the refugees were - and nearly all the *tekedhes* too. He started to do the rounds of the *tekedhes* playing guitar to begin with. His father was a musician from Smyrna, the famous 'Black Cat'. That was his nickname. Can't remember what he played, violin was it? ... *Santouri*? I don't remember. Either way Anestos played guitar from an early age and when I got to know him I set him to learning *bouzouki*. It was me put him on to it: 'You're going to give that up and learn *bouzouki* instead' I said to him and in no time at all he was sitting up there with us in the band. He was a great kid but the heroin killed him. When Anestos left us and became a junky we didn't go near him. So many times we said to him 'Hell, Anestos, can't you see where the others have ended up? You'll get to be like that too. It's a wicked shame! Quit the junk and come back with us so you can get better and work.' I mean we said it all three of us, but he wasn't hearing it. Every evening this woman used to come, called Skolarikou. It was she who'd got him into all that. She was in the brothels, a pretty low type. One time we got him away from her and made him stay with us. We kept guard over him so he couldn't get away. I mean we tried so many things but sadly he wouldn't listen to anyone. He turned into a hopeless wreck and because of that we began to avoid him. We couldn't let the police see us have dealings with him. It was that time when all the great cops of the world had clamped down on heroin, especially in Greece. He died of heroin this guy, along with Skolarikou. Both of them, they hit it with a vengeance and died in the blockade. They found him on the pavement in '43. It was the hunger finished him off and he was still on the heroin. That was how he died, exactly the way he sang it in the song, *O Ponos tou Prezakia*.[84]

| The Junkie's Lament | Ο Πόνος του Πρεζάκια |
|---|---|
| Since first I began<br>to smoke the dope<br>The world gave up on me,<br>I've lost hope. | Απ' τον καιρό που άρχισα<br>την πρέζα να φουμάρω,<br>ο κόσμος μ' απαρνήστηκε<br>δεν ξέρω τι να κάνω. |
| First it was sniffing<br>Then needle and belt.<br>My body soon<br>Began to melt. | Απ' τις μυτιές που τράβαγα<br>άρχισα και βελόνι<br>και το κορμί μου άρχισε<br>σιγά σιγά να λειώνει. |
| Nothing left in the world<br>To do, I'm dead beat<br>Since heroin made me<br>Die on the street. | Τίποτα δε μ' απόμεινε<br>στον κόσμο για να κάνω,<br>αφού η πρέζα μ' έκανε<br>στους δρόμους ν' αποθάνω. |

God forgive him. He was a fine kid when he was with us. Nice, good-looking, okay kid. Back then when I was about thirty he was around twenty two. He'd brought out some records too and they sold well. He didn't have any other job.

Among all the *bouzouki* players I met back then I got to know a fine kid who didn't play that well at first but in the course of time he got to be good and made quite a name for

---

84 'The Junkie's Lament', *chasapiko*, Anestis Delias, rec. 1934.

himself. He was Nikos Karydhakias.[85] I was very fond of him. I teased him and he used to get furious with me. Since I'm a Catholic he used to call me *Frango*. That didn't get a rise out of me but I sure teased *him*, to the point where he was just about ready to kill me. What didn't I say to him? 'Come on Nikolaki mou!' I used to tweak him by the jacket. 'Don't pull me, you'll tear it!' I was crazy about him. He was a great kid and we always went about together. I used to take him along on gigs with our late lamented Yiorgos Batis. Every evening I used to go and find all these dudes, Batis, Karydhakias, Anestos and Stratos, and we'd do the rounds of the *tekedhes* and bordellos, everywhere. People round here knew us by that time. They knew we were a band. They'd got used to us and we were good *chasiklidhes*. We didn't do bad stuff, it was all above board. Everyone knew us and loved us. We weren't looking for trouble and it didn't make any difference to us what the guys around us were doing. So maybe they were thieves or murderers. Whatever they did was fine by us. And if the police were on *our* tails they were after us because we were smoking, not because of anything worse. We just wanted a quiet life, no matter what.

Karydhakias died round about '43 I think. They found him dead in the streets. What he died of I'll never know but I do know that shortly before he died he used cocaine, heroin - those sorts of things. I don't think he had an enemy. He wasn't the sort to bother anyone, a harmless guy, a quiet type. I was so cut up about his death. They stole his instrument and later we found out it was in Corinth. They went there to get it but they never found out who killed him or who gave him that overdose of morphine. He died same way as Anestos died. Those two always went round together because they shared and did the same things. Me and Stratos and Batis, we didn't do that stuff.

---

85 The name means 'Little Walnut'.

So with these guys I was going round all the *tekedhes*, playing and practising, and I got to be perfect on *bouzouki*. Wherever we went I could see I was pulling the crowds. The minute I set foot somewhere and began to play, a crowd would gather. People who wanted to work with me started to come and find me. One of them was an Armenian called Vachram who played fantastic violin, just blew my brains away. He put me on the platform beside him and we played together. Next thing was, I set up the first *Laiki* Orchestra.

The first time I played for money was at Anastasi in Piraeus. It still exists and these days it's called Evyenia, just further on from Ayios Dionysos. This was 1934-5. We played, me, Batis, Anestos and Stratos, in a wooden shack, a little dive called Constantopoulou. We played there five or six months and people came in droves. It was so jam packed you couldn't move! All the world was in and out of that place, people from Athens, from all the neighbourhoods, even the provinces. They sat in there and had a great time. You see it was this new thing that had happened in Piraeus. The *Laiki* Orchestra.[86] First time eh! Quite something!

Before that I'd only played for 'tips'. Some guy with money might say 'Markos, do you fancy it? Get your *bouzouki*, let's hang out in my house and sing. I'll make it worth your while.' But there wasn't much of that. I wasn't running after such things. I didn't want to be seen with a *bouzouki* because like I said, the police were coming down heavy on it. But afterwards when the records came out, 1935 going on '36, we all began to go on tours to Saloniki, to Kavala, to Patras, to Syra, to the Cyclades and Rhodes. That's when the money started rolling in. Constantopoulou is where I launched the song, *Antilaloun oi Fylakes*.[87]

---

86 The *Xakousti Tetras*: 'The Famous Four'.
87 'The Prisons Clang', *zebekiko*, rec. 1936.

| The Prisons Clang | Αντιλαλούν οι Φυλακές |
|---|---|
| The prisons clang,<br>Yedi Koule, Anapli too | Αντιλαλούν οι φυλακές<br>τ' Ανάπλι και Γεντί Κουλές. |
| The clappers clang<br>Parapigmata and old Syngrou. | Αντιλαλούνε τα σήμαντρα<br>Συγγρού και παραπήγματα. |
| If you're a mother and feel for me,<br>Come one day, come here and see | Αν είσαι μάνα και πονείς<br>έλα μια μέρα να με δεις. |
| Your son before they sentence me<br>And weep so that they'll set me free. | Έλα πριν με δικάσουνε<br>κλάψε να μ' απαλλάξουνε. |

It's also where I first played *Kantone Stavro, Kantone, M'ekapses Tsachpina mou*,[88] and *Mia Galanomata, Mia Treli Tsachpina*.[89] I brought out more than twenty songs in that place.

We played every night and I was the highest paid of the whole band, two hundred drachmas in 1934. Sixty-five to seventy-five was the smallest amount of pay, which is what Batis got. Delias was getting seventy-five. I was still a skinner at the slaughterhouse of Piraeus getting between two hundred and five hundred drachmas - we were paid by the piece. But the *bouzouki* was reeling me in. I made a lot of money. I was partying, staying out all night with all sorts of girls both good and bad but mostly bad; because with proper girls I couldn't have such a wild time as I had with the loose ones. I was also the lover of a floozy in Vourla.[90] I was singing everyday and I was stoned every day, like we all were, all four of us, me, Batis, Stratos and Anestos.

I don't remember exactly how we came to split up. The joint was doing good business but the people were wild. We had rows, brawls, knifings, for all sorts of reasons but mostly

---

88 'You Burnt me you Flirt', rec. 1934.
89 'A Blue-eyed Crazy Flirt', rec. 1937.
90 A district famous for its bordellos.

women. The *chasiklidhes*, who they say used to kill for hashish, they were actually the best. A *chasiklis* won't ever kill anybody. Well, he will if he's got a mean streak in his soul, but otherwise, no. Like I said, if he was high he only wanted one thing and that was to sleep. The whole world could go to hell for all he cared. He didn't give a damn what anyone else was doing or saying. That's what they were like these guys, the *chasiklidhes*, I'm telling you now and I can't say it enough times, they were saintly people. Would I go bothering another guy? Say bad stuff about another guy? I'd think twice I can tell you. Sure, there was a sense of honour, like, I say to you 'Whoah! What the hell did I do to you?' Yeah, a guy'd kill you for honour's sake but it wasn't vendetta, not out of any vindictiveness. Those things happened from touchy pride, in the heat of the moment. The lover boys used to come, the ones who were at *Youyoulia tou Youli* where they had the hookers. Our place was where they had out their little differences: 'Why did you steal my broad!' Same old story a million times over.

Brawls happened too because of glass smashing. People considered it an insult and things could get out of hand to the point where guys got killed. They didn't like it. Well why should they? In my time they took care not to break things, not to do stuff like that, swaggering about. The waiters and the manager would come on over: 'No breakages! No this that or the other!' Loads of brawls blew up because of plate-smashing! No one could stand having plates and glasses coming at him. At parties they might break the odd plate or a glass but nothing like the number they were breaking recently till the government made it illegal. A wicked shame! God knows how many glasses poured out of the factories just so they could smash in people's hands. I don't get it, I mean, why this mania for breaking things?

I went one time to Crete in '55 or 56, before glass smashing caught on over here. They were already doing it there and I was stunned the first time I saw it. At Heraklion where I was playing, as well as at Chania and Rethymno it was all smashing and crashing and smithereens! Later I saw it here. In my time though, supposing you broke a glass or a plate, the manager would come up and say politely, 'I'd ask you please not to do that again.' Even if the manager was on a high he had to keep on top of things, stop breakages. If a guy ignored his warning they kicked him out, 'Beat it! Get the hell out!' I mean, from then on I began to understand that this business requires a firm pair of hands. Take Sarantopoulos now, a ferocious thug. He was a guy who had what it took. The minute a fight broke out he was onto it straight away; headed it off. The police wanted a quiet life, they didn't want disturbances.

Later I set up another joint at *Aspra Chomata* with my own funds. Didn't need that much outlay: retsina, beer, ouzo and cognac. The very first band of *laiko* music: me, Evstratios Payioumtzis,[91] Yiorgos Batis, and Anestos Delias, and on guitar the composer Skarvelis, known as Pastourmas. He wrote a number of songs like: *Ti Leei i Mana Sou yia Mena?*,[92] *Kaimo mes stin Kardhoula mou*,[93] *Ergatis*,[94] lots of fine songs, which everybody sang. A great composer and musician.

I can't begin to tell you what a buzz there was round this dive. They were partying the whole night through. It was a big open space where they played volleyball too and lots of cars came. There was space for them to come and park there, no problem. The joint was going along fine but the cops didn't leave me alone. Every evening they used to come and pester me to make me give up and shut the place down. They kept doing searches and of course they rounded up the guys they wanted. There was no way they were prepared to

---
91 Otherwise known as Stratos.
92 'What Does your Mother Say About me?'
93 'The Sorrow in my Heart'.
94 'The Worker'.

let this band go on playing even though everybody had taken such a shine to it. I can't begin to tell you! Even up to this moment of my life right now I have never seen so many people, so many cars get together as in this joint I had then. And I was the guy running the show, the boss.

I did the paperwork so they'd give me a permit for the shop but nine months went by after I opened it and I still didn't have one. Reason was, if I got the permit I'd have to become their stooge and snitch on whatever dirty deals the *manghes* fixed up - all the illegal stuff going on. But was I the guy for that kind of business? The *manghes* would've killed me and I'm not kidding! So I got worried sick about this dive. I ran here, I ran there and where didn't I run in hopes of a permit? But they didn't give it me. Every night while I was playing they used to come and book me. I got summoned on the grounds I was disturbing the peace and so on and so forth. I paid penalties every day. They didn't let me name the joint but everyone called it *Markos*. It was always 'Today' or 'Tomorrow' they'll give me a permit but nothing happened. Nothing.

At that time there was an inspector called Liaromatis in Piraeus. Since I went there again and again this guy knew me and as soon as he saw me he greeted me, offered me a coffee. What I said to him was: 'Why Mr inspector? So many other dives and when it comes to me and my place they don't give me a permit?'

'Markos, I know you very well and I tell you, when you want us to give you the permit you have to become our man. That means that when we come on down and do the rounds, you tell us what you've heard, whether so and so came by your place, who's on the razzle-dazzle with wads of loot … You have to feed us some info like the others do.'

'So who helps you Mr inspector?'

'The guy who owns the *Prasino Mylo*,⁹⁵ the Russian bar for example. What I mean is anyone who's got a joint will have been telling us stuff. That's how we help you to get the permit. But you, Markos, don't do those things. I know very well what you're like. For this kind of work that we want you for, you won't do. Look, pal, here's what I suggest. They're not going to give you the permit but I *will* order the department not to harass you.'

After I left the inspector I walked along the street, thought about what to do and I made up my mind to close down and get shot of it so I could take a breather. Along with all this I'd been recording with the companies and I was running this way and that way like a lunatic. So much effort and it was all going nowhere. I could see by now that the police weren't going to give me the permit. So I closed down.

Meantime, the recording companies had their ear to the ground: 'A certain Markos from Syros in Piraeus, *bouzouki* ... draws the crowds wherever he goes.' That's how it was wherever I went. People knew me. 'Markos shall we play a song?'

'Sure.'

I was in this business just to play you understand. I wasn't being paid in the beginning. It wasn't like a profession. It was just for the hell of it. Sure, people paid for my drinks, like they'd shout 'Make Markos a coffee.' But it's not like I was drinking anything else.

'Bring Markos a beer!'

'No thanks I don't drink.'

The first recording I made was with Columbia where I had a letter of introduction from a guy called Ioannis. The song was *Eprepe na'rchosouna, Manga, mes ston Teke mas*.⁹⁶ Came out with a *zebekiko* solo on the other side. It

---

95 'The Green Mill'.
96 'Mangas, You Should Have Come Into Our *Teke*', recorded with title: *Karadouzeni* 1933.

went the rounds and sold like hot cakes, an instant hit. Something people were thirsty for and they were hearing it now for the first time. I'd been writing songs, my earliest songs from about 1931 onwards, before I ever got into recording. I'd written about fifty. I'd write the words and set them to music and there it was, all done. I worked it out as I went along, playing on my *bouzouki* and memorizing. It wasn't like I'd ever even been to any musician to get him to write out the notes for me. I knew them off by heart.

When the time came to go to the recording studio and play them, they asked me 'Do you sing these?' My answer was no, I wasn't going there to sing. I didn't have any confidence in my voice being okay for singing. But this voice, it turned out - my voice - was just exactly what they were looking for.

So they call me to the studios to hear me play and they say: 'Sing them.'

'I don't know how to sing.'

'What d'you mean you don't know? How did you write them?'

'I've written them like that, but I don't know how to sing. I mean, of course I sing them but it's not any good.'

In the end though, they got me to sing. It was that song *Eprepe na'rchosouna, Manga, Mes ston Teke mas*. The minute I sang it they were speechless. I didn't think I had a good voice because in the singing lessons at school they had me doing second voice, not top voice, and I didn't understand that second voice is also important. I just didn't get it. I'd see all these tenors doing their stuff while my voice was taking the base line. But that was the voice these guys were looking for. So they said to me

'Yeah we'll have this one. Got another?'

'You bet I do.'

'What've you got?'

'I've another *chasapiko, Charmanis Eimai ap'to Proi.*'

'The way you sing it for us here, that's exactly how you have to record it on the machine. Can you do that?'

'If that's how you want it.'

I hadn't the least idea at the time that this ability is gold dust in the business I'd embarked on and of course these guys weren't trying to cheat me out of my money.

'Do it just just like you did it before' they say to me.

'Sure. That's how I'll do it.'

So I made a recording and I was good at it. How can I explain? I mean I didn't need a whole lot of fixing. You see the recording process wasn't that easy. There were people who spent ten hours just to record one song. I'd get it done in one or two takes. In those days they used to record on wax, not like now when it's big business and it's a breeze. I was a natural you might say. I sang everything right and didn't give them any hassle in the recording session. That's how I began to turn out songs and to make money.

Not a day went by without people coming to my house. They came from all over the place to ask me to go and play in their village. I mean, that's the reason I've been all over Greece; it was well paid too. Everyone loved me to bits and looked on me as a great artist in my line of music. I turned into a musician and a big talent. I was writing verses, making the music, playing and singing on the gramophone.

After the *Aspra Chomata* I decided to take Batis, my kid brother Argyiris, and a pianist called Rovertakis, and go back to Syros for the first time in twenty years. I played in a joint on the seafront and every night the place was packed. I stayed about two months and when I got back to Piraeus I wrote *Frangosyriani*[97].

---

[97] rec. 1935.

| | |
|---|---|
| *Frankosyran Girl* | *Φραγκοσυριανή* |
| I've a swelling in my heart, | Μία φούντωση, μια φλόγα |
| A flaming burst of heat, | έχω μέσα στην καρδιά |
| It seems like you've bewitched me, | λες και μάγια μου `χεις κάνει |
| Frankosyran girl, my sweet. | Φραγκοσυριανή γλυκιά. |
| | |
| I'll come down to the shore | Θα `ρθω να σε ανταμώσω |
| So that we two can meet | κάτω στην ακρογιαλιά, |
| And I'd like enough and more | θα ήθελα να με χορτάσεις |
| Of cuddles and kisses sweet. | όλο χάδια και φιλιά. |
| | |
| To Finika, Parakopi, | Θα σε πάρω να γυρίσω |
| I'll take you all round there | Φοίνικα, Παρακοπή |
| Galissa and Della Grazia | Γαλησσά και Ντελαγκράτσια |
| If it kills me I don't care. | και ας μου `ρθει συγκοπή. |
| | |
| To Pateli and Niochori | Στο Πατέλι, στο Νυχώρι |
| As far as Alithini | φίνα στην Αληθινή |
| And at Piskopio romances | και στο Πισκοπιό ρομάντζα |
| My sweet Frangosyriani. | γλυκιά μου Φραγκοσυριανή. |

That record from Labropoulos' Columbia studios is still selling even now. Later on Hatzidhakis recorded it too and sent it abroad. Everyone was running to congratulate me on this big hit I'd pulled off. They all loved me loads in Syros because I was a Syran and that made them feel proud. Every summer they waited for me to go and play there. The whole island went wild partying with me and my band.

## Chapter 13

## I DON'T WANT YOU ANYMORE

But my wife, the bitch was having orgies with that wretched friend of mine I told you about, who took advantage of me being out all night for my work. I was in a wretched state because, like I said, I used to hang out in the *tekedhes* and all the *manghes* in Piraeus knew me. I felt like I'd lost face. It made me moody all the time but I clung on to the hope that someday I'd be rid of the misery my wife had plunged me into. She'd brought so many wrong things into my life. Every so often I'd say to her 'Quit the down-hill path you're on and let's try to live happily' but she thought I was a sap. She knew that I loved her.

But even for me there was a sticking point. That was when she had me at loggerheads with everyone at home, even with my own brother. I began to hate her like I'd never hated any woman. I got very touchy and had rows with my brother. He kept saying 'Get rid of her because it's humiliating for you to have such a whore for a wife. She's made you a laughing stock!' So many people said to him 'This brother of yours, can't he see what's going on? Does he like what she's doing, gadding about with her precious boyfriend!' They made him feel bad, because even if he was in and out of jail he still kept his head held high, had a sense of honour and what was proper in the eyes of the world. Fact was he'd made up his mind to do everything he could to split us up since she'd made a fool of me. He began to follow her and every day he made scenes outside her house about what she was doing with her lover. We were all looking like fools.

One night he saw her somewhere and gave her a savage beating. He even stabbed her in the arm. Luckily she got away because he could have killed her. I didn't want any harm to come to my brother and I was afraid he'd go to jail because of her. I hated her so much by now! The filthy slag ran to the police. She made a statement against him and the next thing was the police were beating him up every time they saw him. Because of her, my brother and I came near to killing each other. I'm talking hatred, beyond all imagining. Frangiskos wanted to separate us and to have me under his thumb. But I was my own man. Didn't need anyone else telling me what to do. He was going after me, sometimes with a knife, sometimes with a gun. Sure, I'd suffered a wrong. I could see that, but I didn't want another person to get mixed up in it. So I said to him 'You keep your own house in order and I'll see to mine. I can handle it myself. Stay out of it. Fine, you're ashamed of the way things are right now, but it's my affair not yours.' The hatred just went on growing in the family.

Just imagine what a state of affairs that was for our mother to see her two sons at each other's throats every day and all because of that whore. We were beating each other up. How she suffered - don't even ask! This thing lasted years until the day of deliverance came. I left her. I divorced her and got far away from her, like I wrote recently in *Xenychti (Atakti,* rec. 1966*)*.

| *The Girl who Stayed Out All Night* | *Ξενύχτης (Άτακτη)* |
|---|---|
| *I needed to meet up with you*<br>*I had some things to say*<br>*And if I couldn't change your mind*<br>*I'd throw my tongue away.* | *Ήθελα να σ' αντάμωνα*<br>*να σου 'λεγα καμπόσα,*<br>*κι αν δε σου γύριζα το νου*<br>*να μου 'κοβαν τη γλώσσα.* |
| *I don't want you, I don't want you*<br>*I don't love you any more.*<br>*I don't want you, Off you go now*<br>*Good luck where you're headed for!* | *Δε σε θέλω, δε σε θέλω,*<br>*πια δε σ' αγαπώ.*<br>*Δε σε θέλω, και πάρε και δρόμο*<br>*και τράβα στο καλό.* |

| | |
|---|---|
| *The sorceresses told me,* | Μου το 'πανε οι μάγισσες |
| *All those coffee-gazing cats,* | κι όλες οι καφετζούδες, |
| *A girl from Egypt told me,* | μου το 'πε μια απ' την Αίγυπτο |
| *The one with those thick plaits.* | με τις φαρδιές πλεξούδες. |
| | |
| *What did I not do for you,* | Και τι δεν έκανα για σε |
| *And all to set you right?* | για να σε διορθώσω, |
| *But you're so wild I must escape* | μα εσύ 'σαι τόσο άταχτη |
| *So get out of my sight.* | στρίψε για να γλυτώσω. |

It took time to forget her and every night I was moody. I took to drinking, I didn't give a damn about anything. She was always on my mind. Although we'd split we still met up secretly from time to time, in some out of the way place where no one could see us, because everybody knew by then I'd divorced her. My brother used to come round and he did what he could to make me forget her, but I loved her too much and it was hard. My brother tried to keep a watch on me because he was afraid I'd take up with her again. But however much I was hurting, however much I loved her, once I'd left, I wasn't going back to this home where I'd been ruined, body and soul. I was wretched and I couldn't forget her but I never thought of sleeping with her again. Never. I'd taken an oath. I was struggling but so what if they saw me run to see her? It was only to *see* her.

## Chapter 14

## TOURS AND GLORIES

I was a musician now and when I didn't have regular work in a club I toured the provinces. I'd be in Larissa, Tripoli, in Githio or on the islands maybe. I went all round Greece. I took Batis or Papaioannou with me. First time in Saloniki it was me and Batis playing *baglama* and *bouzouki* at Papafis'. We stayed for about a month playing in a packed out garden. On another trip to Thessaloniki we played just up from the huge waterfall in Upper Toumba. That was a month too, some time between 1936 and 1938. In Upper Toumba it was me, Batis and Papaioannou, can't remember who else. I've been to Saloniki three times. One time I played at Irini street, me and Papaioannou, at this club in the red light district, for about a month and a half. I also met Tsaousakis[98] at Irini street. Not that he was playing. He was nobody back then. He used to come along every day, climb the railings and gawp along with the rest of the crowd. He was the most troublesome guy and sometimes we had to throw him out as he wouldn't sit still. He pushed and shoved to get in closer, to hear better. He messed people around, stirred up rows and all kinds of mayhem. I'm not sure if he was into wrestling at that time. Later on I heard he was a wrestler. Like I said, the fights followed us around wherever we went.

 I liked Thessaloniki a lot. Beautiful city. I can't think of any other clubs that played *laiko* music because I didn't know them. I only knew the places that took me on for work and that was all. Nor do I remember any other *laiko*

---

98 Prodhromos Moutafoglou, born in Istanbul in 1919. He went by the nickname 'Tsaousakis', i.e. 'Little Sergeant', because he served as a sergeant in the Greek army during World War II. His family moved to Thessaloniki in 1923 after the Catastrophe. Orphaned young, he became a professional wrestler but started singing *rebetiko* during the Occupation; he was the original singer of the famous *Synefiasmeni Kyriaki*, or 'Cloudy Sunday'. Tsitsanis discovered him and brought him to Athens.

musicians there. What really made an impression on me was the market. There wasn't just one. Thessaloniki has three or four. I wouldn't know where to start! It had all kinds of things: fish, meat, pulses, amazing vegetables! At dawn before going off to sleep I used to watch the carts arriving from the outlying areas, piled high with goods. Whatever you wanted you'd find it there. Great bargains and good quality. Very good clothes. I loved everything I saw in the market. Everybody, even the poor folk went about smartly dressed, especially the women - very chic. The men dressed well too. I mean to say, it was a wealthy place, like Europe say, not that I've ever been there. A bit like Rhodes - that's a place I *have* been to. I wrote a song '1912' back then about Thessaloniki (rec. 1936).

*1912*

In Saloniki I had fun.
Took me back to the victory
Of 1912, as old and young
All came running to see me.

To hear my sweet bouzouki strokes,
Enjoy themselves and have a ball.
They're generous and full of jokes.
They sure loved me, one and all.

*1912*

Ωραία την επέρασα,
μεσ' στη Θεσσαλονίκη,
θυμήθηκα το δώδεκα
που πήραμε τη νίκη.

Μικροί μεγάλοι τρέξανε,
εμένα για να ιδούνε,
ν' ακούσουνε γλυκιά πενιά
και να 'φχαριστηθούνε.

In Thessaloniki I also met the famous chief of police, Nikolaos Mouschountis. He boasted that we were his compatriots from Piraeus and Athens, he was mighty proud of us! Such a great guy. I can't tell you how much he loved us. Not just me and Batis but everyone who came from Piraeus and Athens: thieves, pickpockets, you name it, they all had to pass through Mouschountis' office and he'd say to them 'You know nothing. Behave well and stick around here. If you're not staying, take this money and scram.' But when it came to the Thessalonians he gave them a real hard time. He kept them on the rack and hung them out to dry. But then they were a bad lot: thieves, pickpockets, murderers, hoods. He was on *their* trail all right.

When we went the first time to Thessaloniki I slept with a 'girl of loose morals' in her room. In the morning they come knocking at my door.

'Who is it?'
'The police.'
'What do you want?'
'Get up, let's go to the station.'
'Who me, Markos Vamvakaris?'
'So, you're Markos Vamvakaris. Get up, let's go to the station.'

What had happened? The police had sent the officer to pick up someone else. Earlier on, a dead child had been found, smothered, in that room. When Mouschountis saw me there, he says to the policeman, 'Come here you, did you ask this man's name?'

'Yes. Didn't you tell me to bring the man and the woman who were there? I brought the man. I don't remember what happened to the woman.' Mouschountis swore at him and sent him away. 'Get out of here' he says, 'you bloody peasant.' To me he says, 'Take a seat Markos', so I sat down and he offered me a coffee. 'My apologies' he said and told me the story. Some hooker down there had smothered her kid. We sat there chatting for some time. What I mean to say is he really loved us. 'Markos', he said to me, 'I know perfectly well that you do the rounds.'

'Of course I get around' I told him, 'I'm not going to lie to you.'

'You go from one *tekes* to the other.'

'Yes I do Mr Nikos, I can't lie to you.'

'As a favour to you, as a favour to all of you, I'm not going to give them any trouble while you're here. You can feel free' he tells me, 'It's okay, I've fixed it.'

He couldn't stomach the snitchers. There was a guy from Piraeus who owned a *tekes* at Vardaris where the hookers were. His name was Nikos, I forget the surname; Mouschountis was giving him a hard time. Okay, now you're going to ask me why Mouschountis was fighting that guy so much since both of them were from Piraeus. But Nikos had got on the wrong side of Mouschountis. He was a bad guy. A squealer. If he was a squealer he had to be bad! Mouschountis wouldn't give him a chance! Of course we wouldn't care less. We'd go to all the *tekedhes* including Nikos'. We'd say to Mouschountis: 'What do we care if Nikos informs on us if we've got you, Mr Mouschountis, on our side?' So no matter where we stayed, whether at Nikos' *teke* or any other, no one bothered us.

Like I said, Mouschountis only had to hear that guys like us were from Athens or Piraeus and he'd make us a present of Thessaloniki. It was ours. So we strutted round the city, all of us in full feather you might say. But we didn't bother anybody. Only the women. We ran after them. We stayed in a hotel and the broads used to come along every day, do their stuff and leave. That was all we did, apart from the odd *argile*. They knew that. Mouschountis was an enthusiast, he loved *bouzouki* but he didn't smoke hashish. I'd have known if he smoked because he used to take me and Batis to a little *kafeneion* away from the city centre so we could play for him and nobody would recognize us. Well of course they knew who *we* were but it was *him* they mustn't recognize. He actually gave us stuff to smoke and we smoked right there under his nose. 'Come here every day' he said to us, 'Come for coffee.' But how could we go there every day? Us being *manghes* and all? How could we have all the others see us hang out with Mouschountis? We told him how it was. He was smart, he understood. Boy he really loved us! I met his old man Vangelis along with a bunch of nephews, nieces and cousins. The old man came and danced *zebekiko* when I was playing at *Dasos*.[99] He was a huge hulk of a man, a bruiser. We met other policemen too along with Mouschountis - an adjutant, Kostopoulos from Kalamata. Mighty fond of us, came to see us down here. He's probably retired from the army by now with a high rank. I went a few times times to Trikala before the war and stayed about three weeks. They'd turned the fortress into a music venue and it was there that I wrote and launched *Oloi oi Rebetes tou Dounia*.[100] I met Tsitsanis'[101] family there. Tsitsanis has one brother who's helped him a lot. He writes songs and plays a bit of *bouzouki*, but not like Tsitsanis eh? Christos he's called. He drinks the odd glass of wine. He's less well off but made of better stuff than Tsitsanis in my book. Quite a few notches up on Vassilis as far as character goes. Trikala is where they killed Sarkaflias the number one wallet-snatcher of Greece and a beautiful lad, very handsome. I never met Sarkaflias but I met his very ugly brother who was a great guy even if he was a thief. A very easygoing little bloke and a real pal. I mean he used to wish me good day like he really meant it. What happened was Sarkaflias went and played heavy with Antonitsis, his fellow inmate in the prison. He thought he was new in there. But he picked on the wrong guy. Antonitsis was not someone to mess with. He'd already bumped off two or three other inmates; he was a bit crazy. So here's how Antonitsis finished up: he was at some place down near the railway line and he saw a bunch of youngsters chanting:

> Antonitsis you're a shit  Βρε Αντωνίτση κερατά
> You killed Sarkaflias, what a hit!  που σκότωσες το Σαρκαφλιά.

So he caught up with these lads. He had a knife and stabbed them all to death. Then he makes his cross, falls in front of the oncoming train and that's the end of him. Whether

---
99 'Forest', a famous music dive of Antonis Vlachos in Votanikos, Athens.
100 'All the *Rebetes* of the World'.
101 Vassilis Tsitsanis, 1915 -1984, composer and *bouzouki* player, the 'Bach' of *rebetiko*.

that's true or not I don't know. That's what they told me. A powerful guy he was. Ate men for breakfast. That's how I came to write *O Isovitis*. I wrote it at Aspra Chomata, the place where I'd set up that music dive - same time as my wife was messing me around.

**The Lifer**

They stuck me in a jail for life
And all because of you
You watered me, you poisoned me
With misery's bitter brew.

You're the reason for it all,
I'm beaten down with pain
The sufferings and the torments
Spin me round and round again.

I'm launching an appeal
In hope their hearts will melt,
You murderess, you devil,
I'm going to slash your pelt.

Oh to douse you in petrol,
Make you burn in fiery hell!
And then I'd love to hurl you,
Down a dry stone well.

Fine, let them sentence me
To 'Life' times seven.
And hang me at Anaplion,
I don't need Heaven.

Those pretty looks of yours
Led all the judges astray
They sentenced me for life
And so you had your wicked way.

**Ο Ισοβίτης**

Στη φυλακή με κλείσανε
ισόβια για σένα
τέτοιο μεγάλονε καημό
επότισες εμένα.

Εσύ 'σαι η αιτία του κακού
για να με τυραννούνε
οι πίκρες και τα βάσανα να με
στριφογυρνούνε.

Τώρα θα κάνω έφεση
μήπως με βγάλουν όξω
κακούργα δολοφόνισσα
για να σε πετσοκόψω.

Να σου 'χυνα πετρέλαιο
κι ύστερα να σε κάψω
και μέσ' στο ξεροπήγαδο
να πα' να σε πετάξω.

Εφτά φορές ισόβια
τότε να με δικάσουν
και στη κρεμάλα τ' Αναπλιού
εκεί να με κρεμάσουν.

Όλους ενόρκους δικαστές
τους πλάνεψε' η εμορφιά σου
και με δικάζουν ισόβια
για να γενεί η καρδιά σου.

I beat up the battalion man,　　　Με τη ραδιουργία σου
I killed him, don't know how,　　μπουζούριασα το Χίτη
It's through the snares you laid for me　χωρίς να θέλω μ' έκανες
That I'm a 'Lifer' now.　　　　να γίνω ισοβίτης.

There'll be a mighty vengeance　　Τέτοια μεγάλη εκδίκηση
If I get the upper hand　　　　αν την εξεμπουκάρω
And I'll be like Achilles　　　　όπως τον Έκτορα ο Αχιλλεύς
Dragging Hector through the sand.　τον έσουρνε στο κάρο.

I also went to Yannina and played at *barba* Yorgis' place, the one above the lake not the lakeside one. There *were* lots of music dives down by the lake but I only went down there a couple of times to see what it was like. It wasn't like I was there for sight seeing. Wherever I went I had to stay put - hell, I had work to do!

I didn't know any people there. There were quite a few traditional folk musicians but I didn't have much to do with these guys. They were scared of me because when I came out in the record business I was bad news for a lot of them. My *bouzouki* had caught on like wildfire and after that they didn't have as much regular work as before. Some of them loved me and others hated me. I ruined lots of people through the *bouzouki* and the record companies. My records sold in large numbers and these guys who were there before me, before I came out, they weren't recording. Nowadays though, the traditional folk players and the *laiko* musicians are on good terms. The *laiko* musicians love folk music and folk musicians love *laiko* song. That's how it is *now* but back then it was different. When I first came out on records they didn't want me anywhere near them. They called me every kind of bad name, 'Filthy pimp', 'Hashishi bum', not to my face of course, but behind my back. I trod on their toes and it hit them hard, really hard. Even now there's a bit of this still around, a touch of bitterness. But in the end they realized it was pointless and gave up. Why fight us after all?

*Dhimotiko* song is Greek song, since forever. These folk songs were sung by the *armatoloi* and the klefts in 1821.[102] But *laiko* song was born in the hearts of the poor who toil, the workers. *Laiko* song is what the workingman likes.

The only place I didn't travel to was anywhere outside of Greece. They didn't let me go. The hashish was a black mark on my name. They had me down as a real bad guy. Boot's on the other foot now. Turned out later these guys who'd wanted me out of their sight started raising their hats to me, 'Good day Mr Markos!' Police, gendarmes, all these guys who used to chase me! My name was everywhere. It was a big name.

---

102 'Bandits'. The *klefts* were fighters who resisted the Turkish occupation through many generations in mountainous remote areas. The *armatoloi* were originally armed bands put together to defend villagers from the *klefts* but in fact they often collaborated with them against the Turks. Both groups played an important role in the Greek war of independence in 1821.

## Chapter 15

## YOUR BLUE WINDOWS

On these tours I had a lot of affairs with women. They ran after us. Not just me - the others too.

| | |
|---|---|
| *I have seen cuties* | *Εγώ έχω δει κοπέλες* |
| *All whims and caprices* | *με γούστα και με γκέλες,* |
| *I've seen great beauties* | *έχω ιδεί μεγάλες ομορφιές* |
| *That shone like lilies* | *που λάμπανε σα κρίνα* |
| *With dainty little bodies* | *και με κορμάκια φίνα,* |
| *Lots of heavenly brunette fillies.* | *θεόμορφες πολλές μελαχρινές.* |

In Saloniki a Serbian girl fell in love with me. I said to her, 'What do you want with me, you poor soul? You can't be seen going around with me, you're a woman!' I was telling her the truth but all I got back was 'No, no, I love you!' In Thessaloniki I got to know a Soula. With her I toured the whole of Macedonia and in Drama we both went down with malaria. I went back to Piraeus and pitched up at my mother's house. For about eight months, people kept saying 'What's *wrong* with you?' I was in such a bad way they thought I must have TB. Mama was running here, there and everywhere to get me better. One day she left the house to get some medicine. She put a pan on the stove to cook some beans and when I woke, the smell of the food got me wham in the nose. I got up, took a spoon and laid into a piled-high plate of beans. I ate with such appetite, the way a healthy guy eats. Then I fell asleep again. Mama came home and found the dirty plates, gave me a slap for eating. But that food fixed me up, I got better! I waited for the fever, the chills and the sweating I'd got used to every evening, but no. God rolled on a new day and still nothing. No fever, no chills, no sweats. I'd turned a corner. Poor mama, she'd been through hell and high water for me. With her help I began to get up and sit in the sun till I was well again and able to work.

I got shot of the malaria but I had further dealings with Soula who came and lived with me in a house in Baroutadhiko. Her dad was a convict in Yedi Koule. When he got out he began hounding me, sent me a summons to say he wanted money for his daughter. That was a fly in the ointment so I gave her the boot, marching orders toute suite and when it came to court they let me off on grounds of reasonable doubt. That's how I got clear of that filthy slag. A right little piece off the Augeian dung heap!

With all these women I still couldn't forget that tigress Zingoala. I still loved her and I was always moody and troubled. The woman who helped me to forget her in the end was a Bulgarian broad from Thessaloniki. I got to know Ellie in Vardhari in a house of ill fame. She was a hooker; loved me like crazy and I loved her too. She was a beauty, petite but not too small, plump shapely and well dressed. She had money. She raked it in and her mother in Thessaloniki had a huge plot of land too, all her own. She took me to see it and I met her mother, a woman that tall! A beast of a woman! Boy! It's like I can see her in front of me right now. Don't remember where that place was but it was like Ellie was showing off, kind of saying 'See what a lot I've got.' So I took up with this broad. I pulled her out of the gutter and I said to her 'You behave and I'll take you to Piraeus with me.' So I did and we stayed in a house near my brother Frangiskos' place in a room on a hilltop. Meantime I was still eaten up with longing for Zingoala even though there was nothing this Ellie woman wouldn't do for me! How she loved me! She adored me!

| | |
|---|---|
| *I met this Bulgarian dame* | Κάποια Βουλγάρα γνώρισα |
| *I stole her heart away* | της πήρα την καρδιά της, |
| *I ran her out of house and home* | της πούλησα τα ρούχα της |
| *And she was glad to pay* | κι όλα τα έπιπλα της. |

That's as far as I got with this little verse. In fact it wasn't I who made her sell everything. She did it so she could come away with me. We had good times together and since she sang a little I got her onto a recording when we sang *Sto Faliro pou Plenesai.*

**In Faliro You Go to Swim**

In Faliro you go to swim
And turn into a little dove.

In a bathing suit I saw you there
Yesterday Mario[103] my love!

On the beach down by the sea
Arm in arm with another guy.

And not a single glance at me,
Steely flirt you passed me by.

**Στο Φάληρο που Πλένεσαι**

Στο Φάληρο που πλένεσαι
περιστεράκι γένεσαι.

Σε είδα χθες με το μαγιό
γεια σου τσαχπίνα μου Μαριώ.

Στης θάλασσας την αμμουδιά
με άλλον ήσουν αγκαλιά.

Κι εμένα ούτε μια ματιά
δε μου 'ρίξες σκληρή καρδιά.

This is a genuinely Syran *zebekiko,* neat little tune in a major key. I remembered this tune the barrel organs used to play from the time I was a kid in Syros but the words are mine. Ellie and I worked together but I can't tell you what a wretched state I was in. I couldn't sleep at all. I couldn't get that damn first wife out of my head. Ellie knew the story and encouraged me to forget Zingoala because *she* wanted me but not even that kept me from sneaking off at night and tapping on Zingoala's windows. Sometimes Zingoala didn't open up and other times she did. She didn't care if her lover was in there. Not that I saw him, but he could have been. That's the kind of woman she was. That's where the song comes from: '*Ta Ble sou Parathyria*' (rec. 1938).

---

103 Mario sounds like a boy's name but isn't. It's common for girls' names in Greek to have a shortened version with a stressed – o at the end, e.g. Vangelio, the name of Markos' second wife.

## Your Blue Windows

Passing by I saw your face
At the window there, up high.
Then those black eyebrows of yours
Thrilled me and made me sigh.

I roam the streets like a madman
Since you left this part of town
I cry although it does no good
But the misery gets me down.

Why do I try to find you still
By sea or land, oh why?
When you went away and left me
With my heart burnt out and dry.

Rent your house and come on back
To your old neighbourhood.
So I'll see you at the window
And stand where I always stood.

## Τα Μπλε Παράθυρα

Γυρνούσα και σ' αντίκριζα
ψηλά στα παραθύρια
και τότε τα καμάρωνα
τα δυο σου μαύρα φρύδια.

Επήγες σ' άλλη γειτονιά
και εγώ τρελός γυρίζω
με παίρνει το παράπονο
κι ανώφελα δακρύζω.

Πού να ζητήσω να σε βρω
στη γη στην οικουμένη
σαν έφυγες και μ' άφησες
με την καρδιά καμμένη.

Ξενοίκιασε το σπίτι σου
και έλα στη γειτονιά σου
όπως και πριν να σε θωρώ
απ' τα παράθυρά σου.

Sometimes I had rows with Ellie because of course she found out I was going on the sly and tapping on this woman's windows. My brother would say 'Hell, aren't you ashamed? What is it you want? To be a sap and go knocking at her door till she opens up?' Passion! I loved her, just couldn't get over her, I tell you, it had to be her and no one else. It's not like I didn't know loads of other women. Pretty ones, beauties! What! Was she the only good looking broad? Fine, she was a beauty but there were plenty others more beautiful. I was eating my heart out day and night over this thing. How could I throw away all my self-respect? Time went by and I kept on loving that bitch. Just think what the new girl went through from being in love with me; loving me so much as she did, and me loving that whore.

A year went by and I still wasn't over the crazy lovesickness. But maybe I was beginning to forget and day by day, I began to lose that feeling of anguish. Trouble was I felt like I didn't want any woman at all. I wanted to be alone so I made up my mind to split with Ellie as well. When I first hitched up with her this chick was fresh and pretty but now it didn't look like the clothes she had would do for her much longer. Once I'd made up my mind and knew I couldn't bear it any longer, I went down to a shop in Piraeus called *Star*. I bought her three thousand drachmas' worth of clothing and made a parcel for her. I handed her that and two thousand drachmas and put her in a car. 'Off you go now, beat it kid! Take the things and go. Have a good life, but we can't live together.' I was sorry for her because she loved me, I could see that. I sure was sorry for her but who was going to be sorry for me? So I got rid of her and felt calmer. After she left I lost track of her. I dumped her like she was nothing. I can't begin to tell you how sad it makes me feel when I think about this woman who stood by me so bravely and loved me beyond imagining, when all I could think about was that other miserable bitch. Afterwards I sang a *hidjaz*[104] *chasapiko* with some neat words which Evstathiou is about to record again: *M'Ekanes kai Chorisa* (rec. 1936).

| *You Made me Break up* | *Μ' Έκανες και Χώρισα* |
|---|---|
| *You made me break up.* <br> *You were the cause.* <br> *Now I wander alone in the street.* <br> *You vexed me, drove me to despair,* <br> *Now there's no one I want to meet* | *Μ' έκανες και χώρισα* <br> *και συ σουν η αιτία* <br> *και τώρα μένω* <br> *μέσ' στους πέντε δρόμους.* <br> *Πολύ με αγανάκτησες σε τέτοια απελπισία,* <br> *δεν θέλω για να βλέπω πια ανθρώπους.* |
| *Alone up in the mountains,* <br> *Is where I want to be.* <br> *You slut I'll live alone there* <br> *With wild beasts for company.* | *Μόνος μου μέσα στα βουνά* <br> *θέλω να πα να κατοικήσω,* <br> *να `χω τ' αγρίμια συντροφιά,* <br> *βρε άτιμη,μονάχος μου να ζήσω.* |

---

104 One of the commonest *dhromoi* or 'roads' in rebetiko song with a flattened second and an augmented third in the first tetrachord.

I've cursed the hour that ever
I got caught up with you
And nobody came running
To see what they could do,
And ask what you had done to me.

Orphaned young, my lucky break
Was you, you devil. I didn't know
I nurtured in my arms a snake.

Βαριέστησα με σένανε,
την ώρα που `χω μπλέξει,
αρνήθηκα τη μάνα μου για σένα.
Και άνθρωπος δε βρέθηκε
για μένανε να τρέξει,
να μάθει το τι μου'χεις καμωμένα.

Ορφάνεψα από μικρός,
Συ βρέθηκες μπροστά μου.
Δεν ήξερα πως έτρεφα, κακούργα,
Φίδι μες την αγκαλιά μου.

Like I said, my songs are all true because they've all come straight from the heart.

## Chapter 16

## VOTANIKOS

After the tours they were waiting for me down in Athens at Votanikos[105]. Adonis Vlachos had a joint, down there, a bar called *Dasos* in an enclosure by the railway lines. I began to form my orchestra. That's when I took Ioannis Papaioannou for the first time as well as Kostas Karipis and Stelios Keromytis, a fine kid - neat little *bouzouki* player, plus one Stelios with his *santouri*. So we had the *laiko* orchestra, the one and only genuine *mangas* orchestra. Later I had Haskil the Jewish singer[106] and one or two other women singers whose names I don't remember. Our band had seven or eight people, all hand picked. Karipis was a very good singer and great on guitar. He was from Constantinople. Older than me and he'd recorded a lot of stuff: *manedhes, zebekika, chasapika, dhimotika, kleftika*, everything.

Keromytis was quite a lot like me. In fact he even tried to *be* me on the voice a little bit, you know, the gruff *laiko* sound. He was born in Piraeus but his family was Cretan. He was nearly three years younger than me and I got to know him here playing *bouzouki* in the *tekedhes*. I'd heard he was the son of Charilaos. His father was a *mangas* too, one of the old *chasiklidhes*.

We had a fine collection of songs. Karipis had his songs. Keromytis also had songs, three or four that he used to play; I don't remember them now. Papaioannou had some too. I had loads, from the earliest songs right up to ones I'd recently written, all ready for singing. I mean I was writing them all the time: *'Eprepe na'rchosouna Manga Mes' ston Teke mas'*, the first. *'Charmanis Eimai ap' to Proi'*, the

---

105 A district 3kms west of central Athens which takes its name from the nearby Botanical Gardens. At that time it had large forested areas and an industrial zone near the railway.
106 Stella Haskil 1918 - 1954, one of the great women rebetiko singers, born to Jewish parents in Thessaloniki. The family moved down to Athens during the occupation to avoid capture by the Germans. Her most famous song was '*Nychtose choris Fengari*' recorded 1947.

second, a *chasapiko*. '*M'ekapses Tsachpina mou Oraia*' the third, another *chasapiko*. '*Antilaloun oi fylakes*' the fourth, a *zebekiko*. '*I Klostirou*' a *chasapiko*. '*Ego Mori yia to Yinati sou*', a *chasapiko*. '*Dhen se Thelo pia dhen Eisai Oraia*',[107] *chasapiko*. There are lots I can't remember now but I've got them written down. I can't begin to tell you what went on there. The place was heaving every night, everybody packed in, clapping like crazy, partying till five or six in the morning! Every night was a fiesta and that's where I wrote: *Alaniara ap'ton Peraia* (rec. 1935).

**Wayward Chick from Piraeus**

I'll be waiting every night for you
I'll take you to wherever you desire
I want your love, so love me do, you tease!
So you can quench my heart that's all on fire.

Why, little one, d'you want to hear me groan,
And mangas-like, heap curses on your head?
Please try to treat me nicely, change your tone,
Since you're a Piraean – that's what you said.

Since you tell me that you come from Athens
Behave, you little tramp, like one of the crew.
Every night come rendez-vous with me,
And all my love, my chick, will be for you.

Come now stop tormenting me
Give me a break from your caprices,
You'll have from me whatever you want,
Stop, you've left my heart in pieces.

Lady give me healing balm,
Put out my fire, restore my calm.

**Αλανιάρα απ'τον Περαία**

Κάθε βράδυ θα σε περιμένω
κι όπου θες εσύ θα σε πηγαίνω.
Θέλω από `σε να μ' αγαπήσεις,
παιχνιδιάρα,
τη φλόγα της καρδιάς μου
να μου σβήσεις.

Γιατί θες μικρό να αναστενάζω
μάγκικα, βρισιές να σ'αραδιάζω;
Μια που λες πως είσαι
απ' τον Περαία,
να ξηγιέσαι όμορφα κι ωραία,
κι αφού λες πως είσαι
απ' την Αθήνα
να ξηγιέσαι μόρτικα και φίνα.

Κάθε βράδυ ραντεβού μαζί μου
κι όλο εσένα θ' αγαπώ πουλί μου.
Έλα πάψε πια μη με παιδεύεις,
κι από `μένα έχεις ό,τι γυρεύεις.
Άφησε μικρό μου τα γινάτια,
πάψε πια που μ'έκανες κομμάτια,
γιανε μου κυρά μου την καρδιά μου
να μου σβήσεις φως μου το σεβντά μου.

Every night they used to dance *chasapiko* when I sang this one. They went crazy! It was quite something, I can tell you,

---

[107] 'Mangas You Should've Come to our Tekes', 'I've Been Dry since Morning', 'You Burnt me Pretty Flirt', 'The Prisons Clang', 'The Threading Girl', 'Because of your Waywardness you Minx', 'I Don't Want you Anymore'.

one hell of a buzz. All kinds of folk were coming on down. High society folks along with the *manghes* and bums and the party didn't stop till dawn. We had the cream of Athens passing through, the whole of Kolonaki.[108] Those people didn't dance but they sat there.

There were knifings and brawls of course. Those things always went on but the boss of this joint, Adonis Vlachos was a man to be reckoned with. In this kind of business a rumpus is bound to happen from time to time and he used to rush over at once and patch it up with everyone, smooth things over. If a guy didn't step back into line there was all hell to pay. He got a beating and a half. The cops would take him away. Sometimes they let him go, sometimes they'd hand him over to the magistrates in the morning. There were some low down creeps who came just to smash the place up. But like I said, they got thrashed. Anyone who had that sort of thing in mind, he'd better think twice. I still remember one time when this guy who'd killed Pikinos[109] the owner of a taverna in Thisseion, came to our place to swagger about and play the *koutsavakis*. Boy! Don't ask me what happened. Unbelievable! I was sorry for him. I never saw anything like it. They beat him to a pulp, more dead than alive. You think it was only him? There were loads of others like him who played the tough guy and left with their heads smashed in. Every so often though, some hardcore guys used to come. There was a certain Vassilis. The minute Vlachos saw him he'd be on edge. He couldn't say anything to him because this guy really meant business. I mean he was hard as nails and a thorough crook. But guys like him didn't get into a quarrel over just anything. They weren't looking for trouble. Nor did anyone give them any! They'd kill you as soon as look at you.

---

108 A chic upmarket district of central Athens on the slope of Mount Lykabettus where Athenian socialites live.
109 Kostas Roukounas the great singer from Samos, famous for his *amanedhes*, wrote a fine song lamenting the late Pikinos and his musical *kafeneion*.

The women came in droves because of me. Boy they loved me! They'd come and throw money at me, loads of money. I met one woman, her name was Anna, good luck to her - I don't know if she's still alive. She used to come every evening with some big cheese of a tycoon and some guys who were in the movie business. Loaded, every single one of them. She was crazy about me, really I can't tell you how she loved me, you wouldn't believe it! She came with these guys just a few times and after that she dropped them and came alone, hung around near me. She filled my pockets with money. Thousands. I didn't need her of course in that way but that's how she wanted it: 'I'll make you rich.' At some point I took her on a tour of the *tekedhes*. Bit by bit I taught her to smoke as well. I took her to Gravaras' *teke* at Ayi Anargiri. We used to get stoned the two of us and then we'd go to a hotel and sleep together.

This woman disappeared on me, snap, just like that; same way as she came into my life. I'd been looking out for her, waiting for her to come back and hang out in the joint. I knew she went on journeys abroad, France, England and so on. She had this friend who owned the motion pictures. He started coming, this guy, and he'd ask 'Maybe you've seen Anna?' That made me feel pretty shifty. This girl had blown a whole heap of money on me.

| | |
|---|---|
| ***Gypsy, Deal your Cards*** | ***Ρίξε Τσιγγάνα τα Χαρτιά*** |
| *Gypsy, deal your cards. Tell me the truth* | *Ρίξε τσιγγάνα τα χαρτιά* |
| *The sorrow that I feel and all the pain* | *και πες μου την αλήθεια* |
| *That I have in my breast and in my heart* | *θα γιάνει τάχα ο καημός* |
| *Can it be cured? Will I be well again?* | *που έχω μες στα στήθια;* |
| *Or will this grief destroy my youth?* | *Πες μου τσιγγάνα και φλουριά* |
| *Here take my florins, fill your sack,* | *εγώ θα σε γεμίσω,* |
| *The girl who's left me, tell me the truth* | *την κόρη που μ' αρνήθηκε* |
| *Am I going to get her back?* | *αν την ξαναποκτήσω.* |

The efforts I made to find this woman! What happened to her? Did she die? This other guy she'd left behind was just as keen to find her as I was. 'If it's a matter of someone else taking her away from me' he said, 'I'd rather it'd be you.' I couldn't look him in the eye this man, because she'd been getting so much money off him and giving it to me. I'm not an ungrateful man. I didn't want an injustice.

There were loads of other women who came just to hear me and see me. They really fancied me, you know what I mean? I was a pretty fit guy back then. Here's a song I wrote at Votanikos for a girl who used to come there every night, *Mia Xanthia Treli Galanomata*.

### A Crazy Green Eyed Blonde

*A girl with green eyes, crazy blonde*
*Who's full of youth and beauty*
*Sits every night up front and makes*
*Me melt she's such a cutie!*

*So slinky and provocative*
*She comes here every night.*
*Give up your tricks you naughty blonde*
*Embrace me hold me tight!*

*You've got me all confused and you*
*Don't care I droop with pain.*
*You tease! I cannot bear it as*
*The pain I try to hide's insane*

### Ξανθιά Τρελή Γαλανομάτα

*Μια ξανθιά τρελή γαλανομάτα,*
*που 'ναι όλο ομορφιά και νιάτα,*
*κάθε βράδυ κάθεται μπροστά μου*
*κι έλιωσε τα φύλλα της*
*καρδιάςμου.*

*Κάθε βράδυ πάντα μ' ανταμώνει,*
*με τα νάζια της πώς με πεισμώνει,*
*Άφησε ξανθιά την απονιά σου,*
*βάλε με μέσα στην αγκαλιά σου.*

*Μ' έχεις μπερδεμένο δε σε νοιάζει,*
*Πώς πονώ για σε κι έχω μαράζι.*
*Δεν μπορώ ν'αντέξω παιχνιδιάρα,*
*κρύβω μέσα μου για σε λαχτάρα.*

I could see her sitting there but I wasn't going to tell her 'I wrote it for you.' I fancied her. I saw she was beautiful and I used to sing this when she came. Of course she would have guessed I'd written it for her. For sure that's why she came, but she never even invited me to go sit at her table so she could offer me a drink or something. Maybe that's because she didn't come alone. She always had company but she came sure as clockwork.

The ladies of the night, the hookers used to come and they'd send guys over with little *billets doux*: 'Maria wants you' or 'Yannoula wants you' or 'So and so wants you to go meet her in the evening at a certain house' ... I was young then and cut a dash like my son does now - good-looking and a snappy dresser down to the last detail. What didn't I wear! Even now if my wife were to show you my wardrobe you'd have to see it to believe it! Nice shiny shoes, the old-fashioned sort. I wore them on TV where I went recently. I had a cloth cap, a *traiaska* that I was very fond of, the very best sort you could get. Sober colours: blacks, browns, greys. I've still got all that stuff. Shoes, clothes, shirts and I liked polo necks eh? I've got lots of those. The black suits were quite something back then, French-style, tailored, cheviot wool. All English. I *have* got some Greek ones - they're still good suits, but I keep them for second best. I liked the black ones best. Black clothes are serious. In fact it was round that time I brought out a song which the late Karipis sang at Columbia, a little *minore* about black clothes.

| | |
|---|---|
| *Wear your Black Frocks, Wear Them*[110] | *Φόρα τα Μαύρα Φόρα τα* |
| *Since the time you gave up black,* | Απ' τον καιρό που έβγαλες |
| *Don't wear it any more,* | τα μαύρα σου τα ρούχα |
| *The hots I had for you my dear* | έσβησε φως μου ο σεβντάς |
| *Are less hot than before.* | μες την καρδιά που σού `χα. |
| *Wear your black frocks, wear them do!* | Φόρα τα μαύρα φόρα τα |
| *It's mad how they enhance your charms,* | γιατί σου πάνε τρέλα |
| *And when you've put them on one night* | και με τα μαύρα μια βραδιά |
| *Come and run into my arms.* | στην αγκαλιά μου έλα. |

---

110 *Fora ta Mavra, Fora ta*. A song by Kostas Karipis which Rosa Eskenazy recorded in 1936. In 1971 Markos recorded this song in his own arrangement with the same words but to a different tune which closely resembles the *Soura kai Mastoura* of Anestos Delias, originally recorded in 1936 with Delias himself singing,.

| | |
|---|---|
| *That little black number,* | *Τα μαύρα ρούχα μάτια μου* |
| *Mama mia! Please put it on again.* | *να τα ξαναφορέσεις* |
| *Because when you are wearing black* | *γιατί τα μαύρα σαν φορείς* |
| *I seem to go insane.* | *πάρα πολύ μ' αρέσεις.* |
| | |
| *It gives you a coquettish look* | *Σου δίνουνε μια τσαχπινιά* |
| *Makes you look extra sweet,* | *και μια περίσσια γλύκα* |
| *No dowry's needed for the boys* | *που γρήγορα θα παντρευτείς* |
| *They'll snap you up a treat.* | *χωρίς πεντάρα προίκα.* |

I've still got piles of black suit material, just sitting there. I have words with my wife. 'What are you going to do with all that?' she says to me. What'll I do with it? I'll do what I do. Share it out when I die. But if only I could go to America I'd blow them away those Yanks. They'd say 'Hey who *is* this guy?' Back in the day, just like I say it now of my young Stelios, I was a mighty fine young feller.

One night when I was playing at Votanikos, two hookers came in and sat down in front of me. One of them pulled out a photograph and showed it to the other. They both looked at me and said 'Doesn't it look like him?' One of them, the blonde one, came up and showed me the picture. She invited me to their table so they could offer me a beer. I went over, thinking the photo was of me, because the companies had publicity photographs which they gave out. But it wasn't. It was the blondie's boyfriend. We really *did* look very like each other. As soon as I see it I say 'That's not me.'

'No it's not.'
'What's he to you?'
'He's my boyfriend'
'Okay.'
I sit there, drink some wine then I go back up to play.
'Play us a nice little song...'
'Sure. What would you like?'
'Play us a *chasapiko*.' She asked for one I'd recently brought out, *M'ekapses Tsakpina mou Oraia*, (rec. 1935):

### You Burnt me Lovely Flirt

You burnt me lovely crazy flirt,
You scorched me with your heat.
You burnt me and I'm melting from
Your kiss it was so sweet.

### Μ' Έκαψες, Τσαχπίνα μου Ωραία

Μ' έκαψες, τσαχπίνα μου ωραία
μ' έκαψες, τσαχπίνα μου τρελή,
μ' έκαψες και λιώνω ολοένα
με τ' ολόγλυκο σου το φιλί.

After that I did another song, *Yia Sena Rousa kai Xanthia*, (rec. 1939), a *zebekiko*:

### For you Red-headed Blonde

For you, red-headed blonde, the guys
Of all the world are crying
And my soul cries for me as well
Since you ignore my sighing.

Because of you now everyone
Is saying that I'm bad.
Because I sing my songs for you
They shout that I am mad.

### Για Σένα Ρούσα και Ξανθιά

Για σένα ρούσα και ξανθιά
κλαίνε του κόσμου τα παιδιά.
Κλαίει και μένα η ψυχή
γιατί'σαι άκαρδη σκληρή.

Για σένανε, για σένανε,
κατηγορούν και μένανε.
Και με φωνάζουνε τρελλό,
γιατί για σένα τραγουδώ.

She thought I'd written that song specially for her but of course I hadn't! I'd never met her. How would I know her? I didn't set foot in those kinds of places. Even if I'd divorced my wife I didn't go to bordellos. Was I going to go and show my face there so they could say 'Markos was here'? Markos was a big name. Anyhow, these broads were fans of mine and one day they'd said to each other 'Let's go to Votanikos and hear Markos.' Mario's boyfriend beat her. He got jealous when they told him they were coming to see me. They quarrelled a lot and she decided to rub his nose in it every night.

'D'you know how much stick I get because of you?' she says to me.

'Because of me? Why? What's it to do with me?'

'It's like this.' she says, 'My boyfriend thinks I've got something going with you.'

'Hey kid, what are you talking about? Who is he?'
'Mitsos.'

I knew him; he had a *kafeneion* this guy. He took all her money. She worked; he pocketed all the dough; kept her in harness. In no time at all she was sticking to me close. Eh, and I wasn't so dumb I couldn't read between the lines. 'Aha, I'll have her, we'll go somewhere and let rip.' So we had ourselves a fine old time. We had a ball. Went on and on and still she doesn't disappear. So now what do we do? She says to me 'I'll take a room somewhere.' Something along those lines. 'I'll leave that place where I am now.'

'Tell you what,' says I, 'Here's what I've got to say to you: if you behave, fine, I'll marry you, take you to meet all my family. You'll be my wife. That's if you feel you're ready to leave that kind of life behind, the one that you're used to. Because this is going to be different. Can you stick it? Can you handle it?'

'Sure I can.' says she.

'Right then, it's a deal.'

But with this girl Mario I went through hell: first of all with her boyfriend Mitsos who bombarded me with threatening messages; then there was the owner of a wine bar. He had a wife and kids but Mario had driven him out of his mind and turned him inside out. His in-laws were running after me in the hope I'd head her off from him. Then there was a certain Yannis who'd served five years in prison for her. They say she was the reason he lashed out at some guy, stabbed him again and again with a knife and served time in prison. *He* was hounding me too and since I knew he was a nasty piece of work I said to her 'Hold your horses, don't go looking for trouble with that guy.' But I didn't have that much self-control myself and one day I caught him there in Koumoundourou Street and gave him the beating he deserved. 'Take her you bastard!' says I, 'You think I've got her chained up? If she wants to go with you take her! Go on, run round to where she works and have a go!'

But here's the worst thing: she was one hell of a quarrelsome broad! I told her to stop doing that kind of work. Then I'd sign her off the hookers' register and marry her. I took her and we stayed in Mama's house but she couldn't stand the housework. She wanted to be free. She enjoyed that filthy job of hers. 'Markos' she says to me, 'I'm going to leave, I can't do it, I can't take it.' That just about knocked me out. 'Off you go then,' I said, 'leave if you want to.' What else could I to say to her? Later on she got round me and we started sleeping together again in a room she'd taken in Pireos Street in Athens. But she was a very jealous woman, which is why I wrote *Ziliara*, (rec. 1936).

| *Jealous Woman* | *Ζηλιάρα* |
|---|---|
| Ah you wicked creature how you hurt me, | Αχ, κακούργα πόσο με πληγώνεις |
| These games of yours make me feel like a clown. | με τα σκέρτσα σου πως με σκλαβώνεις |
| You made me roam about just like a madman, | μ' έκανες και σαν τρελός γυρίζω |
| You've turned me inside out and upside down. | την καρδιά μου πια δεν την ορίζω. |
| | |
| Ah you wicked creature put away | Αχ, κακούργα πάψε αυτή τη ζήλια, |
| This jealousy and give me your sweet kisses. | φίλα με με τα γλυκά σου χείλια. |
| How you wither me you jealous minx! | Αχ να ξέρεις πως με μαραζώνεις |
| Why do you want to wound me with caprices? | Ζηλιάρα γιατί θες να με πληγώνεις. |

| | |
|---|---|
| Lady since the day | Σαν σε πρωτογνώρισα |
| I first met you | κυρά μου |
| You burnt me up, you left | μου 'καψες βαθιά |
| my guts on fire. | τα σωθικά μου |
| The smallest things they | Ζηλιάρα που όλο θές να |
| put you in a rage | με θυμώνεις |
| To make me angry is | γιατί με το παραμικρό |
| your sole desire. | κακιώνεις; |

She was so jealous and every so often her passion made her go off the rails. Do you know what jealousy means? I'd be talking to her in a nice way and she'd take things all wrong and act in a way that had nothing to do with what I'd said.

| | |
|---|---|
| I am patient too | Κάνω κι εγώ υπομονή |
| Just like the earth - a clod. | ω σαν της γης το χώμα |
| Mouthless I say nothing | που το πατούν και δεν μιλά |
| Just sit there where you trod. | γιατί δεν έχει στόμα. |

One day we were walking together through Omonoia and she had a savage look on her face. I'd done something to her, don't know what and she was furious. We got as far as the square where all the taxis of Athens wait in line. I stopped at a kiosk to get some cigarettes and cast a sideways glance at a girl walking past. She says to me 'What are you waiting for?' Just like that in a nasty tone of voice. I felt like I was going to burst. I said to her 'What kind of a tone is that?' The guy who had the kiosk knew me. It filled me with such fury I just fell on her, slapping and kicking. 'I've had it up to here you filthy whore!' There were some drivers there who knew what she was like. They knew me too. They ran and got her out of my hands. They rescued her and I left her to get home by herself.

Afterwards I recovered a bit. I went home to pick up my things and leave. She was crying and I felt sorry for her. As soon as I fell asleep she takes a bottle of peroxide, which she had for her hair, and pours it in my face. Till the moment I got up and out of that place I thought I'd bust myself. Took some time to get over that. I'd suffered like nobody's business from these low down broads and still I hadn't wised up. I kept going down the same path again. She wouldn't leave me alone, kept trying to make me go back with her. I seized my chance, picked up my clothes and left. It was over.

Five or six months later she came and said to me 'What are you going to do? Will you come back with me? I won't hurt you anymore. Otherwise I'll get married. A guy's asked me to marry him.'

'Why are you telling me this? Did I ever tell you not to get married?'

'I will get married then. I'm going to marry this Armenian. I'll get out of here and go to Russia.'

'What are you waiting for? Don't expect anything from me.'

'Shall I go? You'll let me go?'

'Sure, I'll let you go.'

She married the Armenian and had a baby with him, but even when she was married she used to come and find me. She didn't want the Armenian. But I didn't mess around with her. Nothing doing. 'No, you go with your husband. I don't want you. He'll take you back to your own country. What're you still hanging about here for? Go on, beat it. You're not seeing me again.' She came back time and again, this Mario. I didn't take any notice of her. The time came when the Armenians left for Russia. She went too and I was free once and for all. After so many years, what a life! Now that I'm married it happens every so often that some guy comes over from there and brings me a little letter from her. The husband died but she can't come back here anymore so that finished the business of the Russian girl. That's that.

With all these women I've mentioned, sooner or later I got clear of them and recovered my peace of mind. But with Zingoala, even after I'd got over the pain, even then I wasn't shot of her. The whore – because that's what she was deep down and the others were just more open about it - started suing me for maintenance payments. About that time I wrote *Diaziyio* (rec. 1935).

Divorce

*I gave you a divorce and now*
*What do you want from me?*
*Now you go about and say*
*'what have you done to me?' but hey!*

*In Aghios Dionysios*
*You know I married you*
*And I made you my Missus,*
*All above board and true.*

*You were the one who beat it, you*
*Left me for good and all.*
*At night with little Yiorgos*
*You and he would have a ball.*

*I really should have killed you*
*And set your brains to right.*
*Take your divorce. Be off now,*
*And get out of my sight.*

Διαζύγιο

Σου `δωσα διαζύγιο
τι θέλεις πια από μένα
τώρα γυρίζεις κι όλο λες
τι μου `χεις καμωμένα.

Ξέρεις σε στεφανώθηκα
μες τον Άγιο Διονύση
και σ' έκανα νοικοκυρά
και ποιος να σου μιλήσει.

Κι εσύ μου την κοπάναγες
και μου την αμολούσες
το βράδυ τον Γιωργάκη σου
τον 'παιρνες και γλεντούσες.

Έπρεπε να σε σκότωνα
να `κανα τα μυαλά σου
πάρε το διαζύγιο
και τράβα στη δουλειά σου.

I preferred to pay the courts and not give her so much as five cents. I changed my name with the record companies who were paying me so she couldn't get her hands on anything. I mean instead of Vamvakaris I used the pseudonym Rokos, my grandfather's name. Not so much as a five-cent piece did I pay her. Here's another song I was singing in '38.

### They Made a Fool of You[111]

I understand what's in your head
The bee that's in your bonnet.
My wretched purse is what you want,
You've set your heart upon it.

For sure they made a fool of you
Don't you waste your time my dear
Your teacher taught you wrong since I
For money don't feel pain or fear.

I only spend it where I'm loved.
That at least you ought to know.
I know you're crafty so my advice
Is to be good, I'll love you so.

You haven't learnt the proper place
To spread your nets out wide.
You think you'll burn just every guy
And take him for a ride.

### Σε Γελάσανε

Κατάλαβα την γνώμη σου
και τι καπνό φουμάρεις
το δόλιο πορτοφόλι μου
ζητάς να μου το πάρεις.

Σε γελάσανε
μην χάνεις τον καιρό σου
δε σε σπούδασε
καλά ο δάσκαλός σου.

Δεν τα λυπάμαι τα λεφτά
ούτε και με πονούνε
να ξέρεις μόνο τα χαλώ
εκεί που μ' αγαπούνε.

Το ξέρω είσαι πονηρή
γι' αυτό σε συμβουλένω,
κι αν κάτσεις λίγο φρόνιμα
εγώ θα σε λατρεύω.

Δεν έμαθες τα δίχτυα σου
που πρέπει να τ' απλώσεις
νομίζεις τον καθένανε
μπορείς να τον καψώσεις.

She was having a fine time with her man. Her lover had left his wife and kid. Every day, such scenes outside her house! The wife would come and yell at her 'Hey you! You took my man you husband-snatcher!' And more of the same, but much worse.

So since she never could get even ten cents off me she figured she'd better leave off the law-suit and start working. Her lover never gave her enough money to get by on and she had to work to support her mother. Her mother was an old battle axe who knew everything she'd done, thought it just fine and covered up for her because she'd done exactly the same to *her* husband. An old woman and she had a lover till she was sixty. A shame for their old man! They had a saintly

---

111 *Se Yelasane*, recorded in 1941 - a song of Kostas Skarvelis.

father but the kids he had! Her father was a worker. He had a good job, but he drank. Every evening after work he'd wash, then go to the taverna and drink wine without eating. He was always troubled. He saw what his family had turned into, his two daughters and a son, all a thorough bad lot like their mother. One fine day the poor guy lay down and died with sorrow on his lips.

His only son became a filthy ponce, led a secret life as the team fag. And as for the girls he'd brought up all lah-di-dah, one was the bitch of all time that I'd divorced and the other was separated from her husband and lived with her boyfriend. He loved her loads because she was a beauty but one fine day he stabbed her seventeen times in the heart and they locked him up. Later on I got him off. I went as witness for the defence at the criminal court in Chalkidha. When they heard my statement the court got the message. Like I said, a lot of people knew me. I told them everything about this family and they let him off with only two years in prison. So that was how my sister-in-law finished up. A sordid way to go. She was a stunner, magnificent shapely body. He stabbed her again and again, seventeen times till she was dead. The old *chasapiko*, a very old one from Syros, tells the same story:

Die oh Die[112] | Να Πεθάνεις
---|---
*Die, dammit, die oh die!* | Να πεθάνεις να πεθάνεις,
*With the nasty tricks you play me* | να πεθάνεις
*And the teases that you try!* | με τα νάζια και τα κόλπα
 | που μου κάνεις.
 | 
*I won't die, I won't pass.* | Δεν πεθαίνω, δεν πεθαίνω,
*I'll get in your eye like a piece of glass.* | δεν πεθαίνω
 | και στο μάτι σου γυαλί καρφί
 | θα μπαίνω.

---

112 *Na Pethaneis*, rec. 1961.

| | |
|---|---|
| Die in the alleys, die oh die!<br>For you may all the young girls cry! | Να πεθάνεις, να πεθάνεις,<br>στα σοκάκια<br>να σε κλαίνε, να σε κλαιν'<br>τα κοριτσάκια. |
| Holy Virgin! die please die,<br>So my heart can leap up high! | Να πεθάνεις, να πεθάνεις,<br>Παναγιά μου<br>να ευχαρι- να ευχαριστηθεί<br>η καρδιά μου. |
| Die, Constantina, do please die!<br>Together in a tomb we'll lie. | Να πεθάνεις, να πεθάνεις,<br>Κωσταντίνα<br>να μας θάψουν, να μας θάψουν<br>σ' ένα μνήμα. |

I made up my mind not to get involved with another woman. I hit the hashish and smoked all the time because that was the only way I could forget and find peace. Two songs I wrote at that time show very well what I was thinking and what my life was like. The first is *Bouzouki mou Diplochordho*, (rec. 1937):

| Double Stringed Bouzouki Mine | Μπουζούκι μου Διπλόχορδο |
|---|---|
| Oh double stringed bouzouki mine,<br>You're the only one that can<br>Console me now for all the pain<br>That tortures me, unlucky man. | Μπουζούκι μου διπλόχορδο<br>μπουζούκι μου καημένο<br>μονάχα σύ παρηγορείς<br>κάθε φαρμακωμένο. |
| The pain that I have in my heart<br>You know it and you share,<br>Remember who I was before<br>That hussy stripped me bare. | Το ντέρτι που `χω στην καρδιά<br>το ξέρεις και λυπάσαι<br>πριν να με κάψεις άπιστη<br>ποιος ήμουν το θυμάσαι. |
| Now I see folk avoiding me<br>'Dopey tramp' is what they say.<br>What do I want with such a life?<br>Come on Charos,[113] take me away! | Τώρα με αποστρέφονται<br>με λένε αλανιάρη<br>τι θέλω τέτοια μια ζωή<br>ο Χάρος να με πάρει. |

---

113 In Greek song and folklore Death is often personified as *Charos*, a relic of ancient Greek mythology. Charon is the boatman who took the souls of the dead across the river Acheron to Hades for the price of an obol.

*My double stringed bouzouki, you,*  Μπουζούκι μου διπλόχορδο
*Only you remain in place*  εσύ μονάχα μένεις
*To sweeten my embittered life*  την πικραμένη μου ζωή
*And soothe the frown from off my face.*  να μου τηνε γλυκαίνεις.

It wasn't just that the *bouzouki* was the only thing that had the power to sweeten my miserable life but also I was remembering that time when the *bouzouki* was being hounded. I told you they were chasing us in the *tekedhes*. They were giving us a hard time and they didn't want to hear about the *bouzouki* in any shape or form. But from that time onwards it was unstoppable. It had such power it went all over the place, even to the place where it's at today. The other song was *Osoi Echoune Polla Lefta*, (rec.1936):

**Those Monied Guys**          Όσοι Έχουνε Πολλά Λεφτά

*Those monied guys I wish I knew*   Όσοι έχουνε πολλά λεφτά
*What the hell it is they do*       να `ξερα τι τα κάνουν
*With their money when they die.*   άραγε σαν πεθάνουνε,
*Are they still loaded, hey aman aman,* βρ' αμάν αμάν,
*When up they fly?*                 μαζί τους θα τα πάρουν.

*The small change in my pocket,*    Εγώ ψιλή στην τσέπη μου
*I never put it by.*                ποτές δεν αποτάζω
*And all my sorrows melt away,*     κι όλα τα ντέρτια μου περνούν,
*Hey aman aman,*                    βρ' αμάν αμάν
*Only when I'm stoned and high.*    μόνο σαν μαστουριάζω.

*In the other place*                Αφού στον άλλο το ντουνιά
*You cannot spend or show it.*      λεφτά δε θα περνάνε
*Here on earth it saves your face*  τα `χουν και τα θυμιάζουνε,
*Hey aman aman,*                    βρ' αμάν αμάν,
*But what they don't know's*        δεν ξέρουν να τα φάνε.
*how to blow it.*

I began to spend more time with my mother who was going through a hard time and I tried hard to look after her better. There was Leonardhos too who'd gone mad from smoking hashish, and also my kid brother Argyris. Now it was the turn of the second little girl. She needed protection from the head of the family and that was me, the eldest. I hadn't much book learning but I knew a thing or two on the street. Everybody knew me, just like they knew the other two, the one a head-case and the other a jailbird. So all the family troubles weighed me down and I was ashamed of the state we were in. I put the little girl into a convent boarding school in Syros. She stayed there winter and summer, I mean she was being taught French and Greek, getting an education. This second daughter got away to a decent god-fearing sort of life.

At that time I'd brought out a lot of my own songs on record. I was the first and so far none of these guys who now claim to be this person or that person had yet appeared. It was from my pieces, the ones I first brought out, that all of them learnt *bouzouki*. From my tunes. What we're talking about now is the truth and anybody who tells you different is lying. I gave these guys the first shove, that made them come and take up the *bouzouki*; Tsitsanis, Chiotis, Papaioannou, all these guys… from my songs. And even now I can assure you they still follow *my* 'roads'. The one who goes down his own particular path is Chiotis from Anapli. This guy brought out a more refined *bouzouki*. Really that's not *bouzouki* he plays. More like a mandola, but he's an ace player, I mean he's untouchable. While I, on the other hand, I'm a straight *bouzouki* man. The genuine article. The old guys used to play it thirty, forty, fifty years ago. That's my kind of *bouzouki*. Same with Papaioannou and Keromytis. The working man's instrument. Me and these guys, we keep it simple.

Once I saw that the *bouzouki* had gone up in the world and I was making money from records I decided to stop working in the Athens slaughterhouse once and for all. I downed tools and threw myself into *bouzouki* heart and soul. That was round about '36 or '37. In Votanikos we made good money. I was getting two hundred drachmas a day, Papaioannou around a hundred and fifty, Keromytis and Karipis roughly eighty. The women were getting a hundred and more. Plus we each got a hundred maybe two hundred a night in tips. Not bad, which is why I chucked in everything else. At Votanikos it was Vlachos himself who set up the band. Even if for me the pay was good, it was peanuts compared to what the joint was getting, because every night there was more and more work. It was round that time I brought out the song:

| | |
|---|---|
| *At night at the Votanikos* | *Το βράδυ στο Βοτανικό* |
| *I go and have a ball,* | *πηγαίνω και γλεντάω.* |
| *And what I went through for your sake* | *Και ότι για σένα τράβηξα* |
| *Remember not at all.* | *στο νου μου δεν το βάνω.* |

Like I said the whole of Piraeus, Athens and its suburbs used to come down there as well as people from Larissa, Tripoli and Thessaloniki, the whole of Greece. So Antonis Vlachos made piles of money. But he was the kind of guy who, when it came to money, didn't give a shit about anyone not even his brothers. He didn't care about the people who worked for him in that dive. We were all doing a great job and he was raking it in. Every evening we opened his palms and filled them with money. He didn't look out for us. He just didn't get it. Didn't give us the money he should have. Now you'll say to me 'So why did you stay there? Didn't you think of leaving?' All I can say is, we'd got to know the joint; we'd got to know our public and they were coming there every night; so we stayed. Stratos though, who was big at that time as a singer and he'd even been best man at Vlachos' wedding, still preferred not to work in this dive. He worked at other places.

Vlachos hoarded up sack-loads of money. But in the end we saw how much it did for him. He died dirt poor and his friends buried him. They gathered *him* up in a sack and sent him on his way to the apartment block in the sky.

| | |
|---|---|
| The richest man alive | Ποιος πλούσιος γεννήθηκε |
| Can not cheat Death. | και πήρε βιος μαζί του, |
| His body only needs | μόνο τρεις πήχες σάβανο |
| Three yards of shroud. | κι έντυσε το κορμί του. |
| The rich and poor | |
| Go into the same earth | Ο ουρανός κι θάλασσα |
| See the same sky and sea | έχουν το ίδιο χρώμα, |
| And passing cloud. | οι πλούσιοι και οι φτωχοί |
| | θα μπουν στο ίδιο χώμα. |

I stayed in Votanikos till 1939 when war was declared. That's where we were when we saw the first warplanes.

# PART IV: WAR YEARS AND AFTER

## CHAPTER 17

### I'VE SEEN A LOT

War was declared in 1940. Everybody went off to the army and then it was just me on my own. But after a while the army caught up with the men in my age group, from the roll of '25. They called me up at Goudhi and put me back in my private's uniform. I made up a song, *O Ayimnastos*, (rec. 1940).

| *The Creaky Trooper* | *Ο Αγύμναστος* |
|---|---|
| A lot of people said it | Όσο κι αν το `λεγαν πολλοί |
| But I never gave it credit, | εγώ δε φανταζόμουν, |
| Me, an old guy, elderly, | τώρα στα γεροντάματα |
| Dressed up to look like infantry! | φαντάρος θα ντυνόμουν. |
| | |
| And yet they got me into line | Κι όμως με βάλαν στη γραμμή |
| Into a phalanx of fighting men, | εις φάλαγγα κατ' άντρα, |
| And they double locked me | και με διπλοκλειδώσανε |
| Into the ranks, the infantry pen. | στου πεζικού τη μάντρα. |

The war planes kept coming and so the place in Votanikos closed down. Then things got very tough. The famine devoured us all.[114] Along with the filth, the horrors of war, there was this indescribable hunger. You saw people dropping dead on the street and you pretty much expected next time would be your turn. Once more I had to do some hard thinking: what was I going to do now that things had got really bad?

---

[114] The Red Cross estimated that 250,000 people died directly or indirectly as a result of the 1941-3 famine. Worst hit areas were Athens and Piraeus, which housed roughly a fifth of the entire population of Greece. Working class districts like Kokkinia were the worst affected. The only people on extra rations were grave diggers.

I decided to steady up and stay with my mother. I worked and looked after the house so poor mama had some good times with me. Meantime my fellow Syran Marios Dalezios had opened a new music dive in Omonoia, number 6 Ion Street. I agreed to go and play there in the evenings and set up a band again. It was me, Keromytis, Papaioannou, Peristeris, Karipis and others. I don't remember very well but I do know that just about everyone passed through this joint: Perdhikopoulos, Tsitsanis, Chiotis, Hatzichristos, lots of others. Peristeris[115] was director of recordings at Odeon. This guy played ten instruments. Piano, *bouzouki*, guitar, he played loads. A serious musician. He wrote and recorded lots of songs too, *zebekika, chasapika, vlachika, syrta, tsamika, kalamatiana* and *kleftika*. Just the music, he didn't do his own lyrics. He was from Constantinople but grew up in Smyrna and they came over here after the Catastrophe.

I started living on my own at a hotel which Gatos had, *The Castalia*. A bunch of broads used to gather there in Xanthos Street and get thoroughly plastered in the alley way with the Germans and Italians.[116] That way they could earn some of those loaves made from potato-flour. We played till eleven at night because black-out was at eleven. The English airplanes came and bombed us at night.

I spent the Occupation at Marios' and I did very well there. Some Germans and Italians took a shine to me and they brought me lots of food packages which I gave to my family. The black market was crazy. I knew a lot of black marketeers. Sometimes I got a bread ration or an Italian roll, an egg, an olive or two, a little oil, maybe a piece of donkey or mule meat. Most people were living on a daily diet of

---

115 It has been suggested that it was Peristeris who persuaded Markos to sing his own songs for the first time at the recording studios.
116 The Germans and Italians were joint occupiers until the collapse of Mussolini's government in July 1943. They made uncomfortable colleagues as the Italians were appalled by the Germans' cavalier attitude to the starvation all around them.

boiled greens.[117] That's why they got bloated and died. So many people died and so many were killed. I don't even remember all of them. I was making money all right, loads of money, thousands, millions, billions ... but it wasn't worth anything.

| Bundles of Five Thousand Bills[118] | Ματσάκια Πεντοχίλιαρα |
|---|---|
| You need fat wads of drachma notes<br>Bundles of five thousand bills<br>Just to survive. It drives you nuts,<br>You feel like heading for the hills. | Ματσάκια πεντοχίλιαρα<br>θέλεις να την περάσεις<br>που σου'ρχεται να τρελαθείς<br>και τα βουνά να πιάσεις. |
| You go to the tailor's for a suit,<br>And then you have a heart attack<br>Since you need millions, heaps of loot<br>Just to order a tailored sack! | Στο ράφτη μπαίνεις να ντυθείς<br>σου φεύγει το κεφάλι<br>και θες εκατομμύρια<br>να ράψεις το τσουβάλι. |

Meantime my sister Rosa was sent back from the school in Syra. They were demanding payments from me which I couldn't manage any more. I was saving everything so they'd have food to eat in Kokkinia. I kept pretty much the whole family alive, all my siblings, my brothers in law, their children, plus other poor souls who were starving. I'd see them and say 'Take a piece of bread to eat.' Where would you find bread at that time? I gave them money. If I saw someone was dying I'd take him to a restaurant and feed him. Otherwise what would he eat? Weeds and old shoe leather. Whatever I had I gave them. This song, *Polla Eidhane ta Matia mou*, (rec. 1954) was one I started singing in '43.

---

117 Those with enough strength left went and picked dandelion leaves – *chorta* -off waste ground or mountainsides.
118 *Matsakia pentochiliara*, written 1943, rec. 1947 with slightly different words. The new 5000 drachma notes were issued in 1942 in response to the Germans' impossible levy of 'Occupation costs'. The spiralling inflation meant that between June 1941 and June 1942 the official price of a loaf of bread rose from 70 to 2,350 drachmas. The economy collapsed and barter took the place of money.

### I've Seen a Lot

I've seen a lot,
In foreign lands alone,
I've passed through many
A stormy zone.

Always alone
No friend could I find,
To share the troubles
I had on my mind.

I remembered my mother,
And shed a bitter tear,
In the desert of exile
Year upon year.

She used to say to me
'Life abroad is hard to bear.
For me who brought you up my child
There's double the despair.

### Πολλά Είδανε τα Μάτια μου

Πολλά είδανε τα μάτια μου
κι έχω περάσει μπόρες,
μονάχος μου που γύριζα
μέσα σε ξένες χώρες.

Πάντα μονάχος μα κανείς
δε βρέθηκε για μένα,
που είχα τόσα βάσανα
στο στήθος μου κρυμμένα.

Τη μάνα μου θυμόμουνα
κι έχυνα μαύρο δάκρυ,
στην ερημή μου ξενιτιά
ποτέ δε βρήκα άκρη.

Μου έλεγε, παιδάκι μου,
είναι βαριά τα ξένα
κι εγώ που σε μεγάλωσα
διπλός καημός για μένα.

Meantime I'd got involved with a woman called Voula and she was one hell of a bitch. Her father was a priest. Have you ever heard the saying 'Priest's child devil's grandchild'? She'd been in hospital. I took her under my wing, got her into some decent clothes and she was making money. She always had food to eat and food was a big deal, so she behaved nicely with me. We got along fine. I had her in the hotel where I lived. She was one of those good time girls. She used to go out with the Germans and with Italians too because she wanted to learn Italian. She wasn't the only one doing this sort of thing. Lots of women in Greece wanted Italian and German lovers. It was all the rage at that time. But Voula stopped listening to me. I'd saved her from death and she wasn't straight with me. She did whatever she felt like. She'd got to know an Italian and he was ferocious the way he kept on her tail. On the good side, he gave her a lot of things which she brought back to our hotel. Some of them I ate and the rest I gave to my family. But I had a lot of trouble with this woman. I did so much for her, always hoping I'd get her to go straight, but that didn't happen. She liked this kind of life. I began to think 'What am I going to do with this broad?' Every so often she told me she was going to leave me. The Italian guy had began to cotton on to the fact she had a boyfriend, and the boyfriend was me. One night he started chasing me round Omonoia Square. I'd made friends with an Italian lieutenant called Louis, a very decent guy, so I told him everything and he fixed it so the feller didn't trouble me at all after that. Louis loved me a lot. He started learning Greek and he used to come to Marios Dalezios' place in the evenings. We sat there and chatted in Greek.

I should have left this woman, Voula. So what did I do? One night I met a very beautiful girl called Barbara. To make the other one jealous I brought her back to the hotel to sleep with me. But Voula didn't mind at all. She didn't say a word so I made up my mind to get rid of her. I'd put up with so much from this minx. One fine day I gave her the boot and had some peace. After that I had Barbara who loved me a lot. But by now I'd got sick and tired, because every day I was seeing new women. I began to feel disgusted by them. I decided to take a break and go to Livadeia[119] to work in a music dive in *Panourgia* Square. I played every night for forty days with a guy I found there called Georgios Magnisalis. I earned bread, oil, olives and other things. Sent them to my Mother in Kokkinia and that kept them all going. Next thing was someone came over from Arachova[120] and hired me to play there. I went and found a *lyra* player called Labros so we sat and played together every night in the *kafeneion*. Meantime I'd left Barbara because her family came looking for her and I had problems with this guy

---

119 The capital city of Boeotia in central Greece, 116 km north-west of Athens.
120 A town on the southern slope of Mount Parnassus 26 kms west of Livadeia.

Petros, a grocer she was engaged to. It was time to get clear of her because I didn't want to be put through the mill on her account.

One day in '41 my brother Leonardhos died of hunger. He couldn't get by on one *oke* of bread a day so he shut his eyes and died. He'd been off his head for years and at last he got to rest from the torments he suffered. He used to go missing sometimes and then we had to run round the police stations or psychiatric wards to find him. The tortures my mother went through for that kid, God forgive him! I was sorry for him with all my heart, because, like I say, he'd lost his youth. He'd been like that since he was a kid of seventeen. And I can tell you, when a crisis took hold of him he sure was scary. He lived at mama's place in one room which he shared with his fourteen year old sister and eleven year old brother. I was afraid for the kids, Rosa and Argyris, but it seems like he just loved them loads. He never did them any harm. Far from it. He was always very affectionate with them. One time in a crisis he bit my mother on the lips. He was very violent. I had to pin him down and tie him up with a rope. I gave him a slap with the rope and I guess that brought him to his senses. Then he said to me to me 'Why do you hit me? I'm a dead man already.' That just broke my heart, I can't begin to tell you. I let him go and I went away crying. We were both crying, both of us. He had times when he was a bit saner and you'd get some sense out of him. Poor mama. The number of doctors or 'wise old women' who said they'd do magic on him; she ran to all of them! But God made an end of him.

After the death of Leonardhos it wasn't long before mama died too. She was crushed by all this misery. She died in 1942 from the dreadful illness they call dropsy. So I found myself being papa to the two kids Rosa and Argyris. It was the Occupation and people were dying on the streets every day. Terrible times were upon us. People were starving and frozen, in a state of utter wretchedness. I thanked God I was able to scrape by and look after my family, my brothers and sisters who I felt for. I could see people dying from hardship and hunger and I did my best to look after them. Like no other brother. Because I can tell you, in the game of survival it was every man for himself, just trying to stay alive. I took them whatever I earned in the way of food. I had a sense of duty and it was my habit to feel responsible for everyone. I found a good safe place for the children to stay, a room in 79 Menander Street, in Athens. I rented it from a musician called Michalidhis and the price wasn't too bad - 30,000 drachmas a month. I stayed in a hotel and my sister Rosa cooked and washed clothes for me and the boy.

Since I had him near me, I began to train the kid, Argyris, in my own line of work. He was ten years old when he first touched the instrument and in the space of a year, he got to be ace. Looked like he'd end up a famous player and sure enough he did. I looked after his education and sent him to the Piraeus Odeon which is still there today. I was doing my bit for the kid and as for the little girl, I kept her like a lady. Even if they didn't have a mother, I was their guardian and better than a mother. I got clothes for them and kept them well dressed. People knew they were my siblings and I didn't want anyone saying mean things about me. I did my duty. I didn't begrudge the money I was spending on anyone. Only thing was I used to say one day they'd be helping *me* out.

My brother Frangiskos killed some guy round about that time and was on the run from the law. He was a skinner like me in the Piraeus slaughterhouse. The butcher he killed had failed to pay some money he owed to Frangiskos. Result was he ended up dead. He fancied himself a tough guy and didn't listen to anyone. Frangiskos used to come at night and hide in the room I'd taken in Menander Street. In the morning he'd leave to go to a friend's house. The Piraeus police force were hot on his tail.

As for me I was staying in Lavrio now and whatever I took home to my kid sister she squirreled away and took to our sister Grazia who had four or five kids and her husband wasn't working. He didn't know what to do. The life had gone out of him.[121] He didn't go out or run around looking for ways to make money, the black market for example. He just sat there and the family was facing terrible hardship. With all my heart I was glad to let the kid take what we had to her big sister. She had to get by somehow with her children. That was how things were and every day the grim reaper swallowed up more people. We were longing for the liberation to come so we'd have some peace.

The Occupation went on and on and I wasn't getting any younger. My sisters said I should get married and settle down. There was a girl in the neighbourhood, a friend of my sisters, and so I promised to get married. But I'd had that disaster with my first wife and I didn't really want to marry. Not one bit. I was scared. Why should I marry? I suffered what I suffered. Did I want to go through it all again? Seemed to me all women were the same. But later on my sister, the older one, starts on at me and says 'Vangelio is a good girl and our mother wanted it to be her when she was alive. She's so and so's daughter, a very decent girl, you'll be happy.' Then I began to think what'll become of me later on? Maybe I should settle down with someone, think ahead to when I get older. Her family and my sisters were all in favour of it so I made up my mind to give it a second chance with this girl. We'd met but I hadn't had much to do with her, what with me being married. Besides, I was much older you know. Sure, I'd been with a lot of different girls in my life but what would I have to do with *this* girl? Vangelio

---

121 Hopeless lethargy was a typical symptom of malnutrition as recorded by observers during the worst of the famine in the winter of 1941-2.

worked in a dried fruit shop. I popped in from time to time, met her there and we talked a bit.

| **Years around Piraeus**[122] | **Χρόνια στον Περαία** |
|---|---|
| I've been years in the Trouba,[123] <br> Mega mangas, loose and free. <br> You should first investigate <br> Before you marry me. | Χρόνια μες στην Τρούμπα <br> μαγκίτης κι αλανιάρης, <br> ρώτησε να μάθεις <br> κι ύστερα να με πάρεις. |
| I'm a clever kid <br> And I play the bouzoukaki, <br> And everybody loves me <br> As I'm a Syrianaki | Είμαι παιδάκι έξυπνο, <br> παίζω και μπουζουκάκι, <br> όλος ο κόσμος μ' αγαπάει <br> γιατ' είμαι Συριανάκι. |
| On the street where I grew up <br> They all gave me respect <br> Cos I'm a damn smart mangas <br> All present and correct. | Στην πιάτσα που μεγάλωσα <br> όλοι μ' έχουν θαυμάξει, <br> γιατ' είμαι μάγκας κι έξυπνος <br> και σ' όλα μου εντάξει. |
| The manghes pay attention <br> Take heed of what I say <br> And when I come among them <br> They get love-sick and we play. | Οι μάγκες με προσέχουνε <br> κι όλοι με λογαριάζουν, <br> όταν με βλέπουν κι έρχομαι <br> μαζί μου νταλκαδιάζουν. |

My first marriage was a problem. I'd got married in a Catholic church even though my wife was Orthodox and as is well known, our religion doesn't give divorces. But I had a friend at the bishop's headquarters, a great guy, Yannaki Kalysi, God rest him - a car killed him one day as he was crossing the street. He was fond of me and somehow, goodness knows how, he fixed up the paperwork and got me the certificate which said I'd married an Orthodox even though I was a Catholic. When they saw this the Catholics said to me 'Go and get your wife.' My answer was: 'Which wife do I go and get? Didn't I tell you this woman is a whore

---

122 *Chronia ston Peraia, zebekiko*, rec. 1936.
123 One of the sleaziest districts of Piraeus, notorious for its bars, cabarets and brothels.

and screws around? How am I supposed to take this woman? You take her!'

I got married one Sunday in 1942 and I invited my fellow musicians to my in-laws' house, the band I played with, Peristeris, Papaioannou, Keromytis, Kostas Karipis plus other musicians too. That was my wedding with Vangelio, my present wife. Vangelio was good and I wish I'd had her for my first wife. Then people would have pointed at me and said 'There goes a lucky man!' Such a good wife and mother, this woman I've got now. With her I began to bring children into the world, something I'd given up hoping for. I was much older than her but we lived together happily.

I was lucky in this second marriage but then I had trouble again with my sisters and that upset me a lot. One day the elder sister, Grazia decided to take Argyris away from me. Rosa, the younger one, took her side. She had her own reasons. She wanted to marry the man that *she* wanted and I didn't approve at all! So they broke up the little family I'd set up, you know, me, my wife and the two kids. They couldn't wait to get their mitts on him and within a fortnight of our getting married they took the boy. By that time, you see, the kid played *bouzouki* very well. He was capable of making a living all by himself and he began to go round the villages and play. He used to go to Markopoulo, to Liosia, to Liopesi and to Spata. He made money because he was a kid and everyone loved him. They knew he was my brother and they looked out for him. Everyone used to say 'Hey that's Markos' kid brother.' They've gone on saying it ever since. The first thing my sisters did was ruin the boy. He left the Odeon. If he'd stayed he'd have been one of the great pianists by now; among the best. That upset me a lot. I got hold of him and talked to him, tried to get him to stay with me but he wouldn't listen. I wrote this for Argyris.

Markos and Vangelio, newly weds.

## Those Cruel Words[124]

| | |
|---|---|
| The words you spoke last night | Αυτά τα λόγια τα σκληρά |
| Too cruel by far, | που μου πες χθες το βράδυ, |
| Have left upon my life | μες τη ζωή μου μείνανε |
| A permanent scar. | παντοτινό σημάδι. |
| | |
| The things you say about me, | Να σκέπτεσαι το καθετί |
| Just think about them first. | όπου θα λες για μένα |
| Don't use these bitter words | μη μου πληγώνεις την καρδιά |
| To make my heart burst. | με λόγια πικραμένα. |
| | |
| Listen kid, and do your best | Άκου λοιπόν αγάπη μου |
| To shape up and be wise, | κι αν θέλεις συμμορφώσου |
| Cos I'm the one who brings you joy | πως η χαρά σου ειμ'εγώ |
| Brings light into your eyes. | εγώ'μαι και το φως σου. |

## Αυτά τα Λόγια τα Σκληρά

My sister Rosa who wanted to get married kept making terrible scenes. I was harsh and every time she made me a scene I wouldn't forgive her. So one day she got her stuff together, went to Grazia's and stayed there. But not for long because she soon married this guy and that was the end of it. I was left high and dry by everyone.

From '42-'43, not only was I not going hungry, I was earning pots of money. After Marios' I got work at a joint called *Amphissa* in Ion Street, as well as another joint next door called *Evvia* run by a guy called Kornaros. The place wasn't really his. It belonged to some Israelite. Those people had to hide from the Germans because they were picking up Jews and sending them to Germany where they burnt them in an oven. I played there too every evening. I was a regular for many years. They had women in this place. The Germans used to come, Italians too and they'd take their pick. That's what the place was for. Not for families. It was all ne'er-do-wells, pickpockets, ponces, all kinds of sleazy folk. There were good clients too, but mostly it was the

---

124 *Afta ta Loyia ta Sklira*, not recorded until 1966.

seedy sort and they pinched things from the Germans and Italians.

That's where I made another conquest. I made friends with a girl who worked there, Yorgia from Patras. She was separated from her husband and had a little boy. Her mother worked in the same joint. So began happy days with Yorghia. I loved her. She loved me. She knew I was married but at that time with the state things were in, nobody was looking further than how to make a crust and get through it. That was all. Nothing else seemed to matter. They loved me in this joint because I pulled in the customers and they looked after me well. They put in a piano and it was me and Argyris. I never stopped helping him so he'd grow up and be a good player. I remember a time when he got something wrong with his eyes, and me and Batis took him to the eye-doctor to make him better. I looked after him and felt sorry for him; he was such a young kid. I poured money into making him better.

All the *bouzouki* players went through *Amphissa*. Kostas Kaplanis among others. Michaelidhis gave him lessons and I took him on to work with me. Michaelidhis, whose house I lived in, was from Constantinople, a first rate pianist. He was a teacher, but his colleagues gave him the cold shoulder. Their kind of music was the 'European' stuff. The fiddlers played light music and foreign tunes, and they never took him on for any work. He had a rough time, because he really was a musical giant but cranky too, so they kept him at arms length. He was old, he got drunk, he chased women; pilfered money sometimes. I caught him red-handed once or twice. He was touchy and jealous too. He got envious when he saw the girls treating me to a sweet, you know, those war time sweets made from carob nectar or maybe some wine or tasty titbits. He was a very sickly guy. He had TB for years and the minute he drank wine, even one little glass, he got drunk and couldn't play. His tongue ran away with him and he started fighting with everyone. Every month that went by he raised the rent. I mean I'd taken the house for thousands and he turned it into millions and in a short while to billions.

Every night he and his wife Persephone were at each other's throats because they had a son who'd gone mad and the old man was at the end of his tether with the poor kid. Before he went mad the son had been a jazz band maestro and toured all of Europe. He was a first rate musician like his father but then he got ill. His wife had left him and his parents had him at home. He was always in and out of clinics and psychiatric wards. He didn't know what he was doing, poor guy, and when he did something out of order in the house, his father wanted to stick a knife in him. Good thing I was there with my wife. We had to pull them apart and make them calm down. I mean the life I had with this family! My nerves were in shreds, my wife's too. It was hell. Meantime I was waiting for my wife to give birth. It was the first child I brought into the world.

The Occupation. People were dying like dogs every day. That's how it was. I was looking after my family and my wife and I brought into the world this first child, a boy. I baptized him and called him Dhomenikos, my father's name. I can't tell you the joy I felt but after about nine months he fell ill with double pneumonia. What I went through to save him! I spent a fortune and in the end I couldn't do anything. If I could have given the child penicillin I'd have saved him. But it was the early days of penicillin then and the hospitals kept it for the army. We lost him.

Time went by and I brought a second child into the world, a girl. And again I felt the joy but she wasn't fated to live either. Grief for the child who'd died was eating into me and I told myself it was my fault for having got involved with Yorgia the girl from Patras. It had brought bad luck. That was my conscience talking. But what could I do? I'd got involved with her and every so often I'd take her to the doctor for an abortion and I can't tell you what anguish *that* caused me. I just didn't know what to do. She loved me so much. Our affair lasted a long time and I should have ended it because she had no future with me. I was married and for all the stuff I did with other women I loved my wife because she loved me very much and she was a great wife. I wasn't going to trade her in for any woman. She was a real gem.

Every evening we had Michaelidhis brawling with Persephone and it was the poor kid Vassilis who got it in the neck. I mean, he'd really lost it, the old man. He didn't know where to take out his rage and he'd be yelling at him. The old woman loved her boy. On summer evenings she'd get him out of the house for a walk maybe to Omonoia or to Syntagma to make him feel less gloomy, because he wasn't completely nuts. He had times when he talked quite normally. I mean he was a very sad case. But I used to have some fun with these people too. Michaelidhis' wife was afraid the hookers round there were driving her old man crazy. She'd come every evening and peer through the windows to see what he was doing. Whatever *was* the poor geezer supposed to be doing? Just a poor piece of old rag! They squabbled night and day and sometimes, just for the hell of it I'd stir them up to a frenzy and then I'd separate them. I was laughing. What could you do with this old girl? She'd fly at him: 'Have you been running after the women again?' Fat chance! He couldn't even walk! They'd be at it hammer and tongs. I used to tell the girls to put lipstick on him. And then, sure enough, all hell broke loose in that house. My wife used to say to me 'Aren't you ashamed of yourself?' But that was how I kept my spirits up. I'd forget all the things that were going on, the starvation, the round-ups, executions, stealing, informing, all of that. What with the work and this guy and his old lady I got through a bad time. A song I was singing around then is *Tha Spasei to Bouzouki mou*, (rec. 1940).

### My Bouzouki will Break

My bouzouki, my only friend
Is going to break apart,
It's breaking from the sadness
That I feel in my heart.

Remember how I lulled you
To sleep on the divan
And sang you lullabies at night
The sweet-bouzouki man.
It doesn't care to spend the night
All alone with me,
Now there's no hope of playing to you
Our daily melody.

Who now will sing sweet serenades?
Who, my sweetiepie?
Who now will sing the 'nani nan'.
The pretty lullaby?

### Θα Σπάσει το Μπουζούκι μου

Θα σπάσει το μπουζούκι μου
η μόνη συντροφιά μου
απ' το μεράκι το πολύ
που νιώθω στη καρδιά μου.

Θυμήσου πως σε κοίμιζα
τα βραδιά στο ντιβάνι
με το φτωχό μπουζούκι μου
σου 'λεγα νάνι-νάνι.
Βαρέθηκε να ξενυχτά
κι αυτό κοντά σε μένα
χωρίς ελπίδα να χτυπά
μερόνυχτα για σένα.

Καντάδες όμορφες, γλυκιές,
τώρα ποιος θα σου κάνει
ποιος θα σου λέει μικρούλα μου
γλυκά το νάνι-νάνι.

An Italian tango had come out at that time called '*Naninani*'[125] and I put together this lullaby from that. I talk about 'serenades' because it fitted this song but of course the *manghes* don't do serenades on *bouzoukia*. Serenades went with guitars and mandolins. People from Corfu, Kefalonia and Athens played them. The *manghes* didn't do that stuff. A *mangas* wasn't going to go and sit outside a girl's window and do serenades. Can you imagine them doing a thing like that? No, they went round on tiptoe. I mean they flitted. Man, how can I put it? These are guys who look for every possible way to keep out of sight, so people won't see them going for a smoke. They went furtively to their secret places, they'd do anything not to be found out. They were scared of the police, really scared!

---

125 *Nani nani* is the Italian equivalent of 'lullaby'.

The Germans and the Security Battalions[126] came in every evening. They were searching the *bouzouki* joints for the boys off the mountain.[127] One evening at the *Amfissa*, the *Komandatura*, the German police came in. They had a Greek with them who spoke German and he was called Markos too. This guy helped the Germans with whatever they wanted. He hunted the hookers and he hunted insurgents, whoever came down from the mountains. He was a terror, wherever he set foot. They locked the doors so that nobody could get in or out. A lookout kept guard while the others searched the joint and anybody suspicious they took away to Merlin Street in Kolonaki. That's where Commandant headquarters was. After they'd combed the joint and rounded up prisoners, along comes the officer, with this Markos fellow and says to me 'You'll come tomorrow to Merlin Street round nine in the morning.' 'What d'you want with me?' I reply, 'What business have I got over there?' This was a terrifying time because there were the communists too. People were stepping up their activities against the Germans and I can't tell you what a funk I was in about their wanting to see me the next morning at Merlin Street. It was a place of horror, last stop before the firing squad. They took people off from there and shot them. Once you were in you'd be lucky to get out. It was pretty much a death sentence.

I told my wife when I got home and we didn't sleep that night. I had so many fears running around my head. In the morning I say to my wife 'My dear Vangelio, I'm going now to see what they want from me.' I walked along the street like a man on his way to the guillotine. What else could I

---

126 In the last year of the occupation there was a proliferation of Greek collaborationist battalions. They were formed to counter the threat posed by the Greek resistance - EAM/ELAS, the largely 'communist' 'National Liberation Front' and 'National Popular Liberation Army', which by that time controlled about two thirds of the country. For more conservative Greeks, fear of a communist take-over had by now come to outweigh fear of the Germans. These Security Battalions were notorious for their brutality.

127 The *antartes*, Greek resistance fighters who fought in the mountainous regions of Greece with *ELAS*. To 'go to the mountains' was synonymous with going off to fight as an '*antartis*'.

do? I put on a brave face, turned my heart into a rock. At Merlin Street there were sentries all over the place. But at that time, even among these sentries, there were guys who were communists. They'd planted their own among the men who kept guard for the Germans. The minute they saw my face they shouted 'Markos, Markos, what are you doing in this place? What d'you want here?' What was I to say to them? A German guy opened up two massive doors with lots of locks and bolts and let me in. I was shaking like a leaf. On one side there was a very large underground space and it had small locked cells packed with people. As I went past them towards the stairs they were shouting 'Markos what are you doing here? Come here!' But I couldn't, I was so scared. The place looked like a slaughterhouse. I saw blood on the walls and some of them were shouting 'Come back, come here, we need to speak to you. Go to our homes. Tell them tomorrow they're going to shoot us. Kiss my children for me, my wife, my little brothers and sisters…' And me, poor devil, hearing these things, boy was I sorry for them! Especially knowing as I did that they were shooting about fifteen or twenty guys a day. I got to a big door. Markos was waiting for me.

'You came?'

'I did.'

'Hang on I'll go and see if it's a good time to present you to the officer.'

I waited on a sofa and after a while we went into a sitting room. I had never seen a German army lieutenant before. He was smiling cheerfully and talking to me in German. I didn't understand a word of it but he was very friendly and he was telling Markos what they wanted to say to me. I was on pins till I'd heard what they wanted. Man, what I went through! 'First of all', he says, 'we'll make you a coffee.' It was two or three years since I'd drunk coffee. Where would you drink it? There wasn't any! The Germans had good coffee. So he makes me a coffee and I drink it. 'Right Markos,' the interpreter says to me, 'Listen, the reason why they've brought you here to this place is you're going to be helping us.'

'What! How will I be helping you? I'm just a guy who plays *bouzouki*? Other than play *bouzouki* what am I supposed to do? You want us to go on a spree and have fun? Fine, that's something I can do.'

'Not that' says he.

'Eh, what d'you want then?'

'A lot of people come in the evenings to the place where you play. They dance and they get drunk and maybe you know who they are.'

'Who?'

'These guys who come down from the mountains. Various communists, I don't know. You must know them.'

'Listen chum, how would I know them? How the hell am I supposed to know them?' In fact that very night when they came to the *Amphissa*, and told me to come the next day, you wouldn't believe what a beating they gave to one guy they caught. They beat the shit out of him and took him away. A strong guy and he was never seen again. Gestapo.

'This is what you'll do for us. You'll tell us everything. We'll give you whatever you fancy, bread, food, all kinds of good things and we'll pay you.' What was I to say? I nodded yes to everything they said to me. 'Yes, yes, yes, yes,' just to have done with it, clear off and get out of there. As soon as the conversation with the Gestapo was over they took me out a different way, not the same way I came in. As I was leaving, the driver of this German lieutenant spoke to me. He was one of those undercover communists. He says to me 'Hey pal, how the hell did *you* come to be here? Mother of God, who brought *you* in, of all people?'

'Who brought me here? Why, this Markos fellow brought me here. He came to the place where I play every night and he told me to come here the next day. So I did.'

Afterwards my only thought was how to make myself scarce. I mean, was I going to do these sorts of things when the Greeks all loved me no matter what party they belonged to? They'd come and they'd give me money and things for my family. Once they treated me to a car-load of three and a half tons of grapes which I shared with everybody. I got back to the rooms I was staying in with the old guy Michaelidhis and I figured it was time to leave town. Luckily it was the time when the Germans were coming apart and after I came down to Piraeus, not even two days went by before they took to their heels and left.[128] They were in a great hurry to get away and save their skins. That's how I got out of the tight spot they'd put me in. The day they left I wrote a four liner:

| It was on a Thursday, | Ημέρα Πέμπτη ήτανε |
| The 12th day of October, | δώδεκα Οκτωβρίου |
| They smashed the head | που σπάσανε την κεφαλή |
| Of the savage robber. | του άγριου θερίου. |

After that I went back to the *Amphissa*. There we sang all my songs from before the war and I wrote some new ones too. One that went down very well was a *zebekiko* called *Chaidhari*. Chaidhari was a prison camp where they assembled the prisoners. They took them there from Merlin Street and that's where they killed them. We sang this a lot but I didn't record it.

| *Chaidari* | *Χαϊδάρι* |
| Mother run as fast as you can | Τρέξε μανούλα όσο μπορείς |
| Oh mother run quickly. | τρέξε για να με σώσεις |
| From Chaidari's prison block | κι απ' το Χαϊδάρι μάνα μου |
| Run and set me free. | να μ' απελευθερώσεις. |
| Because I'm under sentence | Γιατί είμαι μελλοθάνατος |
| And I'm about to die, | και καταδικασμένος |
| A seventeen year old | δεκαεφτάχρονο παιδί |
| In iron chains I lie. | στα σίδερα δεμένος. |

---

128 October 1944.

| | |
|---|---|
| They'll take me from Sekeri Street | Απ' την οδό του Σέκερη |
| To Chaidari today. | με πάνε στο Χαϊδάρι |
| Hour by hour I expect | κι ώρα την ώρα καρτερώ |
| Charos to take me away. | ο Χάρος να με πάρει. |
| | |
| Mama just look at the sword | Να δεις του Χάρου το σπαθί |
| Charos' sharpened knife | μανούλα που θα φέρνει |
| That he'll be carrying in his hand | και τη ζωή του καθενός |
| As he takes each man's life. | μάνα πως θα την παίρνει. |
| | |
| Talk to the other mothers | Κι όταν με δεις μάνα νεκρό |
| When you see me dead. | να πεις στις άλλες μάνες |
| With sufferings even greater | γιατί πονέσανε κι αυτές |
| Their poor hearts have bled. | με πίκρες πιο μεγάλες. |
| | |
| Tell them I saw their children | Πως είδα τα παιδάκια τους |
| In prison clothes ill-suited | στα σίδερα δεμένα |
| Manacled in iron chains | με την κατάδικη στολή |
| Unjustly executed. | αδικοσκοτωμένα. |

In the midst of all these things that happened to me I hadn't forgotten Yorgia. I still had her with me. We were always together. She was a great girl and I really felt for her. I couldn't just abandon her. I didn't spend even so much as a cent on her because she worked but I always had a weight on my mind. I wasn't being straight with my wife as I had this dishonest thing going on. I was always drawn towards these girls and singers. That was my world, it was where I worked. What could I do? It wasn't even as if I had anything to complain of at home. I felt bad about it all the time because I had no excuse for treating my wife like that.

At home with Vangelio everything was calm. She didn't know anything and she was eaten up with grief over the child we'd lost. She cried night and day because she was a very devoted mother, as she still is now with our three boys. The Patras girl used to come to the house and sit there chatting with her as if nothing was going on at all. My wife was very innocent. It never crossed her mind that anything like that could happen, that I might have Yorgia for my lover. My conscience wasn't clear but I guess at some point I'd decided that all women were the same, I mean, like the first wife. So to hell with it I'd have as good a time as I could. Anyway I always did have a roving eye.

After *Amfissa*, I moved on to the next place, the *Kare tou Assou*[129] near Ayios Pavlos. I played there every night for seven or eight months with Peristeris, my brother and some other guys. There were communists who came there too and they were always on the look out for their enemies the *Chites*[130] so once again we had some ugly bust-ups, pretty much every night. The communists used to come to me and say 'Hey you've got to stop singing these songs about hashish.' Chaos, death and destruction all around us and these guys wanted me to stop singing my hashish songs! They were dead set against them. 'We'll send you into exile, we'll drive you out. Don't sing these songs!' They were squeezing me on both sides. The *chites* would come along. 'Go on Markos, sing them. Don't you mind anybody, we'll protect you.' The *chites* and the communists, boy, that was one hell of a business. No picnic. The *antartes* wanted me to play my stuff but *not* the hashish songs. The people mustn't get to know about this kind of thing. These guys were serious. They wanted me to be serious too and sing serious songs - I don't mean their insurgent songs because how would I know those songs? But the *chites* used to say 'Play whatever you like. Nobody can stop you.'

They were hunting each other down, killing each other. They had battles in the street, right outside our joint.[131] It

---

129 A hand of four aces in poker.
130 Members of the 'Organisation X' founded by Georgios Grivas. Very similar to the other security battalions, its symbol was the Greek royal monogram, a pair of crossed Gammas which looked like the letter *Chi*. They were dedicated to fighting communists and fought alongside the Government forces and the British in the *Dekemvriana*, the December insurrection of 1944.
131 From the summer of 1944 to Jan 1945, Athens was a battlefield. Corpses swung from the Acacia trees and people were surprised if they *didn't* hear gunfire.

was a savage struggle. I had to try and keep on terms with everyone. Of course I wasn't going to show whose side I was on. And I *wasn't* on anybody's side either. Neither the *antartes* nor the *chites*. I was a Greek through and through. I loved my country and I was just waiting for the time when we'd be set free from this anguish, from *these* guys on the one hand and *those* guys on the other. I minded my own business. I worked day and night at the *Kare tou Assou*, I got paid, I did my job.

Like I said, the Germans had left and Greece was on the brink of falling into the hands of these communist guys. The others, the *chites* I mean, did at least help to stop that from happening. There I was in the middle of it all, keeping my cards close to my chest because I didn't want either side to kill me. So many times they beat people up, even at our joint, and I'd get in there:

'Hey guys, it won't do. It's a sin. We're all brothers!'

'Keep out of it Markos!' they'd say to me - whether they were *chites* or *antartes*, 'Don't you get mixed up in these things.' So I sat tight because there was nothing else I could do. I had to do what they said. That's how things were at that time, until we got shot of this misery and the whole damn lot of them went away. Our army got to work and sorted them out.

After the *Kare tou Assou* I went to *Vangelas'* in *Patission Street* for a while, till the building was demolished. They had women in there. Down below was the restaurant where we played and upstairs it was a bordello - short-stay room rentals. Guys would take the women upstairs, do their thing, go away. A cheap, seedy joint. It had food, drinks, everything. Of course I had stuff going on with the women. Affairs with the hookers in there. The broads loved me. I didn't give them any trouble; and if ever it happened that some guy tried coming over heavy on me, or tried to fool me, I'd say 'Hey get lost! Outa here! Before I set the hookers onto you. They'll skin you alive!' I only had to say a word to the girls and they'd be onto him like a shot.

In that place I was getting a hundred drachmas a night and maybe another two hundred in tips. A lot of people passed through this joint. Tips were good. The women, you see, made these guys dance and get drunk and throw money about like nobody's business. Vangelas provided food and put down insurance stamps for us. He was a great guy; good-looking too. Later on he got ill with diabetes just like me. I don't know whether he's alive or dead but I can't tell you what a great guy he was. The diabetes turned him into a rag. The great Vangelas ...

The records meantime had come to a standstill when war was declared. The factory shut down as soon as the bombing began. Whatever records of mine the factory had, they sold. But they weren't making new ones. I wasn't getting money from the records any more and I simply had to have an income. After some time I went down to Trouba to a place on the seafront, *Linari's*, and every night it was me playing with Argyris, Batis and one Stefanos Makronas. Sailors used to come. A lot of people came in because it was where the hookers lived. We made money, and all the time I was still seeing Yorgia.

After about three or four months, year 1947, Papaioannou came to Trouba from Tzitzifies. They'd set up the *kentro Kalamatianou*, and he says to me, 'Markos, how about you come on over and we'll put a band together. We talked it over and set up the band: me, Papaioannou, Rovertakis, Karipis, Chatzichristos, Keromytis and Peristeris. Every night the world went crazy! Everybody was coming down to Tzitzifies to get cool and have a wild time. The anguish from the communists and all that had cleared up and we were normal Greeks again, true Greeks. Down there in Tzitzifies, that was the business alright. The whole world descended on that place. It was the only joint that was running in that area and it was us who got it going, me and Papaioannou. I started making records again with all the companies, Odeon, Columbia, Parlophone, His Master's Voice and all the other companies that started up at that time. They became smash hits. Every night I was singing my new songs and people loved them. I was singing, Papaioannou was singing, Keromytis was singing, Chatzichristos and Karipis too, we were pretty much all singing. Some of these guys are still alive.

In Tzitzifies you see, there was only the *Kentro Kalamatianou*. Later, Marios Dalezios opened up a place too. He was a fellow Syran, also a Catholic. From Ion Street he came down to Tzitzifies and I left *Kalamatianou*. I went over to Marios' and then it was me and Papaioannou at one joint and Manolis Chiotis at the other. But our place was doing good business. We had every kind of person in there, professionals, classy types, and working folk, all having a great time. Jam-packed every night. Here's a song I wrote then, *Kolonaki Tzitzifies* (rec. 1949):

| Kolonaki - Tzitzifies | Κολωνάκι Τζιτζιφιές |
|---|---|
| They set off from Colonaki<br>To get down to Tzitzifies<br>To hear a little bouzoukaki<br>With the sweetest of 'penies.' | Ξεκινούν από το Κολωνάκι,<br>για να κατεβούν στις Τζιτζιφιές,<br>λίγο για ν' ακούσουν μπουζουκάκι,<br>με τις πιο γλυκύτερες πενιές. |
| You'll see luxury motor cars<br>And famous ladies, take your pick,<br>Fine aristocratic gentlemen<br>And many a slinky sexy chick. | Βλέπεις κούρσες τις πολυτελείας<br>κι όμορφες κυρίες ξακουστές,<br>κύριοι της αριστοκρατίας.<br>νόστιμες κοπέλες ζηλευτές |
| They're all yearning for the sea shore<br>And our magical 'penies'.<br>Our bohemian songs fill all<br>The world with joy and loveliness. | Όλοι νοσταλγούνε τ' ακρογιάλι<br>και τη μαγική μας την πενιά,<br>το μποέμικο μας το τραγούδι,<br>ομορφαίνει όλον τον ντουνιά. |

In that place I had yet another conquest. A girl from Syros came one day with her sister. Rita was her name and it was the start of an idyll, an overpowering passion. The minute I saw her I was swept off my feet. She was a twenty year old girl with 'long hair' as the saying goes 'and little brain.' I was head over heels and little by little she made me forget Yorgia, the girl from Patras. I'd recently brought out a *chasapiko*, *Kaloyeros*, (rec. 1946):

| The Monk | Καλόγερος |
|---|---|
| I'm fed up with girlfriends, | Βαρέθηκα τις γκόμενες |
| I'm getting in a funk. | κοντεύω να τα χάσω, |
| Because of that I've made a plan | γι' αυτό και τ'αποφάσισα |
| To go and be a monk. | για να φορέσω ράσο. |
| | |
| Although I made a heap of dough, | Οσα λεφτά οικονόμαγα |
| I haven't saved a franc. | φράγκο δεν αποτούσα, |
| I blew it all with girls and now | μαζί μ' αυτές τα χάλαγα |
| There's nothing in the bank. | και ρέστος τριγυρνούσα. |
| | |
| Rows and dramas, sleepless nights | Μπελάδες και τραβήγματα |
| Bruises and kicked shins, | ξενύχτια φασαρίες, |
| Regular horrors I've endured, | και ταχτικά τραβιόμουνα |
| A high price for my sins. | και πλήρωνα αμαρτίες. |
| | |
| But now I'm going to change my life | Τώρα θ'αλλάξω πια ζωή |
| They won't call me a mug, | δε θα με λεν μπατίρη |
| Cos I will go and be a monk | και πάω για καλόγερος |
| In a monastery snug. | σε κάποιο μοναστήρι. |

Rita told me later on that she'd been in a convent when she heard that. She'd planned to become a nun but when she heard it she packed it all in and went off to Kolonaki to work as a maid in someone's house. Later I wrote this song for her, *Ap'Oses ki'an Egnorisa*, (rec. 1948):

*Of all the girls I ever Met*

I've got incurable longings
Deep down in my heart,
They always see me now at night
Sitting moodily apart.

Poor devil that I am I met
A lovely girl and she
Has stolen my poor heart away.
Now I live in misery.

Alas the only thing I think
Of now is how to get her,
So that from love's fiery grip
I'll escape and feel better.

A sweet and dusky little flirt
She's such a slinky air.
Of all the girls I ever met
She's the most rich and rare.

She knows how much I love her,
And that I'm all on fire.
She trusts me when I truly say
It's love not just desire.

But if I cannot have her
I surely will go mad.
Can't see the point of living
Without her to make me glad.

*Απ' Όσες κι αν Εγνώρισα*

Εχω καημούς αγιάτρευτους
βαθειά στα φυλλοκάρδια
και πάντα μελαγχολικό
με βλέπουνε τα βράδια,
για μια κοπέλα όμορφη
που γνώρισα ο καημένος,
μου έχει πάρει την καρδιά
και ζω δυστυχισμένος.

Και σκέφτουμε ο δυστυχής,
πως να την ανταμώσω,
κι απ' το σεβντά που μ' άναψε
πως πρέπει να γλυτώσω,
είναι γλυκιά μελαχροινή,
καμωματού τσαχπίνα,
απ' όσες κι αν εγνώρισα,
αυτή 'ταν η πιο φίνα.

Το ξέρει πως την αγαπώ
κι έχω φωτιά στα στήθια,
και με πιστεύει, πως εγώ
την επονώ στ' αλήθεια,
μα `γω τρελαίνομαι γι' αυτήν
κι αν δεν την αποκτήσω,
τι να την κάνω τη ζωή,
τι μ' ωφελεί να ζήσω.

At first Yorgia didn't know about Rita, but she saw that I was avoiding her. She cried and cried: 'You don't love me. Looks to me like you've got someone else!' Meantime my wife found out about Yorgia and you can't imagine the wailing that went on in the house. 'She was pretending to be my friend and all the time she was digging my grave? What a fool I am!' Yorgia never set foot in my house again. All the time I was looking for ways to smooth things over or get Vangelio to shut her mouth because she wouldn't keep quiet. I mean she had every right to complain. I did have three kids with her after all. I still hadn't broken with Yorgia and on top of that I'd got involved with Rita! I shouldn't have done the things I did to Rita. A girl from Syros too, my compatriot. I mean I was in the wrong. Good people don't do those things.

'Ach!' was all that would come out of my mouth. I couldn't stop at home because my wife never quit complaining. To get any peace I had either to be asleep so I couldn't hear it or to be out. One day I got on the bus to Tzitzifies and they were both on it, Yorgia and Rita! They had a row and I left them to it; got away on another bus. These kinds of things were happening all the time. In the end I said to myself Now's the time to get free of Yorgia. I reckoned maybe she'd go and find her husband that she'd split up with and they'd get back together. I couldn't bear any more after all that had happened. Now my wife had found us out and on top of all that there was Rita as well. So we parted. But Yorgia never lost my good opinion. She never talked ugly. Probably she loved me too much. Either way I close a chapter with this woman and it was with her that I spent the toughest time of my life, the Occupation. She looked out for me; kept me out of harm's way. Bless her wherever she is.

## CHAPTER 18

## IN THIS BAD WORLD

Here begins the drama with Rita. Like I said she was a maid in Kolonaki and when I'd finished work at Tzitzifies I used to go to the place where she lived. She let me in by a little window. There was another maid there too but I got her on side and she didn't tell tales. I'd get in there and spend a few hours and after that I'd come home again, back to the complaining. I kept telling my wife I'd ended it with Yorghia but she didn't believe me because I still didn't get home at a decent hour. The kids kept falling ill so I had to keep getting in doctors. What with that and my wife scolding 'You bring us bad luck and our kids are getting sick', I didn't have a single pleasant day at home. She didn't even know I'd got tied up with Rita! *I* was remembering my kids as well, the ones who'd died, and I told myself I was to blame. But what could I do? After all I kept the household going. It wasn't like I was running away and not giving money every day to my wife. The medicines and doctors cost a lot.

Like we said, by now I was working with Papaioannou at Tzitzifies and the passion with Rita was growing, to the point where I actually went to her family home. I mean I acted like I was a free man when all the time I was married! The lengths I went to with this Rita! Meantime I was telling them 'I'm separated from my first wife. I'll get a divorce and then I'll marry Rita.' I mean I was telling lies to these people! I shouldn't have done that. But it didn't take them long to find out the truth. Then things got really tough for me. After about nine months had gone by I went all the way with Rita and don't even ask! She got pregnant in the first month. She didn't say anything to me and I didn't get it, not until she was nearly due to give birth. What didn't her folks say to her then! They threatened to take me to court, but she stood by me; she was very firm. She didn't let them because really she felt she'd suffered more from her parents than from me. From an early age they'd shut her up in a college for juveniles and she'd been through horrible times in there. She didn't want to see her parents. When they said to her 'Leave that lying rascal, we'll put him in jail' she fought them off and didn't want me to suffer any harm. In the end they had to come and take her away by force and keep her under guard. But she kept running away and coming to find me. She used to let me into her home just like at Kolonaki. I used to sleep with her and a little sister they'd put in there to keep her company, all in one bed. But she fixed things, I don't know how, and the little mite didn't tell on us. I used to leave at the first sign of dawn so as not to be caught. But then one day they *did* catch me. They wanted to take her to the police but they couldn't because she was of age by now. So they turned her out of the house.

    I got a room for her in the orchards at Aghia Eleousa in Kallithea. I looked after her, paid for the room and made sure she was okay. She gave birth to a little girl who got to the age of about fourteen months and then became very ill. I took her to the children's hospital but after three or four days she died. I'd baptized her and given her my mother's name Elpidha. I'd registered her birth along with my other children. Meantime my wife found out this new exploit of mine. But like I said, what could I do? It was all down to the line of work I was in. I had to have a woman.

    At Tzitzifies we were getting 150 drachmas a day and we just about doubled that on tips, plus I was making a lot of money from the records. But later on my star began to fade, I wasn't top of the tree any more. After *Kalamatianou* had come to an end I took Rita and we did a tour of the islands. We took the boat and went to Ikaria and to Fourni, a little island just next to it where I had an old pal from army days. I played there three or four days in a joint owned by a guy called Ismail. Sounds like a Turk but he wasn't, he was Greek. This island Fourni was all fishing folk. They did their fishing in Africa and we arrived at the time they were coming back so they had some money. I had Rita with me and we worked together. I had her singing with me on the platform.

After we'd finished there I wanted to go across to the Dodecanese. A caique was going there from the Cyclades. It came from Paros all loaded up with potatoes and went round the islands selling them until they ran out. I met the captain of this boat when it came to Fourni and I said to him 'How about taking me to Patmos and the Dodecanese? Shall we get in? The woman too?' 'Sure I will' he said.

So in we get and off to Patmos. To Patmos on that day of all days! We'd scarcely gone one or two miles when a storm blew up. I can't tell you what that was like! The captain was scared. 'We'll go back.' he said, 'We can't go on!' We came to a little desert island piled high with shells of old lobsters, and crayfish, a dismal looking old heap of rubbish. We sheltered there for a bit then went back to Fourni and stayed there for two or three hours. 'We'll try again' says the captain, 'We're going to get there dammit, let's try.' Eh ... we were saying the storm had settled down. We set off again. We arrived at the same place as before and the sea catches us out. Really bad. The captain lost it. Same with the mechanic he had with him. I lay on my back and didn't say a word. Only Rita seemed like she didn't mind and she wasn't afraid. She was singing! All the rest of us had gone grey with fear. A terrible storm. The captain kept saying 'We'll get to Patmos if God wills it.'

By the skin of our teeth we *did* get to Patmos. In the harbor the captain hurled the caique into the mole and half smashed it. All in all it had suffered quite some damage by the time we got there. I went to look for a place where we could stay and do three or four days' work before heading on.

I found a place. The guy invited me to stay and we struck a deal. Then me and the woman were summoned to the police station to sort out our permit. As soon as we got there I saw the policeman, a sub-lieutenant of the regional police force. This guy had his eyes on the woman. You can guess the rest. He fancied her and he started saying any old nonsense, this that and the other, like: 'What's your plan? You have to take out a license and I'm not sure I can give you permission to play.' He piled it on thick and it was all about the woman. I acted dumb and instead of calling him Mr Policeman I called him 'Admiral'. It was all 'Lord High Admiral' this and 'Lord High Admiral' that. The guy knew me but he pretended not to. I just kept giving him the 'Lord High Admiral' treatment.

'Markos I am *not* in the navy. I'm in the police force. Why are you calling me an admiral?'

'Ah, so you *do* know me.'

'Won't you stop it with your Admiral this and Admiral that?'

'So I'll stop,' says I to him, 'and then what, Mr Policeman? I tow *your* line? Since you *do* know me, you do know who I am don't you? What kind of an act are you putting on for the woman? She's not for you. The woman is mine. What is it you're after? Do you feel like letting us play? If you do that's fine and dandy. If you don't, we'll leave tomorrow morning. On to the next place. End of discussion. But since you do know me, you'll know that I don't put up with this kind of bullshit. I'm not just any old mug. If I have a woman with me it means that she's mine and I'm fully concentrating on the *what* and the *how*.' Some time back, me and this guy, we'd hung out together at Marios'. We'd done goodness knows what in all sorts of other places besides. 'Well,' he says he to me, 'I'll give you the permit to play up to four days.'

'Now you're talking. Good. But if you're not willing we'll leave. It's not like we're twisting your arm' says I to him. 'Of course you couldn't've banished us from here since we're travelling artists. That's what we do to earn our bread. We don't steal, we don't snatch, we don't do anything. You *have* to give us the permit. Isn't that so?' And after that we became friends. Of course he understood those tricks wouldn't do. I gave as good as I got. What else could I do?

He gave me the permit, I played two or three nights in a *kafeneion*, made some money and the time came to leave. The caique had sold the potatoes and was ready to go to Leros. There too the sea was torture. Rita was okay but not quite as okay as she was on the way to Patmos. A gale was blowing and for all the harbor at Leros was so enclosed, it still hurled us onto some rocks. Anyhow we made it and dropped anchor. The main town of Leros wasn't much good. There were some restaurants, that sort of thing, but we didn't want those sorts of places. We wanted to find tavernas that sold wine and all those kinds of things. So we headed for the Upper Chora. There we met one Vassilis, a tall guy who used to be a waiter in Marios'. His father had hotels and since we knew him from Athens he was keen to find us a place to play in Leros. He took us to this joint. We went in, sat down and the owner brought us a glass of wine. Vassilis did the introductions: 'An artist to play music in the evenings' ... 'You bet!' ... 'Be delighted to play' etc. etc. Blah blah! Off goes Vassilis and leaves me with the manager.

'So how much will you pay me to play each day?'

'How much do you want?'

'For me, together with the woman, 500 with food included.'

'Isn't that a lot?' says he.

'How much can you afford to pay and still make a decent profit?'

'For now I'll give you three hundred.'

I had to stay and make do with the 300 drachmas because we were broke. We'd been stuck so long in Patmos, not earning any money, and that was the reason they got away with it. In the villages they set up the megaphone and they kept shouting 'Tonight at so and so's place Markos Vamvakaris, the sweetest *bouzouki* in Athens and all of Greece will play.' Towards nine in the evening I went there taking Rita with me. The minute we got in we saw a huge crowd waiting: 'Markos, welcome to our village!' they shouted - so many people that even *I* was in a daze.

I started solo, playing *bouzouki* and singing. The people who'd come didn't have room to sit. They were standing up and they'd already polished off all the food. There weren't even snacks or drinks. Complete chaos. So the joint closed and we sat down to eat. Along comes the boss and says to me 'Mr Markos, I wasn't expecting so much business. That's why I was a bit cautious, but tomorrow I'll fix everything, I'll go to the police, get them to give me an all-night permit and you can play for as long as there's work.'

'No we're leaving tomorrow, we're going to Kalymnos. They've been waiting a month for us to come and play. Let's gather up our stuff, get the instruments together. We'll be off now,' says I to Rita.

'Why?'

'Because the money you give me isn't enough.'

'Why?'

'Because it's a ridiculous amount. Me, the artist. Markos. With the woman too, to be getting three hundred drachmas!'

'How much do you want?'

'A thousand per night if you want me to stay. If you want me to play four or five days.'

'But it's a lot.'

'It's not much at all considering you take ten thousand each night. What? And you give us three hundred!'

'How much do you want?'

'A thousand.'

'But it's a lot.'

'It's nothing. You'll pay me a thousand. If not, I take my things and leave in the morning.'

So, dragging his feet, he says, 'I'll give you eight hundred.'

'Not eight hundred,' I say to him, 'you have to factor in the three hundred drachmas for the woman and that's not much. You'll give me the thousand.'

In the end, gritting his teeth he paid it.

'Pay me three thousand up front.'

'Okay, here you are.' He pulls out a wodge of money.

'Three nights plus two ... five' he says.

So I did pretty well. I mean in five days I made 8,500 *drachmas* and I stayed on an extra day without pay since I was getting so much in tips. I hadn't stopped sending money back home because I had the kids and they were small. Whenever I got some money I sent a telegram: 'I'm sending you money.' Sometimes a thousand, sometimes two thousand. Either way I was very regular with family payments because I felt for my kids.

We went to Kalymnos, found a place and fixed up a deal but the guy who ran the joint was a scumbag. When he saw the woman he thought he'd take us on and buy the woman too. But he was a guy that people didn't like. They hated him and didn't come to his place. We worked six or seven days but we didn't make anything, even though, as I well knew the people there had a great appetite for these things. They knew me in the Dodecanese because I sold a lot of records there. In Kalymnos, Symi, Rhodes and Kos a lot of records were selling. It was big business and I was getting a percentage. So there I was, working at Panormitis' and the owner, who was married with kids, had gone nuts over this woman I had, Rita. Every night as soon as we finished work he made a scene. He demanded, for instance, that we must go from table to table with our instruments, that sort of thing. One night he was trying it on. He wanted to take Rita from me by force. He said to me 'Get lost now or I'll throw you in the sea and drown you.' But I wasn't leaving. I got hold of Dimitros, the pal who brought me to this place and I said to him 'Hey chum, how come you didn't know he was such a louse?'

So there we were, working in that place and no question but he took the both of us with the sole idea of running off with the woman. 'Hey, you're not having the woman' I kept saying to him, 'You can't have her.' In the end I had to go to the police. They knew what kind of a rat he was. He'd stitched up a lot of people round there. He'd been hand in glove with the Germans when they were around and all the locals, at any rate the good ones, hated him. But they feared him too. His wife was scared of him because he used to beat her and she didn't talk at all. Not only his wife but nobody said a word to him. Even the police had been turning a blind eye, but now there happened to be a new guy in charge. So the police called him and said 'If you give any more trouble to the woman with the guy we'll beat the shit out of you and lock you up. You'll be sorry.' But he was some *koutsavakis!* A proper little hero, he strutted about like a lion. Who did he think he was? Pitiful specimen ...

People came to hear us. They paid money, but what can you do? I wanted to get away from there. I *had* to leave. It was a big worry, the business of this guy. I had to leave before I got hurt. Somebody was sure to get killed, either him or me, because I was crazy bitten with this woman and I'd made up my mind to stick a knife in him and kill him. The woman was fine. She loved me, no way was he going to take her. What would I have said to her folks if he had? So we left and came to Kos. When we got there it was another little drama.

In Kos we found a joint to stay in and play. This guy comes along with fancy moustachios, an old geezer like me, but older. People said he had a passion for nice clothes, for being dapper and fussy about personal grooming. If I was fifty this guy was seventy five. He had children, sons-in-law, family and he played *laouto* in those parts. He was a musician so he comes up to me and says 'How about we join forces and I'll play with you here where they know me and I'm a local? Together we'll get in lots of people. We'll make a packet.'

Sap that I was! But how would I know he had his own plan? I should have kept my head screwed on. I said to him 'Come in the evening and we'll play,' so that's what he did. Damned if I knew what the *laouto* had to do with a *bouzouki*! But never mind, for luck, let's say, and to beef up numbers ... One day this old guy says to me 'Let's go to my house. Come and meet my family.' 'Sure.' He lived a bit further on from the place where we were staying. 'Let's go to his house' I say to Rita, 'He's invited us for lunch.' He introduced his daughters to me. He had two sons who were musicians too but they weren't around. Just the girls. Lovely girls. What a great 'family man'! Sure, and meantime this guy tried to make out with Rita behind my back. She told me everything. She didn't have secrets from me.

'What's he been saying to you?'

'He wants to go and get some clothes for me.'

She didn't need clothes. She was working, getting money, doing fine. 'He wants to take me to a shop where they make watches, bracelets, that sort of thing - to get a ring made for me.'

'Oy oy the old goat! Hell! doesn't he understand that when you get up to go I'll ask you where you're going?' So, the upshot of it was he takes her along to a shop and has three outfits made for her and puts fifty liras into her hand, gold liras! He gets her a ring. How much it cost I don't remember. About two thousand I reckon. She put it on and came to me like that, all dressed up. 'What's this?'

'The guy who plays with us', she says, 'See, he gave these things to me.'

By now I was feeling sorry for his family. In fact his own wife told me he was a rogue. 'There's nobody worse than him' she says to me. So many sons, so many daughters and sons in law and this guy, the last word in snappy dressing, every hour of every day, even to the point of dyeing his hair and his moustache. 'You know what?' says I to her, 'Pah! we're not going to waste the money or the rings or the clothes. We'll leave,' says I, 'We'll go to Rhodes and we'll take them with us.'

'Okay.'

We stayed some time, till I couldn't bear it any longer. I didn't want to end up laying hands on him. 'Piece of shit!' says I, 'What do you expect from a scumbag?' I had words with him, something along the lines of 'Shame on you! I took you on, I had you playing beside me on the platform, so you could sit there and rake it in and all the time you're trying to steal my girlfriend! Take her then! Think you're up to it? Take her!' I didn't say anything else. I didn't mention the gifts or anything. So we got out of there and went to Rhodes. Not two or three days go by before ... would you believe it? There he is in Rhodes! Right there. I was playing at Baboulis' and I see him coming to greet me. 'You know what?', I say to him, 'We'll be finishing in a minute. Hold on. Let's head back to the hotel together because I need to talk to you.' When we'd finished and got to the hotel I started in on him: 'Hell, aren't you ashamed? Dammit you old rascal!' says I to him, 'How can you do such things? Giving a small fortune to the woman! What's this woman to you that you give her money and clothes? First and foremost you're old! Get it? She's a young girl. What are you up to? Don't you think of your family? You still have unmarried daughters! As well as married ones and sons-in-law and goodness knows what. It's a disgrace you should want the woman, a total disgrace. What can I say to you? Be grateful you're seventy years old, because if you weren't I'd get a stick and whack you on the head with it. You'd be in deep shit, that's for sure.' Then to the girl I added 'Come on, give him back all this money he gave you, be quick about it, the clothes and the ring. Take them you old troll! Get out of my sight! Scram! Back to your donkey field and your kids! To think you sat there doing business with me. Did you think you could take my woman? Not bloody likely!'

What could he say? No, this guy didn't have a leg to stand on. 'If I were some low down pimp I'd take your money' says I to him, 'but I can't take it from you. First of all because you're a musician, at any rate you *act* like you're in the same business as me, and second, because of your family. I'm sorry for your children dammit. If you think my girlfriend is the sort to say 'Come along then', you've got another think coming! You think she's just any old tart who'll say to me 'Hell, what's it to you?' No, you've got the wrong end of the stick. She's not that kind of girl. How can I make you get it? She was brought up with money. She had a respectable family. They took care of her. If she were just any old baggage that'd be another story.'

We stayed in Rhodes for three or four months, at *Bapoulis' Kentro*. We agreed I'd play every night and the manager would give me 300 drachmas for the two of us. He didn't have other musicians and he paid for our hotel and the food we ate, midday and evening. We stayed in a hotel kept by an old Italian woman. I got on very well with this old lady and she used to tell me about her children and all the troubles she had with them. When I didn't have work we passed the time of day in there. We'd sit and chat with her. Every night, thank God, we made money, sometimes six or seven hundred or even a thousand a day. I was sending home cheques at regular intervals as well as things for my wife, like clothes which were cheap over there. A rich place, Rhodes, it feels really like a European city, only I didn't like the people there so much. Not the way I liked people in Kos. They are wonderful people in Kos. The best. I used to sit there in the marketplace every morning, whenever I had time to loaf around. I bought all sorts of things there. We wanted, me and Rita, to send parcels on the boats. This wasn't allowed of course but it was okay for me because wherever I went, people on the boats knew me. There'd be some sailor, a mechanic, maybe one of the stewards, even captains.

Meantime, with the death of that little girl I'd had with Rita, there wasn't anything left to hold us together any more. I kept telling her: 'You've got to leave me. Find someone else. Go on, scram! As far as I'm concerned, my wife's a good woman and I've humiliated her because of you. Beat it, kid. I can't go on.' It really was time for her to go and find someone. In fact she *was* looking for someone, But she just wouldn't leave dammit! In the end it was Vangelio who chased her away.

When we got back to Piraeus Vangelio was upset and jealous. She sure put me through it. She thought I'd thrown her over. But I hadn't. I felt too much for my kids. She raised one hell of a rumpus to make me and Rita split up. She got the police onto me, did all sorts of things. I was up to my eyes in trouble. It looked like me and Vangelio were on the verge of getting divorced and she was pregnant at that time with Dhomeniko. She was eight or nine months pregnant, about to give birth. When she found out about Rita she went to the police and they said to her 'Do you know this woman?'

'Sure do!' says she.

'Don't try to catch her yourself. We'll send a policeman. You can point out her house to him from a distance and afterwards come here. Don't you worry.'

So that's what happened. Vangelio went to the police station and waited for them to bring me and Rita there. Ach! What a brawl! But what could I do? I still carried on the affair with Rita. I said to Rita, there in front of the policeman, that we'd separate. But *how* did I say this to her, eh? It was 'Yes' but not with my whole heart and soul. Just to keep appearances. Because you see I felt I had an obligation to Rita. I'd taken her virginity, we'd really gone to town and I felt for her. Then we'd had a child too. If she'd lived I would have put her with my own kids, the ones I already had. I'd have taken her to be brought up by my sisters and later on I'd have sent her to the nuns over there in Syros. I'd have baptized her in the Catholic rite and paid for her education so she could get on in the world and do well. What she did after that was her own business. I saw that as my duty. Sure, maybe not to feed her in my own house but to provide for her and pay for schooling. She was a great looking girl, Rita, and the child's death hurt her a lot, but she never blamed me for it. Not at all. I never heard her say a word of complaint.

At any rate, later on I stopped having anything to do with her. We didn't meet up. I avoided it at all costs. Because it was *not* a good thing to do at all, this thing I did, you know, and I had a stain on my soul and in my heart because of it. A heavy burden. Like I said, when we got back from Rhodes my brain was full of how can I cut loose, how can I get some peace? But it was an affair of over ten years. Luckily she found a good guy and began to live like the well brought up girl she was meant to be and everything was alright between her and her father. I had to cut loose the way I did and I got some peace. She came to me in the end and said there was this guy and 'He has to marry me. Do you approve?' She asked me first and it went ahead. They'd been writing to each other even while we were in Rhodes. Not behind my back - I knew about it. He was from Piraeus, a solid, respectable, wholesale grocer. But they didn't have children. All this happened up to and after 1950.

After we parted I didn't see her again. Not at all, and I didn't ever want to either. Wouldn't want to rekindle an old flame. What would be the point? You've got to be kidding! She's married, I'm married ... that flame was all gone out. Strike up again? Well you know, I had a strong feeling that if I'd said 'Let's do it' we might have. So it was better not to. Right up to this very moment in time, so far so good. I haven't seen her and I didn't go near her. She left the platform, didn't sing again after she got married. This guy set her up in his home and made her his wife. Of course, now after so many years I can't know what her life is like. But probably she's happy because her husband was quite an altogether sort of guy; not just anybody; and even knowing what he knew about her he still loved her, because she was a beautiful woman.

Up to this point I'd been earning good money. Good pay, plus tips and I'd brought out a lot of records. But from Tzitzifies onwards ... what can you do? I went and got ill in 1954. Terribly ill with arthritis. I was laid out sick on my bed. I couldn't walk and my hands were all clenched up. I was a wreck from head to toe, don't even ask! The state I was in made work impossible. The misery was beyond anything. I can't begin to describe how awful it was! What could I do? Not a single one of my relatives came to see me, not even my siblings, or any of my wife's family. They left me to die. Later I wrote this song, *S'afton ton Kosmo ton Kako,* (rec. 1960).

| | |
|---|---|
| ***In This Bad World***<br><br>*In this bad world I don't expect,*<br>*Anything good, just ask Who pecked*<br>*Your eye out? Answer: family*<br>*Ach, and it's pecked out thoroughly.*<br><br>*Your friends and your relations, they*<br>*Will throw you over, give no quarter.*<br>*Ach! For sure they'll find a way*<br>*To drown you in a sip of water.*<br><br>*Those you helped*<br>*When you saw them suffer,*<br>*When they see you begin to bleed,*<br>*The moment that your life gets rougher,*<br>*Won't know you or hear your need.* | ***Σ' Αυτόν τον Κόσμον τον Κακό***<br><br>Σ' αυτόν τον κόσμον τον κακό,<br>καλό δεν περιμένω,<br>ποιος σου ῾βγαλε το μάτι σου,<br>ο συγγενής, αχ<br>κι είναι βαθειά βγαλμένο.<br><br>Οι φίλοι σου και οι συγγενείς,<br>κοιτάζουν να σε ρίξουν,<br>μέσα σε μια γουλιά νερό,<br>όταν σε βρουν,<br>ααάχ, ζητάνε να σε πνίξουν.<br><br>Κι αυτούς που εβοήθησες,<br>τις ώρες που υποφέρουν,<br>σε μια σου δύσκολη στιγμή,<br>όταν σε δουν,<br>αχ, κάνουν πως δε σε ξέρουν. |

I fell on my bed and waited for *Charos* to come and get me. It was around then that an uncle came to see me, my father's half brother. The minute he saw me the guy was overcome. He took out 300 drachmas and gave them to me to go and take the waters at Ikaria. In Ikaria I bathed in the Spring of Moustafa. The level of radium in these baths was 360 degrees and I had twenty-two sessions. There was a relative of mine there, Kostas. He'd only just got married, and as soon as he saw me he took me to his house, told me to sleep and eat there. But I didn't. I found a room where I paid ten drachmas a day. I'd spoken to this guy who was running the baths as a business and arranged to play *bouzouki* every midday and evening at a hotel called Zachiris'. That way I made a little money to send home. I was ill. I was in a lot of pain, forgotten by everybody.

Out of sight and out of mind.

*Who in the world will hear me*
*When I tell the pain I feel?*
*A little sympathy I want.*
*Is that too big a deal?*
*Such tortures and such miseries*
*Have worn my poor heart down.*
*My lips by now've forgotten*
*How to smile, they only frown.*

*I've found no comfort anywhere*
*The grief will never let me be.*
*Pain's crushed my heart for evermore*
*I wrestle with agony.*
*This life is such a sham, its tyranny*
*Is more than I can bear*
*   and my last shout*
*Is let me die one morning, and be free,*
*And forever let me be rubbed out.*

Σε ποιον να πώ τον πόνο μου
στον κόσμο λίγη συμπόνοια
ψάχνω για να βρώ.
Τα βάσανα τα τόσα τα μεγάλα
μου τρώνε την καρδιά τόσον καιρό.

Τα χείλη μου δεν γέλασαν μια μέρα,
δε βρήκα πουθενά παρηγοριά.
Τα βάσανα, οι πίκρες και οι πόνοι
μου πλήγωσαν για πάντα την καρδιά.

Παλεύω κάθε μέρα μ'αγωνία,
σε τούτη εδώ την ψεύτικη ζωή.
Δεν την αντέχω πια την τυρανία,
ας έσβηνα για πάντα ένα πρωί.

Just across from Ikaria is an island called Fourni where people knew me. So when I left Ikaria on my way back I stopped off there. They'd invited me, so I went and played one or two evenings and made a decent amount of money. I had a friend there from the time when we were soldiers together. He had me to stay at his house and threw a party; gathered a bunch of people together and they showered me with cheeses, honey, beans, figs, lots of things I was able to take back to the kids.

I got better and went to Samos. It was my first time there. On the seafront a guy called Nikos saw me and recognized me. We knew each other from Piraeus. A worker in the port, very poor with seven children, he helped me find a joint and I played there together with another port worker who played *santouri*. I played every evening and began to make some headway. He got out programmes and scattered them all over Samos and people began to come in the evenings. I toured all around: Karlovasi, Mestos, Vathi,

Tigani, Kalabachxe Metapodhia, Marathokambo, and other villages. Everybody knew me and loved me but they didn't have any money. I played sometimes at music dives and sometimes in private houses. I showed them a good time and put them in such a good mood they plugged me with money and all good things. One of them, the biggest householder in Kalabachxe, gave me five or six *okes* of *touloumotyri*[132] the like of which I've never found anywhere else, as well as olives, oil, beans, chickpeas, and soap. Holy Mary and praises be! He put them into a case and sealed it up all ready to send to my wife. I found a number of people there - I knew them from Piraeus and they were always having me to stay in their houses and getting out the fatted calf. One shop-owner dressed me up in stuff from his daughter's wedding trousseau just for night clothes to go to bed in! In Marathokambo I drank a coffee *alla Turca*, from a big copper bowl with enormous handles. The coffee was ground then boiled and I drank it. Lovely coffee! Unforgettable.

Samos has a lot of music. There were two brothers, the Kaltakis brothers, very good musicians. They played *santouri*, violins, clarinets, everything. Over there they loved the heavy songs, the old *zebekika*. They were terrific dancers. They loved the *taximia* that I played, eh? We used to play some *syrto* and the *santouri* player helped me a lot with local songs. He'd play them and I followed his lead. I learnt a whole lot of songs I didn't know from this guy and whatever *he* didn't know, same again, he'd learn by tagging along with me. I mean, he wasn't, you know, that great a musician, but later on, I heard he had a son who became a musician and was very good on the guitar. I sang all the hashish songs and they liked those. They were people who loved the *instrument*, the *bouzouki* - liked what I played. They danced, they partied, and they were generous, open-handed people, happy to part with their money.

---

132 Cheese wrapped in goatskin.

I toured the whole of Samos doing solo *bouzouki* and that was a godsend. One fine day I decided to come back to Piraeus for some peace and quiet, even though I was on my own in Samos. When I got back to Piraeus I had to work so I decided to to go and play in Arta, taking with me Batis, a guy called Kostas on *bouzouki*, a guitar player and Rita who hadn't yet got married. My wife had forgotten by then the whole business with Rita, but suddenly she found out and I had fearful rows. Indescribable! So I had to cancel this tour, likewise another tour I went on with Panagopoulos, Georgios Papadhopoulos, the father of Lela Papadhopoulou, and Stefanakis on *bouzouki*. Afterwards I went on working with this orchestra but I got rid of Rita and had some peace.

Performing in public had become very difficult by now. I wasn't in demand any more from the joints that used to want me before. I was all washed up and that lasted till 1960. I survived by running off to the islands, to *paneyiria*, to Arta, Preveza, Yannina, this place and that place, all over the shop. I'd leave home and tour for months at a time, here today, gone tomorrow. I didn't go to Thessaloniki though. It was only before the war I played there and now recently. On these tours we were usually a band of five or six. Lela Papadhopoulou used to sing the *laiko* songs, all of them but she was no slouch on the other stuff: European, *zebekika*, *chasapika*, light popular songs, she played everything. She's the big time accordion player these days. She sings too and above all as a dancer of *zebekiko* she's unbeatable. Wherever we went we made a stir. We had Lela's husband Vlachos with us, singing *dhimotika*. He sang them correctly, beautifully. Still does. Vlachos is very good but he hasn't made many records. He's trying to do that now. He went to America and now he's back. He made some money over there which he's used to set up his own studio to make records. He got my sons together and they've made a first recording of four or five pieces and started to sell them. He was Lela's husband at the time we did the tours, but later on, when they went to America, they split. They've got kids who sometimes go with their mother and sometimes with their father. They still work together even though they're separated. I had another guy with me, Stefanakis, another *bouzouki* player. He's ill now, on his sickbed poor devil and can't get up. Been like that seven or eight years now ... 'the great Stefanakis'. I mean when I was playing down in Piraeus and I was *the* 'Markos' he was there too in Athens. I was bigger, though, even if I was in Piraeus. He didn't sing you see. He only played, while I had everything. I was singing, making up the music, writing the lines, *and* playing.

With this band we went all round Messolonghi, Yannina, Preveza, Epirus, and further up from there as far as Aiyio staying three or four weeks in each place. I got on well with the band. We didn't fight, not at all, and they all listened to me. We travelled on the public buses. We'd leave Arta and go to Yannina where we knew so and so had a joint. I'd go find this guy and say to him 'We're available to play in the shop, and this is how much we want to be paid,' so we'd fix it up and get to work. Sometimes he'd pay a fixed price for the band or otherwise he'd fix it at twenty per cent of the profit he made. But we had tips on top of that. They danced a lot of *zebekiko* there, *kalamatiana*, all sorts of things, I mean whatever you wanted you'd find it there.

As far as performing went, in the years 1955-57 I vanished from the scene. I wasn't playing any more. All this misery was my brother's fault. He didn't care about me at all. All the things I'd done for him didn't seem to count for anything. I didn't get work any more and I was suffering. If he'd been a good brother he would have said to me 'Here Markos, my brother, I'll see to everything,' and I'd still be the same Markos. Instead he dug my grave. Thankless brute ... when I got ill all those people I'd had with me at

Tzitzifies left me alone. Each one of them got his own band together and they went on working.

When I got back to Piraeus after the touring I was in a lot of pain. I went and found my brother Argyris. I said to him, 'Hell, why did you leave me to die? Weren't you sorry for me? Aren't you sorry for my boys?' So then - I don't know how he made the money - we opened a joint right there in his house. A woman called Anna got seventy thousand together. We gave it the once over and played every night. We were beginning to make good, but Argiris made my life hell. He did whatever Anna said. He ate whatever he fancied from the shop while I wasn't allowed even an olive to snack on. He didn't give me enough money even to shave so I was always whiskery. People would see me and say 'What's wrong with you Markos?' What could I say? Plenty of times my wife was cooking up bones that the butcher had given me. She made soups. That's what my boys lived on, poor kids. I remember one of them took sick and became so weak I had to take him to a foundation, the Sikiaridhion. He stayed three months. Went in a tiny kid. If you'd seen him you'd have said 'He's not going to live', and he came out huge. Hard times.

I'd exhausted all options. I figured I'd better get cracking and find some way to make a living. So I toured again with Papadhopoulos and Lela. We went to Larissa and Volos, to Trikala and even Macedonia. We made some money and where didn't we go together! But I feel sore about the fact that after so much, I ended up not being able to work in Athens. Of all those guys I taught and had playing with me none of them took me on for work. Whoever I asked they'd say 'Why doesn't your brother take you?' I suffered a lot. I had to suck up to the same people who at another time I'd given jobs to, playing with me. Now these guys are millionaires. I don't care. But if only I'd had my wits about me I'd have been a sight better off and have as much as I want now.

## CHAPTER 19

## I LIKE HEARTS LIKE MINE

Later, back here in Piraeus, I did short stints at a number of dives, maybe Baroutadhiko, then Balta, then back to Baroutadhiko, after that to Allach's. A bit here and a bit there. I used to play at another place too in Kavala St. I wasn't as famous then as I've come to be now again. I was still *the* 'Markos'. I was famous but I'd gone down a bit. At that time I was working for anything between a 100 to a 150 drachmas a day. Tips could be anything from twenty-five to 300 drachmas. Now in our old age me and Stratos were working together again at the music joints. They wanted us both. Whoever wanted me wanted Stratos too. I work well with Stratos even if he's always been a strange guy. Very different from me. Chatterbox. Big mouth. He used to say it would just be him and nobody else, and since it was just him and nobody else he took a hundred *drachmas* like me. The 'just me and nobody else' guys get a lot of money. But still, we worked well together. Since then, you know, after 1960 when they started calling me and I went back to playing the joints, I've been paid well. Here's how it happened.

From 1950 the recordings pretty much stopped and I began again in 1960. Perpiniadhis recorded a piece of mine with his own words and he sang it without asking me. This guy thought that since I was a poor old dude with a cash flow problem, that meant it was a free for all. So 'Hey, you,' says I to him, 'I want a word. Did you ask me before you recorded this song?' 'Mr Markos' he says to me, 'Here, take something and we're done with it.' So he gave me something. It was peanuts. You know, he brought it out under his name. But what can you do? I stopped him. But ever since that time when he started doing it I got the fire in my belly too. This song was *Dhen Paizo Zaria pia*.[133]

It was straight after that, Columbia called me. 'Markos, bring us songs.' So I took along a batch of ten songs which Bithikotsis sang. I took ten more and again he sang them. Later I got going and produced sixty, sixty-one, sixty-two, sixty-three, right up till now. Not just with Columbia, with other companies too. Since 1960 I've had this other source of income from songs, because I brought out my old songs, my earliest 'hits'. I was also writing and still am writing new songs all the time. For example *Mana Otan me Yennises*:

| Mother When You Gave Birth to Me | Μάνα Οπού με Γέννησες |
|---|---|
| *Mother when you bore me,*<br>*Why did you not say*<br>*The world has pain,*<br>*Sweet mama, loads of grief.* | Μάνα μ', όταν με γέννησες,<br>γιατί δε μου το είπες<br>πως έχει ο κόσμος βάσανα,<br>μανούλα μου γλυκιά<br>πως έχει ο κόσμος πίκρες; |
| *Best to have died*<br>*Before being born that day,*<br>*Not to know pain*<br>*Would be a sweet relief.* | Καλύτερα να πέθαινα<br>προτού να γεννηθώ,<br>να μη γνωρίσω βάσανα<br>και να μην πληγωθώ. |
| *Your heart was hard*<br>*When you gave birth to me*<br>*And made me the most luckless*<br>*Of your brood,* | Μάνα μ', όταν με γέννησες,<br>σκληρή 'ταν η καρδιά σου<br>και μ' έκανες πιο δυστυχή<br>μανούλα μου γλυκιά<br>απ' όλα τα παιδιά σου. |
| *Destroyed, mama,*<br>*By friends and family.*<br>*My bitter lips don't smile.*<br>*They never could.* | Μάνα, με καταστρέψανε<br>οι συγγενείς και οι φίλοι<br>και δε γελάσανε ποτέ<br>μανούλα μου γλυκιά<br>τα δυο πικρά μου χείλη. |

---

133 'I don't play dice any more'.

This one is new. Bithikotsis sang it now in 1965 and then I recorded it as well. A fine song of pain from all the hard times I've been through. At this time of my life I wrote many songs of pain, not just one or two. Loads. That's all I was writing about. Another is *Apelpistika*, (rec. 1960):

| *Despair* | *Απελπίστηκα* |
|---|---|
| What endless suffering is mine, <br> When others want life <br> I wish I were dying. | Τι πάθος ατελείωτο <br> που είναι το δικό μου, <br> όλοι να θέλουν τη ζωή <br> κι εγώ το θάνατό μου |
| It's hard to bear, <br> Mama I despair. | Απελπίστηκα, μανούλα μου, <br> να υποφέρω, |
| I'm tired of living life <br> In search of Death. <br> Dark as the night is, <br> So's my heart and breath. | κουράστηκα μες στη ζωή <br> τον Χάρο να γυρεύω <br> Όσο' ναι η νύχτα σκοτεινή <br> έτσι' ναι κι η καρδιά μου <br> και σαν τη σιγανή βροχή <br> τρέχουν τα δάκρυά μου |
| Like silent rain my tears run down, <br> I'll find in rocks and earth some hole, <br> And there I'll leave my bones, <br> Life, body and soul. | Θα πά' να εύρω μια σπηλιά <br> με πέτρες και με χώμα, <br> εκεί θ' αφήσω κόκαλα, <br> ζωή, ψυχή και σώμα. |

When the music dives saw that the radios were blaring out every day *Markos Vamvakaris* and then more *Markos Vamvakaris*, it couldn't happen anymore, me playing for a pittance. I went to Patras for instance, just two years ago, for 1,500 *drachmas* a day. I played here at *Xenichti* for 1,350. They had me in the *Plaka*. I played there two or three nights for a 1000 *drachmas*. I began to catch on. The students helped towards this. They came out on the streets big time. Not just here but also when I went to Thessaloniki. The whole student population turned out. Seemed like they knew my story, they knew who I was. They loved me a lot. I mean, wherever I go now I have students with me. They just turn up.

This began when we did a concert with Nearchos Georghiadhis and Kiki Kalamaras in a big private house. We weren't paid - it was a concert for friends, but the enthusiasm of the students was something else again. There was a second concert for students at the Kentriko. I took my boys, Stelios and Dhomenikos, with me to both. The guy who organized this concert was some down-at-heel, professional guy called Tasos Schorelis. More recently he wanted to take me to Agrinio.[134] He kept coming round here, '*barba* Markos' this and '*barba* Markos' that, and so on and so forth. We did the concert over there and it was big. A lot of people turned out for it, lots of musicians, a very good crowd. They paid me 2000. That's how the sixties began, what they call in the magazines 'the second career'.

I went to Patras in 1965 and stayed fifteen days. I don't remember the name of the joint. It went down well. Afterwards I came back here. At this point I wasn't so bothered if I didn't have work, because the boys were working by now. Money wise, things were better somehow and I didn't worry so much. I wasn't going in search of work. The kids didn't let me because I wasn't well. They were saying 'Take it easy' - same as what they say now, you know. 'Take it easy, don't worry!' I didn't do much here in Athens. I went to Thessaloniki last year in 1968. It was spring time but they had snow. I played at the *Neapoli* in that place where the Barracks of Pavlos Melas[135] is, Yiorgos' place at *Vendetta*. Various locals played with me in the band, good musicians, great guys - they loved me. I went with Stratos for 1,350 drachmas plus bed for the night; stayed in the best hotel in Thesssaloniki, in Kamara. A new

---
134 The largest city in Aetolia-Acarnania in Western Greece.
135 A famous hero in the Greek struggle for Macedonia against the Bulgarians and Ottomans who died fighting in 1904 - also a distant relative of his namesake Pavlos Melas, the present publisher: see Greeklines.com.

hotel which somebody had built near the Exhibition Centre. I got to know the guy who ran the hotel. I liked him and he liked me and we talked every evening. He'd heard me back in the old days and wanted to sit and chat with me. The hotel staff just couldn't do enough for me, like I was a saint! I mean they loved me a lot, the educated folk, and as for the women who did the cleaning! Every hour, every second they came in to check whether I needed tidying, to see how I was. In fact I was a bit unwell and when I got back from there I went right downhill. I was in a fearful state. My right foot ... the two little toes are still swollen; it hasn't got better.

In 1965-6 I went to Syra for a month; played in a dive down in Ermoupoli. I didn't get a whole lot of money, 300, 450 a night. I was *the* 'Markos'. I brought in the whole island, but they didn't have money poor devils.

Somehow this decade's been better. My kids have grown up and I also make some money. We're better off. You came to the house and saw how we were in 1967 and now you see the difference.[136] All this happened with work, and with the kids. Now my youngest boy has left. He used to come over here and whatever money he made he'd give to his mother. Same with all my kids. And my oldest boy? Even now, whatever he earns he brings to his mother. And this other one, the middle boy, he got us a TV and so on, which the older one pays for. Now we've fixed up to build a house. It'll be quite something, always supposing God lets me live. The great thing is to be well, because these things only happen when there's good health. That's not just me. Same the whole world over. Health. With God's help the boys will work and I'll work too and now we'll build a very fine house down there at Ofriniou.

God be thanked, I'd say this decade is the best of my life. Praises be ... and of course if I were going to America it would be even better because I'd make a lot of money there.

---

136 'Now' means 1969. See Prologue of A.V-K.

Not from the university but I'd make appearances, I'd do concerts, and I'd be paid the right amount. I'd say to them 'This is how much. You'll pay me that? Well and good. Otherwise I'm not coming.' If Tsitsanis took 600,000 drachmas for six months, I'd ask a million drachmas for six months. And not to work like he did either! Hell, no! Fine, so maybe he was able to, and he worked like a skivvy, but me, I'd work on my own terms. If they didn't pay me I wouldn't play. I feel sure they'd want me to play once my name has started getting about. Once I was there it's impossible they wouldn't get me to play and we'd make some kind of a deal. They'd pay me alright. Because 'Markos' would be singing and they'd know that this guy singing is the 'Commander in chief' of *Laika*. I'd be able to write songs all in one day over there. If I could just get there I'd write five to ten songs and I'd sing them. I'd give them the 'world premiere' every evening. American inspiration. I mean I have the capacity to do that. This ability is something other people don't have. Or they may have it but they'd be slow writing the songs. Me, I can do it in a week. That's not to say I'll write fifteen new songs ... eh ... maybe three. Even now I have faith, God will make me well and I'll get to America.

I feel calm now that my kids have grown up, turned out well, and I'm very happy that two of them have followed my profession. Because if these two reach my level, knowing, as they do, more letters than me - because they've finished elementary school with extras and languages, French, this that and the other, they're bound to turn out first rate. I'm quite sure the youngest one will become a great musician. An all-rounder this one. Give it a couple of years and he won't be touching *laika* at all. It'll be European, the great music. He writes it, he reads it, he goes to the *Odeion*.[137] He's well on the way to becoming a maestro this one. The other's

---

137 *Odeion Athinon*, Athens Conservatoire.

following *my* path and he also writes very beautiful songs like nobody else has written. He's got fifty or sixty songs that I admire and I'm a composer. They're a million miles away from these writers who are writing now. He follows *my* line. While the other one's going for the big guns. He's going to be a pianist. Of course since he's going to be a musician, whatever instrument he picks up he'll play it. If he sits down to it for five days, ten, twenty, a month or two, he'll learn the violin. If he sits down for another two months, three, four or five, he'll learn the saxophone. A real great musician! And if it's *bouzouki* we're talking about, do you know what it would mean now if they invited him abroad, to Vienna for instance, to Germany, where they invite the maestros, the big names? Suppose they invite him and he picks up the *instrument*, the *bouzouki*. Suppose he performs some pieces on the *bouzouki, and* plays on the violin or piano too! Do you know what a thing that'll be? Do foreigners know about these things? No they don't. How will this look to them when they have an orchestra with say fifty instruments and in the middle of it all will be the *bouzouki*, and the *bouzouki* will pull into the lead, eh? ... Play solo? How its stock will rise! Now he plays from these books that they give him, but he also plays my stuff. All these new ones I make up, he writes them down for piano.

 The oldest, Vassilis is a sailor. He's a quiet kid. Do you know how much I feel for him? I feel for all my kids but day and night he's never far from my thoughts this boy who travels the sea. Even if I'm not a sailor I have a sad feeling about the sea. From all the songs other people have written, people who came before me. I feel for him because he's such a great kid and he loves us. I didn't want him to do this line of work. There weren't any sailors on my side of the family. On my wife's side they're all sailors. Now if a guy works till he's thirty and becomes first captain he'll be getting a lot of money. So this kid too will be earning a lot. Of course it goes without saying, whatever money he brings we don't spend it. His mother hides it in the bank so it'll be for him. Same for Stelios. The one who hasn't put anything in the bank is the young one. Now as soon as he's released from national service and starts to make a bit of dough we'll get him going with the bank too so he'll be like the others, on a level.

Dhomenikos is young, but he's been making good money already. We were doing very well because I also have this plot of land. Now that I'm not working, the oldest one is beginning to pay. The other one too, now that he'll be going to work, begins to pay rent for the house here. The rent's 2,500 so whatever's left is for food. As for me, *my* money he takes to the bank and it's for the future, for the boys. I mean whatever one gets, the other will get too, but with the difference that the eldest one will take charge, because he's very good with money. So is the younger one but the eldest is the lynchpin. I mean for every important piece of business I send this kid along and he sees me through it. The minute he comes into the house, everything's okay. He takes an interest, he's prepared to sort things out and take action. The others don't so much. Specially the middle one. Nope. He's not interested. The youngest one is more like the older one.

All three of them are great kids. I just pray to God and the Holy Virgin about the women they're going to marry. Because when it comes to women I've been through a lot. I wonder, will they find wives as good as they are, so they'll live well, not quarrel, have children? I worry. What kinds of women will take these boys into their arms? Women ... I'm scared of them. *I've* suffered agonies. You see, the two of them who go out to work at night see all kinds of things. I guess at least they'll have got that out of their system now. When they get around to marrying, they'll leave all that and settle down. So long as the wife is good, a decent woman.

The husband has to be good and behave well to her. Let the woman have everything and be good in the good times - but also good in the bad times as well. If they don't have good wives they won't do anything.

Like I said, from the money point of view, these days, thank God, I'm doing fine. But I don't feel good about the fact that I, Markos, who started all this business of the *laiko* song, didn't benefit from it. Not like all these *bouzouki* players that we see strutting about now, so big and important! Since the time I came out on records I sang two or three years at *Columbia*, two or three years at *His Master's Voice* and from 1936 to 1950 and beyond, I had an exclusive contract with Odeon. At first I was happy because they treated me right but later on things changed and they pushed me to one side and didn't bring out my songs any more.

Now of course, with this, you know, 'second career' of mine, *Odeon* called me up and they say to me 'Let's make an exclusive contract.' My answer to them was 'For me to stay with you I want you to pay me a million drachmas for two years, and then I'll stop with all the other companies. For me to stop singing with the others and sing only for you that's not a whole lot of money, I can tell you.' If I were being paid a million, or even seventy or eighty thousand I'd go. But Matsas[138] didn't say anything to me. Worse players than me have taken that much money. All these 'great players' were taking eighty thousand a day. How about that? All of them. What *were* these guys who got paid so much money? I was '*Markos*'. That was *me*.

Columbia made no mention of making a deal with me for an exclusive contract. Only I *did* record stuff. I recorded and Bithikotsis recorded. As for Labropoulos I can't understand what it was he had about me. He was the sort of

---

138 Minos Matsas (1903-1970), the recording executive of Odeon-Parlophone who wrote rebetiko songs under the pseudonym Tsamas. Being Jewish he spent the Occupation hiding in the house of his fellow composer Yiannis Papioannou.

guy who if I went to him and said 'Give me this thing' he'd give it and wouldn't take a cent. I mean he loved me. But when it came to work, voice recordings and so on, nothing. Now and again I bring out some little piece. In fact, just now I hear Xarchakos has recorded my songs again. But nothing more. That's why I don't have a contract now. It's because they weren't paying me what I'm worth.

In the last year I made a 100,000 from songs I'd written and from performances I took another 30,000. It's little, very little compared to what others get and what I'm worth. Still, thank God, I never was a money-grubber. Whatever I wanted to do I did. I *am* 'Markos'. My house, this house of mine right here is the fount and source of all truth about the *bouzouki*. However many others sing and strut their stuff they're not going to know what *I* know about the *bouzouki*, because I've suffered for this instrument. That's something all these big shots know too. They know I've suffered all the terrible things in the world. I lost everything. I didn't care about myself or about anything else. What can I say? Sure, maybe I did have money and maybe people were saying to me 'You're going to lose it'. I don't give a damn. But it *is* a grievance. And I have another bigger complaint. All these great and famous *bouzouki* players are ungrateful. All of them. They should have kept a candle burning every day at the feet of 'Saint Markos'! Because I can tell you, if it weren't for me where would these millionaires be? Fine, these guys are good, I don't doubt that. But I was the first who spread the table for the feast and said 'Come on, sit down, let's eat'. These guys filled their bellies and I went hungry. I got ill and nobody came to ask how I was. Nobody. Would you believe it! Hell ... your teacher dammit! Eh! Whatever you do, whatever you say, I *am* your teacher. I led the way. Didn't we say that these guys who came after, learnt from my 'roads'? *After* me, I say, because I filled the world with my records. These guys appeared and they were playing and learning from *my* pieces on the *bouzouki*.

There are singers who became big names by singing my songs. Later they left me and went to other composers. I'm talking about these guys, you know, who are millionaires and say 'We made money and we've given it away.' They give it away? Like hell! I didn't see so much as a brass farthing from any of them for all that they'd promised so much and so much to me. If it had been me and I'd got such loads of money as they have, fine, I would have looked after my kids but then I'd have fixed up an old folks' home and put all the poor old dudes with no money in it. I'd give that money heart and soul if I had, say, ten or fifteen million like these guys do. For me to have given two or three million to fix up a thing like that for poor guys who haven't got a roof over their heads, wouldn't take any skin off my nose.

They've been ruined by so much money. It's money that ruins people's characters don't you think? If you have money do you ever feel shame? I know very well that you don't. It's the poor dude on his uppers that feels shame. I know one guy - let's not mention any names - they say to him, 'You're getting fucked.'

'I am', says he, 'and I'm proud of it.'

'Dammit you old faggot, you fat arse you're getting fucked!'

'Proud of it mister.' That's what he replies.

There's just one guy, Keromytis, a poor guy. He's a good quiet man, a proper dervish, handsome too, and he's my friend. I have a lot of respect for him and my kids love him. The others are rascals without exception. All of them. But you'll say to me 'So you're the only decent guy?' But I *am* decent. I never bothered a soul, I helped people and right up to now, this very second, I still do. I make money with the companies, I fix things.

There in Xenichti where I was playing together with Stratos, Papaioannou and Lafkas, we had some dames up there on the platform and they weren't giving them their share from the tips. Of course we were getting wages as well. But hell, not to give them a share? Eh! If they did that to you what would you do dammit? Everyone shares these tips out equally from the highest to the lowest. Equally. For me as long as I was on the platform, that's how it was. So one night I says to them 'Hey how many are we?'
'Sixteen.'
'And the tips money is divided into how many shares every night?'
'Fourteen'.
'No,' says I to him. 'from tonight there'll be sixteen shares. The ones who haven't been getting tips *will* from now on.' Even Kokkotas who gets 8,000 a night gets tips. But this guy ought to pass on his tips to somebody else, some poor sod who's getting only 300.

Just lately one of these singers came, one of these guys who sing songs about Sunday's joy and Monday's misery - they've been making millions. He came to choose six songs to record for his company. I gave him *Sta nera tou Sikouana*:

| *In the Seine* | Στα Νερά του Σηκουάνα |
|---|---|
| A storm gets up wherever you go<br>Lightning flashes, a thunderbolt,<br>Pelting rain and typhoons blow.<br>Whoever sees you, Drowns - your fault!<br>Blonde and crazy Parisienne. | Όπου περάσεις θύελλα<br>κι αμέσως καταιγίδα<br>σαν αστραπή και σα βροντή<br>και με βροχή νεροποντή<br>που πνίγεται όποιος σε ιδεί<br>ξανθιά τρελλή Γαλλίδα. |
| I've drowned, Sweet Mama,<br>In the waters of the Seine. | Πνίγηκα γλυκειά μου μάνα<br>στα νερά του Σηκουάνα. |

| | |
|---|---|
| You have the kind of body | Έχεις κορμί που όποιος το ιδεί |
| Drives a man out of his mind. | χάνει το λογισμό του. |
| That skin of alabaster | Σαν κάτι θέλει να σου πεί |
| Shows a path he cannot find. | το αλαβάστρινο κορμί |
| Torments, miseries, all thronging | βάσανα πίκρες και καημοί |
| Make a man die of his longing. | πεθαίνει απ'τον καημό του. |
| | |
| What beauty have your two bright eyes! | Τι ομορφιά τι τσαχπινιά |
| What mischief they release! | έχουν τα δυο σου μάτια, |
| A girl that's like cold water streams | κοπέλα σαν το κρύο το νερό |
| And I haven't got the means | και που ν'αντέξω δεν μπορώ |
| Of bearing it. I can't endure, | δεν υποφέρω σε βαστώ |
| I break up piece by piece. | εγίνηκα κομμάτια. |

A nice one that. The guy was shameless. I've written a world of songs and he says to me 'Polish it up could you?' Hey, come on! Get lost!' When they say polish it up they're complaining about the whole song. He didn't say this verse or that verse. I didn't take anything out. Did I deign to? Even if it had been a bad song, if he'd had any kind of a conscience, this guy, he should have told me '*barba* Markos, you know what, I don't like this one. Give me something else.' He should have said it clearly, and not said 'Tidy it up, fix it, give it a comb through.' Dammit, what's this guy talking about? Who does he think he's talking to! One time at a recording we happened to be doing together, both of us at Odeon, he had a fifteen line song and he'd sing it till he got to line eleven and then he kept drying up. Then one of the Odeon guys shouts out to Minos Matsas and says to him 'Mr Minos, let the contrabasso sing it.' By contrabasso they meant me. So when he called out to me 'Do you know it?',

'Of course I do' I said, 'I don't need rehearsals. Let's go.' I recorded it in five minutes. At that time of course this guy was a beginner, but what I mean to say is, he doesn't understand a thing.

That's why I help people who are just starting out. They come along here wanting to take my songs and record them.

Since I've got a lot of songs - and when am I going to record these songs after all? - I give them to whoever comes along. You saw this poor kid, the one who came by? He just got out of the army and he came to see me. 'How you doing *barba* Markos? Can I take that and record it?' Yeah, well, of course I'm not going to give songs to anyone who can't sing them. I always make sure he's got a good voice. And then there's the other thing too. If the company likes him and he's good, then he'll sing. If not they'll say to him 'You won't do, kid, and that's that.' Now you'll say to me 'Is it a good thing for a composer to have his songs sung by a newcomer? Why don't you chase up the more established singers?' Reason is they've got above themselves. These guys, you can't ever explain anything to them. They've got their noses up in the air because they're loaded. Besides, didn't I say, as far as I'm concerned they're a bunch of scumbags. They don't *need* me. If I give one of them a song he doesn't give a damn. They're all the same. While the young guy on the other hand, coming to it fresh, you set him to work till he gets it together, till he learns, till he becomes a name. Somehow he gets through eh? But if you use these famous guys what are you going to get? The best thing of all would be if I could sing them myself, not need anybody and not give a toss about any of them, and that goes for *all* of them. My voice, my very own, is something none of them can do for me. There *is* a guy who's been trying to do it lately, this Evstathiou. He recorded some of my songs. I mean he gets near it but it's not the genuine *Markos*.

From the money point of view, of course it *would* be better for a big name to be singing the songs because the big names sell records. But like I said you can't get near them, and what's more, nowadays they've turned into songwriters themselves. They find a guy in one place, they buy a lyric. They find another guy. He gives them the music and off they go, they've written the song - that's how these guys become 'songwriters'!

When the song is good, no matter who sings it, it'll catch on. Big name or not it'll have a good run. If it's good the world will latch onto it, play it on the radio, and it'll sound good to everybody. The guy that's going to sing it can sing however he likes. Of course it would be great if a big name were singing, but even the big names have had to start somewhere! Isn't that so? The good songs make the big names and then the big names help the songs.

As for these guys who run the music dives *they* don't know what they're doing. Take last year at Xenychti. They put Lafkas in charge of Papaioannis, Stratos and me. How can Lafkas tell us what to do when he's younger than all of us and we taught this guy, all three of us, you know, and turned him into a songwriter and *bouzouki* player. Was *he* going to keep us in line and tell us what to do? No way. And you know what? Lafkas was taking more money than all of us. And Papaioannou was getting more money than me. That's something I found out. I didn't take it lying down. I asked for the same amount and they gave it to me. Lafkas was getting 1,800, maybe 2000 drachmas. Papaioannou was getting 1,500 and I was getting 1,300 drachmas. Stratos was getting 600 drachmas. The difference was that I wasn't sitting there all evening. I made my appearances and sat at my own little table. When I discovered that Papaioannou was getting this amount and the other was getting that, I was pretty upset. 'Now look here' I said, 'since I can see I'm the one with the pulling power...'

All of them were good, but I was in a different league. But there we are, that's what I'd agreed to. Just that. But the first night he gives us only half. The second night he gave us a bit less than half. 'Ah, is that what you're like?' says I. I gather up my *bouzoukia*, my bits and pieces and I was out of there, gone. Hell, that was pitiful! I'll teach you a lesson I thought to myself. I let a week go by. Business slackened off massively. It collapsed. 'What's going on Markos, did you leave the joint?'

'You'll have to pay me what you said you would and then I'll come back. If you don't pay me that amount I won't stay even one hour.'

'You'll come tonight, though, won't you?' He gets round me.

'Fine. You'll pay me my money.'

He didn't say anything to me. Not 'No', not anything. So off I go that evening, second time around. The evening's over, he gives me 600. So I get hold of him. 'Dammit, didn't I say I'm not hanging around for that kind of money? Why did you get me in here? What were you thinking of, coming to my house, interrupting my peaceful life and taking me on for a job? No not a penny less. And now you'll give me 2000.' I'm going to take more than any of these guys here. Otherwise I'm not coming. I'm taking my *bouzouki* and I'm outta here.' Then we go through the whole rigmarole again!

The people he sent to talk to me! '2000 or nothing' was my reply. I didn't want to leave but I had to show him what I was worth and make him get it. So I left and the place shut down after one month. It's still shut.

I know my own power. This guy Leonidas who came by the other day called me and I went and played two nights at his place. It was packed out. And now I come to mention it there's this other guy, Alekos Stamatelis who writes outside his place 'The songs of Markos Vamvakaris are sung here.' He's a sweet kid. How about that? See what they've ended up writing on the walls! My son Stelios says to me 'All the old songs, all the good ones are yours. At the *kentro* everybody wants them. They don't sing anything but your songs. The old songs.' This one, Stelios, is *laikos*. He plays my songs. He knows a lot of my songs and that's something that makes me happy. 'Have you been out performing on the platform kid? Just singing my songs is a full time job!' They're all after me to get my songs. I've got him for my stand-in. There's no joint where they don't play the *chasapiko Frangosyriani*, or where there isn't a request to dance *zebekiko* or they'll sing *Antilaloun oi Fylakes*, *Ta Dhyo sou Cheria Pirane*, or *Yia sena Mavromata mou*.[139] I mean, even the '*yeah-yeahdhes*'[140] dance to my tunes. They invited me to play over at the Hilton one night along with my kids. I took Stelios and Dhomenikos to the concert and they announced me as 'Markos Vamvakaris the *Commander in Chief* of *laiko* music. I played just four or five songs. I wasn't very well back then.

On the ninth of August this year I played on TV. They called me up and came here to get me. Such a great show! I got congratulations from the TV people. Nothing like it had ever happened before. Everybody kept telling me they'd seen it. And now they're still coming to invite me. As soon as I'm well. Only God knows if I'm going to get well. Yeah ... of course I'm old now too, and I'm not like I used to be. But I still have the heart for doing it. Now just let Evstathiou's record come out, hey? Vendetta took two records of mine which I've sung in the last two years, which they'd rejected before.

| | |
|---|---|
| *Winter's over. Now the summer's here.* | Πάει ο χειμώνας πέρασε |
| *You told a thousand lies to me I fear.* | κι ήρθε το καλοκαίρι |
| *You said the two of us would be a pair.* | και μου'πες χίλια ψέματα |
| | πως θα γινούμε ταίρι. |
| | |
| *Lies as big as that cannot be found* | Τέτοια ψέμματα μεγάλα |
| *Not anywhere,* | μες τον κόσμο δεν ειν'άλλα. |
| *In all the whole world round.* | |

---

[139] 'The Frankosyran girl', 'The Prisons are Clanging', 'Your two hands'. and 'For you my Black-eyes'.
[140] Markos' way of referring to pop music fans and hippies who were rocking to the Beatles: 'She loves you Yeah Yeah Yeah...'

Then I have a *chasapiko*, *Ach ta Emorfa sou Matia*,[141] a nice one. I have songs ready to come out on *Odeon*, *Vendetta*, and *Lyra*. Any day now they'll be bringing out the record where I sing some *zebekika* myself, and some *sabah*.[142]

Even now, old and ill as I am, I still look after my work. Even with all these illnesses I've got. I'm an old hand at this business. Hey, just take a look at all the hits I've written: *Frangosyriani, Ta Matokladha sou lampoun, Ta Emorfa ta Galana sou Matia, I Atakti, Kantone Stavro Kantone, Antilaloun oi Fylakes, M'Ekapses Tsachpina mou Oraia, Yia Sena Mavromatia mou, Kathe Vradhi tha se Perimeno, Chronia sti Fylaki, Imouna Mangas mia Fora, O Isovitis* - a fine *chasapiko, Oloi oi Rebetes tou Dounia,* and *Tora tin Kalokairia Mikro mou.* It's a lot of songs. These songs I wrote, my first songs, were all, every single one, outstanding. Especially my heavy *rebetika*, the ones they call the hashish songs. Very good. I had very few failures among the songs when I was writing them. Most were smash hits. That's why the companies are bringing them out again now.

These songs of mine have to be played. They mustn't be lost, they have to be out there. They need to be remembered by everyone. They're Byzantine and their 'roads', their tunes are ancient. What the old guys used to play. Now they're recording the old songs again because the original discs don't exist. If we had the master recording we'd make new copies but they were destroyed in the war. They got burnt. You can imagine what was going on in all that mayhem. What did they care these guys? They busted their way into all sorts of random places. The storm took everything away. Now they're bringing out the songs with new singers. But when it comes to the *laiko* song as I understand it and the way I present it, right up to this very moment in time I've not come across anybody else who's like me. There are these fine

---
141 'Ah your Beautiful Eyes'.
142 Songs in the sabah mode, which is one of the 'roads' or *dhromoi*.

fellers who lord it about nowadays with my help and with my songs. That's why I told you these guys started out from the secrets, from the things I wrote myself, but now they've destroyed the *laiko* song. They don't produce pure *laiko* songs. They bring out pure *pop* songs, '*yeah yeah*' songs. These guys now who write songs and are at the top of their game are the '*Yeah Yeah*' brigade; that's the kind of thing they do. Not one of those songs is *laiko* like mine. That's why … did you see the kid who came by the other day? And another like him and another and another. That's why they write 'Here we sing the songs of Markos Vamvakaris'.

I was quite some guy, I can tell you kid, a proper wild beast, and see what I've turned into with these illnesses. It's not just one illness, it's three. Diabetes, high blood pressure and kidneys. Now more recently my heart as well. The heart seized up about a month ago and it's brought me to a complete standstill, this illness. My hands began to lose all feeling. When I put those pills under my tongue and sucked, it got better. But then I ended up taking twenty a day to get rid of the numbness. Even now it still bothers me but not too much, it goes away by itself. Now I'm okay far as the heart goes.

Two or three years ago I quit smoking. I was in such a bad way, I couldn't walk. I was a wreck. Whenever I walked, fap! I fell over. Five or ten steps and bam! Flat on my face. Now that I've cut it out I realize what a mistake it was to smoke cigarettes. I mean, not to be able to move? How could this happen to me? Not be able to walk! It was from cigarettes I got that. The doctors were telling me 'You'll have heart trouble.'

Let me either die or get better, I've had enough. I've lost my strength. Don't talk to me about health. How did I get to be in this state where I torture my family, everyone in this house. How did I? It's not what *I* want either. I got ill and it seems to me like I won't be able to get well. I'm not too bothered about the diabetes. I take it as it comes, it goes up, it goes down, whatever, but I worry more about the *urea*, and most of all about the blood pressure. Oh boy! Day and night they don't pipe down, my ears, they whistle. They don't stop for one hour. *Gouzz gouzz gouzzz*. Right now I'm alright but come the evening they start up again. I've been to all the doctors. I mean I'm regular in all my visits. I don't neglect any tests. I run around for my health. Whatever the wife tells me. Okay fine. It's not like I'm saying 'Leave me alone I don't want to.' Health and home.

Every day the wife says to me 'What do you fancy that I can make for you?' She looks after me. She brings me all sorts of foods to eat, but all unsalted. And since it's unsalted it's not for me. It's for chucking. I don't want to eat. I can't eat. I wish I had the strength to eat it but it makes me sick. Boy! Unsalted food. It upsets me, turns me into a wreck. Of course I don't want her to throw a *ton* of salt into the food, but just a little … enough for me to feel that it's salted.

I lead a quiet life now. What more d'you want? I sleep, I get up regular hours. I sit for a while over there in the shop, at the grocer's on the corner. Shall I tell you why I go there? It's because it has a telephone. I go along and lots of people phone me up. The kid rings me, Dhomenikos, who's still doing his national service. He's young and I feel for him. Round six in the afternoon I go to this shop. At a quarter to seven I'll be back here waiting for the milkman. This guy comes along and he asks me 'How's your health Mr Markos?' I don't know how interested he is but anyway it's nice of him to ask. Then I ask him back. He's crippled too, with a stomach complaint. I sit around here. I go to the shop where this guy comes along and he's fond of me. I pass the time. The cheese-pie seller comes by and every evening I sneak a cheese pie, even if this isn't in the diet. If Vangelio or the kids catch me there's all hell to pay. When I was still at school I read a poem.

*Whoever's been a starving lad*  
*Never says I'm weak and sad.*  
*But from afar he eyes the bread*  
*He looks at it and cries instead.*

Όποιος επείνασε πολύ  
πεινώ ποτέ δε λέει  
κοιτάζει μόνον το ψωμί  
από μακριά και κλαίει.

It's not that I'm well and only *pretending* not to be. But when it comes to that little bit of food I'm going to eat, just let me enjoy it! I don't need more than that. When I was well, I used to eat herrings, sardines, olives and garlic. I used to eat garlic by the handful. I ought to eat garlic now for the blood pressure. But I can't. Every morning when I get up, d'you know what my mouth is like? 'Can I give you some water melon? a little fruit?' says the wife. I'm a wreck. I just haven't got much of an appetite. These days with a *faskomylo*, I manage to get something down. She gives me a little rusk and this special sugar for diabetics but in the end it seems like just one more thing that sours my life. It's all pills now - this pill and that pill, seven or eight pills a day. Maybe all this medicine I take disagrees with me. Who knows, maybe God wants me to stop taking it. What can it be doing to my stomach? I can't take it any more.

For a couple of days I've been putting a drop of salt on my food, I mean just enough for me to know it's there. I ate it all up. Seems to me like its the weakness makes me ill. Hey, this feels quite a bit better! So maybe all this tottering about ready to keel over, is really due to starvation! I don't want to end up dying on my feet from hunger. I'd be eating my bones. It's not just one day or two we're talking about. It's all the rest of my life. Do you see how I've perked up the two or three days since I've been doing this? Now since I ate something my innards have got themselves together. I walk more easily, more of a spring in my step.

Yesterday we had a row. The wife caught me with the salt. My mouth is a crazy thing. That's why I nibble something and then my wife yells at me. But I have to. It's for this mouth of mine, to cheer it up a bit! I have no sense of taste at all. That's why I can't manage unsalted food. No way. I'll have my guts out first before I eat the stuff. Being in the state I am, don't I just want to die and be done with it? Get it over with. I don't ask for many things, you know, just a bearable sort of life, where I can eat more or less the way I used to eat. It's not like it was a *lot* of food. Just the odd olive, a sardine, a bit of herring. I like pulses, with a little onion, eh, green or dried. I love that. I'm not a big eater, not like those guys who can say they'll eat two or three plates and a loaf of bread. But you know, you sit there and you want to drink a coffee ... eh ... to drink a coffee, one or two a day. I just want to get well so they'll invite me to some joint to play music.

*Far Away From the World*

If I sat on a rock
Far out in the sea,
A few of my pains
I'd wipe from memory.

Far away from the world
Forever on my own,
To see no living soul again,
My sorrow would be gone.

The waves would break upon me
And the winds would blow,
Isn't it a shame, My God,
I should be tortured so?

*Από τον Κόσμο Μακριά*[143]

Να 'βρισκα σ' ένα πέλαγος
μια ξέρα να καθίσω
κι από τα πολλά μου βάσανα
λίγα να λησμονήσω.

Από τον κόσμο μακριά
και πάντα μοναχός μου
ανθρώπους να μη βλέπω πια
να μου περνάει ο καημός μου.

Να με φυσάει ο άνεμος
να με κτυπάει το κύμα
έτσι να βασανίζομαι
Θε' μου δεν είναι κρίμα;

If I had some way of being in a monastery ... I've been through anguish. In this world I didn't find a person after my own heart. All bad people. The world never gets to be good. But you'll say to me it's not possible everyone's bad in this world? All I can say is, from the life that I've lived, from

---

143 First recorded by Bithikotsis to the tune of *Rixe Tsingana*, rec. 1960.

what I've seen and heard, I don't have much faith, not even in my own self. Only in God. I just want to go and be alone. Of course there are my boys. Let them live happy and let me enjoy being their father, but I want to be alone. No matter if I'm a filthy, pitiful old tramp and altogether wretched in there, just let me have some peace and quiet on my own, and die one day. In peace. I've been thinking about this monastery for a long time. Ask my wife. For years now, for three or four years I've been looking into it. I mean, I'm not saying that I'm going to go and be a monk now. No. But that's the kind of place I want to wind up in. I'd go and say to the Prior, 'You know what Father? I've repented of the life I've lived and I've come here to put it behind me. Just give me a plate of food till the time comes for my soul to depart, and I head off down there.' That's how much I long for peace and quiet.

Just seven or eight months ago Rita came to my house and asked my wife to forgive her. I had a photograph of our child who died. She asked me for it so I gave it to her. She took it and left. From time to time, you know, my wife says 'You've still got a roving eye.' These days nothing doing! 'Eat the fish with your eyes and your guts can go hang' as they say. When I married Vangelio the Church excommunicated me for some twenty or thirty years. Now more recently the Catholic bishop from Aghios Dionysis up in Athens gave the order that 'You must at all costs let this man go to mass. Give him the Holy Sacrament.' This happened a year or two ago in 1966. The Catholic bishop, a fellow Syran, heard my name, Markos Vamvakaris. With all the fanfare that goes around my name, the church authorities pricked up their ears - these guys take notice of this sort of thing. You know in Syros they've named a street after me, Vamvakaris Street? That's quite something. The priest summoned me to the church here and he says to me 'We'll give you Holy

Communion, only you mustn't go near a woman. Not even your own wife.'

It's two or three years now since I got ill and ever since then I stopped everything with women. I can't sleep with a woman. I'll die if I do. It's the asthma. So these things, fine, let me give them up with God's help and so on and so forth, you know. Well of course, I'm only human, I see beautiful chicks and I like them, because I'd got used to being with a lot of women. I can't tell lies. But if women say to me 'Let's go and sleep together', I don't. They *do* ask me. Even now some women come and hang around me, because of the kind of work I do you know. Loads of them still want to do it with me; don't they just! I've had enough of them though. I've had enough. I sit quietly at home. It's not because the priests said to me 'Don't.' Pah! You think I buy that sort of thing? Let's not beat about the bush. It's because of my health I don't go with them. That being the case I obey my religion. So these guys now who gave me Holy Communion, they asked me: 'Did you go with a woman?' 'No' I said to them and it was the truth. But if I had done it I'd still have told them 'No.' I would have told a fib.

Now you'll tell me that even this is still better than the monastery. But no. You become a dead weight. Even in your own house. Let me go and work in a monastery that has some nice orchards, trees, that sort of thing where I could sit and eat and some days just not get up; be lazy. You'll say to me one week of that kind of life and I'll have had enough of it. But let God show me the light. I liked letters, as I said, and music and flowers. Ah yes, the flowers. Even now, down at my niece's I have pots of jasmine, roses, carnations, all sorts of things. Up there on the plot of land I got, I've planted stuff too. I've maybe five rose trees, all different kinds, and outside I have three olive trees. Don't even get me started, I love flowers so much! When I was well I could still do something on my own but now I pay a guy to go and water them. Now in the winter it doesn't need watering but before long I'll do some hoeing to churn up the soil. This field I have for the house, I've got cherries in it, and apricots.

We took this piece of land with the kids in mind. Thank God, now I've got my kids and they're grown up, eh ... they begin to bear fruit, to work. Not that I don't pull my weight. More, in fact, than anyone. But after all, what do I need money for? What would I do with it? I don't go out of my house. Like I said, even if I were well I wouldn't go out. I don't want anything to do with the world. Just let me hang out in some place by myself and let me die there on my own. But you'll say to me 'Can you bear to be without your wife, the good woman who keeps you nice and tidy?' What can I say? I'm better off in filth and squalor if I can just be on my own and have some peace. Of course I'll want to know that my kids aren't going hungry, that they're in a position to work and make a living. That's everything. And that bit of land over there, maybe if I get better later on and I'll turn it into a little pad. To go and be by myself there instead of the monastery. Go there and potter about; and you know, it's not far away either. It's in Kalamaki, just above the airport, in the district of Argyrios. As God wills. That's the main thing.

The minute I lie on my bed I'm at peace. I fall asleep. However ill I've been, whatever's wrong with me, I've always slept like a baby, thank God. Even with so many sins you'll be saying? I haven't got any. I've never robbed anyone. Take this moment in time, say, if I have a cent I give half of it away. I'm not interested, and my kids are the same. The one thing I did do was women. I chased after them as a young man. I liked them. I haven't done anything else. These are the sins I've committed in my life. And the Almighty will judge me accordingly. Still, I believe my soul is pure. I didn't do harm to anyone. Whatever was bad I struggled to act on it and fix it, to make good. Right up to now, at the recording companies where I go, I can't speak any harm of anyone. What can I say? Everyone knows me. Wherever you go everybody knows me. I'm a name. I never thought I'd arrive at such a point. I never expected it with the *bouzouki*. The *bouzouki*! I had a black mark on my name and they didn't let me go to America to make money. Not that I'm in love with money of course ...

| | |
|---|---|
| *Ah pots of money do no good* | *Α! Τα λεφτά τα πολλά* |
| *When all is told,* | *δεν ωφελούνε* |
| *And all the many love affairs,* | *ούτε κι οι αγάπες οι πολλες* |
| *They leave me cold.* | *με συγκινούνε.* |
| *I'll tell you, little one,* | *Μ'αρέσουν οι καρδιές σαν* |
| *What is more in my line.* | *τη δική μου,* |
| *Hearts that are full of feeling,* | *που'ναι γεμάτες από αίσθημα* |
| *Hearts like mine.* | *μικρή μου* |

That's how it is.

## CHAPTER 20

## THE MUSIC, THE WORDS, THE SONGS.

The decade from the mid thirties to the forties was a golden one for me. It's when I wrote my best songs. The one great thorn in my side was this business with my first wife. That was chewing me up. But still, discomfort helps me in my work. Somehow I write better, more easily, when I'm upset. And I was, of course, stoned the whole time. I always wanted to be alone. I did everything I could to be alone. I felt like I *had* to be either writing verses or humming music no matter where I was. I had songs coming out of my ears! The inspiration back then, I can't tell you! It was coming to me in spades. I wrote the words first in an exercise book - I always carried one around with me - and then I'd put in the music after. I kept the music in my head. Now of course I have Prokos my fellow Syran and he writes it down for me. Prokos is a musician. I mean, he knows how to read and write music. He came over from Syros, came to find me and I tried to help him get work. Now he's writing out the music for various composers. He does well out of it. He plays piano too, on the platforms. Since I found him I've properly got cracking. I was afraid of forgetting stuff. Time ticking by, you know. A lot has escaped me. The tunes I mean. Not the words. *They* weren't getting away from me. Nice pieces, I remember them. Or at any rate I remember them well enough to know that I'm forgetting them!

    Images, words, and feelings - they all go into the lyrics. This happens even now. How can I describe this thing? I might go and lie down say, with the idea of going to sleep, and then what happens is I don't sleep. The odds are my brain will be busy 'writing'. Mostly writing. But sometimes, even in my sleep I do the music too, and if it's the music I get up straight away and pick up the *instrument*, the *bouzouki*, and play it. I hear it like a song in my sleep. I sleep and I dream this song. I wake up and start mouthing the words and the minute I pick up the *bouzouki* I find it straightaway. It just comes to me you know. One time I'd written a tough verse and I started singing:

| | |
|---|---|
| *I'm not some fancy poet* | *Εγώ δεν είμαι ποιητής* |
| *Fitting words to songs.* | *τραγούδια να ταιριάζω* |
| *It's the arghile that brings them,* | *και μου τα φέρνει ο αργιλές* |
| *Puts the word where it belongs.* | *και τα κατασκευάζω.* |

They come just like that, ready formed. I've never had any trouble writing a song. But I do find that if I'm in a state, a little bit worried, things turn out better both in the words and the music.

For me there's no problem, no difficulty when it comes to composing. I'll make up a piece of music and these days I have the tape recorder in front of me. So I'll play it on *bouzouki* and record it. Done. When I record it I sing with pretend words, just any old words that come to mind, so as to see what words this song is drawing out. 'I love you', 'I like you', 'I feel for you', 'I'm sad for you' and so on. Later I put in the right words. I sing the dummy words just to get the rhythm of the song, to see what words to write. I count the words and the syllables to see how many go to each line. At some point, the time will come to write the proper words. Not the 'right time' exactly but whenever it comes to me. I listen to the music again and I think: What words does this song want? And frap! I catch it and set it down.

Every so often I hear a good word. It might be you who says it, or my wife or some kid out in the street. Ah, this'll be a word I *have* to put in a song. For instance yesterday I was sitting up there on my bed and I was singing a song I didn't finish:

| | |
|---|---|
| With kisses and caresses | Και με φιλιά και χάδια |
| You've wounded my soul | μου'χεις πληγώσει την ψυχή |
| With so many stresses ... | με τόσα πολλά ζαράρια. |

I was going to have *rimadhia,* ('ruins') but I liked *zararia,* ('stresses'). There are some words that do nicely for songs, like for instance, *anghelokamomeni mou,* ('my angel-made beauty') or *lampadhochyti mou* ('my shining light') - you know, the glass shade of the lamp.

The *bouzouki* and its *taximia,* its mysteries - these are things not everybody knows about. They're not written about in books either, because how's the other guy going to get it unless he hears it the way I'm going to do it for you now on the instrument? Still, whatever you understand, write it down. Those who have the passion for it will understand something, and they'll see that the *bouzouki,* which the police were hounding for years like it was a crime, is one hell of a big deal. It can't easily be grasped by just any old person. I learnt all these things bit by bit from the old guys in the *tekedhes,* because I had a great passion and my life was all *bouzouki.* Like I said, I sacrificed everything for the *bouzouki.* It took me over - but it also took me up in the world, way up.

Back in the old days in Syros the old guys were playing *bouzoukia* but not like the ones we play now. No, the instruments they played were called *tsivouria* and *gonata.* The *tsivouri* had a longer neck and wooden pegs for tuning. It had the strings and intervals of the *bouzouki* but with gut frets. I did get to play those *tsivouria* but not for long. They're what *bouzouki* players were using fifty or sixty years ago. The *gonato* was more narrow and smaller than the *tsivouri.* They used to make them from mulberry wood and the *tzouras* they made from the wood of lemon trees. The *tzouras* was a little tiny instrument, half the size of the *baglama* with only seven frets and three strings. These instruments are regarded as ancestors of the *bouzouki*. The *saz* too, like the *tsivouri*, was a bit bigger, with more strings than the *tsivouri* and the *bouzouki*, and a bigger range. All of these were Turkish or maybe Egyptian. I remember round about 1921 I saw a picture of the Petrobey[144] and he was dancing to instruments like that. I don't know the details of how the *bouzouki* came into being from those instruments.

The guy that can make the perfect *bouzouki* so that the fingerboard and the scale are just right, has still to be found. They haven't got it yet. I can hear it, this thing, where it falls short. Course I can. However much you tune it the tuning never comes out right. You can get a *bouzouki* for 450 drachs and you can get a *bouzouki* for 15,000 and 20,000 but as long as it's made by a good technician, the only difference between these *bouzoukia* is the pretty patterns they put on it. Guys in prison used to make *bouzoukia*, both for themselves and to make money for their cigarettes. They made all sorts of things. They had the know-how and the tools. They carved out *bouzoukia*, or *gonata* as they called them. They were carved out of one piece of wood, not glued together. These *gonata* came out of the prisons and they're made from mulberry wood, the best wood.

One of the first *bouzouki* makers I got to know was a fellow Syran Konstantis Delis who'd done twenty years in prison. This guy brought out the best *bouzoukia*. He was the best. Even now this guy's *bouzoukia*, if they're found they get snapped up like Stradivarius violins! This guy made *gonata*, but he also made the sort that you glue together piece by piece. There were lots of other guys who made instruments, both guitars and *bouzoukia*. I met Delis after he got out of jail in 1930, here in Piraeus. He pitched up at Karaiskakis,[145] you know, in that big open space where they

---

144 Petros Mavromichalis 1765 – 1848, a Maniot leader and hero of the Greek War of Independence, 1821.
145 Plateia Karaiskakis, one of the landmarks of old Piraeus, now the site of an enormous football stadium in Neo Faliro on the coast, named after Georgios Karaiskakis, a hero of the Greek war of Independence, who died near there in 1827.

have the cardsharpers, the floozies and God knows what else. He set up a very small shop and there he started making instruments. He took an apprentice, a young kid called Joseph, and began to teach him the tricks of the trade. Five, ten years went by. This guy died but the skill didn't die with him because now Joseph has it. That's where the best *bouzouki* players go to order their instruments. These are the more expensive instruments. Beautiful *bouzoukia*. I mean he's a master craftsman. I've got one of Delis' *bouzoukia*, and my kids have a *bouzouki* made by Joseph.

I used to have lots of *bouzoukia* made by Delis but I sold them. At the time when I was still giving lessons, people used to come here and say 'Will you teach me *bouzouki*?'

'Sure I will.'

'Do I have to buy a *bouzouki*?'

'No I've got one here you can use.' I used to sell them and get new ones. I haven't kept them. Now it's five or six years since I stopped buying those Delis instruments. You see, I got this piece of mulberry wood from a Turkish mosque. I brought it back from Andros where I went and played. I saw a woman there who was cutting up this wood every day and taking pieces away.

'What's this?' I said to her.

'Just look at it,' she says, 'it was in a Turkish mosque.'

Huge. Ten or fifteen metres long I promise you! It was still good to use, thousands of years old. These *bouzoukia* here, the red ones are made from very old wood, black mulberry. The older the wood the better. With enormous difficulty I managed to get a piece from her, and when I got here I made six *bouzoukia* out of it. Six! Some of them Joseph made for me and others were made by Grigoris. He's from Asia Minor. There are loads of guys who make *bouzoukia*. There's an Armenian guy ... and another one I got to know later on here in Chiotika in Piraeus, who had two kids and they learnt his trade. I've forgotten their names.

They were from the Dodecanese, from Asia Minor. They made *bouzoukia* and guitars. Good craftsmen. But not as good as Delis. In Athens too there were three or four guys who made *bouzoukia.* The same craftsmen make *baglamadhes* too, but most of those are carved out in prison by convicts. They last many years.

Can you believe it? It's twenty years now since I picked up a *baglama*! And boy what a *baglama* I played! Who could get anywhere near me when it came to playing *baglama*! I used to tune it up myself and off I'd go. The stuff I used to play! I couldn't do it now. I turned the *baglama* into a whole piano! And I had quite some nails too, you can't imagine! I played with nails on the *baglama*, absolutely never with the plectrum. All these guys who play *baglama* now are playing *baglamo-bouzouki*. These aren't *baglamadhes*. The *baglama* had seven frets, or *berdedhes*, and within these seven frets you'd play all the solos, whatever it was you were playing. While these new ones now have the scale all the way up there! You think they're playing *baglama*? The *baglama* was played with the nail. Of course there were others higher up than me when it came to *baglama*. There was a guy called Antrikakis in Syra. The minute he touched the *baglama*, it was unbelievable what he played! It had three strings, his *baglama* - thin like this, and wooden tuning pegs.

Now we have the European style tuning, *re-la-re* (DAD). This came from the piano. The *bouzouki* used to take the re from the piano. Since the time when the new *bouzoukia* appeared, since the time when I came on the scene for instance, I was trying to keep it tuned to the piano so that it could play along with me. But when I first began to play *bouzouki*, they were playing all those *baglama* tunings we were talking about. Later I learnt from this guy Manetas to tune the *bouzouki* re-la-re. Where he learnt it now I don't know. Anyway he was playing more in the European style than the *laiko* style. Batis too tuned his *baglama* re-la-re, always. Whenever we went to play with a band that didn't have a piano it would have a *santouri*. I used to say to the *santouri* player: 'Give me your re.' He'd give me the re, and we'd tune up to the European style. Same with the guitar. Like I said, the *baglama* they play now isn't a *baglama*, it's a *half-bouzouki*. The *baglamadhes* of that time were made with seven frets. They were the *tzouradhes*. These weren't tuned to re-la-re. They were tuned to the *karadouzenia*, *syriana* and *arabienne* tunings - the *baglamodouzenia*. Those *douzenia* were played by the old *bouzouki* players. I was in time to hear them playing with those *douzenia* - but nowadays they do European style. From the time that I began to lay my hands on a *bouzouki* that's when the European style began. Or maybe a bit before, let's say 1920-25. Manetas and Zoumaritis played in the European style, but I was the one that made it catch on. And afterwards all these other *bouzouki* players appeared and played with the European tuning. Very few people are left now who've learnt the old *baglamodouzenia*, and those people are: my brother, my kids - I'm teaching them now - and Keromitis. They know about these things. But the new guys who've appeared on the scene now, they don't know a thing about it.

Most of my songs are *niaventi*. A beautiful 'road'. All the 'roads' are beautiful, but, I don't know, I guess this one just suits my voice. For me no 'road' is difficult but the best and sweetest one is this 'road', the *Niaventi*. But you think the *kiourdi* is ugly? No it's a beautiful thing. *Ta ziliarika sou matia* (rec. 1938) which I wrote in about 1930 is *Niaventi*.

*Your Jealous Eyes*

Those jealous eyes of yours
Have made me rave.
I didn't count on palaces,
But now I am a slave.

*Τα Ζηλιάρικά σου Μάτια*

Τα ζηλιάρικά σου μάτια
μ' έχουνε τρελάνει
δε λογάριασα παλάτια
σκλάβο μ' έχουν κάνει.

| | |
|---|---|
| I droop | Μαραζώνω |
| And like a burning candle melt. | σαν το κεράκι λιώνω |
| Since you don't love, you torture me, | με παιδεύεις |
| A cruel hand you've dealt. | γιατί δε μ' αγαπάς. |
| | |
| I loved you – that's the truth. | Σε αγάπησα στ' αλήθεια |
| I cry for you, | και για σένα κλαίω |
| My heart's ablaze I tell you, | έχω φλόγα μες στα στήθια |
| Listen do! | άκου που στο λέω. |
| | |
| Your glance, your heart, | Η ματιά σου |
| So fickle and unkind, | η άστατη καρδιά σου |
| Have made me lose | μου `χουν πάρει |
| My miserable mind. | το δόλιο μου μυαλό. |
| | |
| To leave me all alone to pine | Είναι κρίμα να μ' αφήνεις |
| Is a stain upon your soul. | μόνος μου να λιώνω |
| For company all that you give | μαύρη συντροφιά μου δίνεις |
| Is pain, a deep black hole. | μοναχά τον πόνο. |
| | |
| I worship you, make much of you, | Σε λατρεύω, σε χαϊδεύω |
| Don't turn it all to bad. | μην κακιώνεις |
| For if you do I surely will go mad. | γιατί θα τρελαθώ. |

Most of my *chasapika* were in *niaventi*. It's the 'road' that suited my throat and so that's what came out I guess whenever I was singing. With my voice I tend to sing from *re* (D). When I was first bringing out my songs I used to sing the *chasapika* from *Re minore* (D minor) and the *zebekika* from *re majore* (D major). It was a bit on the high side, but in the course of time the pitch lowered and I came down to *Si minore* (B minor) and then I was singing comfortably. None of the singers who've followed me, not one of them has managed yet to take my place. This guy Evstathiou went some way towards achieving it but he couldn't because I do the middle stuff and I go high, right up there, the high voice. I go up and up and all at once I drop right down, straight on the level. Contrabasso and spot on.

Among the 'roads' *niaventi, sabah, kiourdi,* and *ushak* are minor. *Hidjaz, houzam, peiraiotikos, rasti, hidjaskiar* are major. Depending on what songs they're singing, a guy will pick up his fiddle or whatever instrument he plays and say 'Play a song.' It starts off. He understands whether it's major or minor - he gets it from the tune. You see there are songs in the major key but in the 'road' of the song there's also minor key. That's how we play. It's a mixture.

From the moment I started with the *instrument*, I've always been writing songs. And even now that I'm ill and old, these things are still what I keep myself busy with. But in that decade, the thirties I was writing all the time. Most of the songs I've mentioned in this book, my life-story, were written in these ten years more or less. I wrote for the companies and I had a lot of hits. I was obsessed. Like I said, my songs came out in a rush just like that. Mostly I can't remember what prompted them. Something happens, I see it and I write. That's it. Later on another thing took hold of me as well. That was the idea of writing histories and books - and my life story that I began. I started my novel too, *The Condemned Benefactor*. There's a huge lot of songs and I've forgotten so many but now I'll sing as much as I can remember. Here's one I recorded in 1949, *Dhen thelo Plouti kai Lefta*:

| **I don't want Riches** | **Δε Θέλω Πλούτη και Λεφτά** |

*I don't want riches or great wealth,*  *Δε θέλω πλούτη και λεφτά,*
*Dear lady, just your charms.*  *μονάχα σε κυρά μου,*
*To make you sleep with kisses,*  *να σε κοιμίζω με φιλιά,*
*Hold you warmly in my arms.*  *μεσ' στη θερμή αγκαλιά μου.*

| | |
|---|---|
| To have you in my lodging house, | Να σε `χω στο κονάκι μου, |
| In my yard a flower, | λουλούδι στην αυλή μου, |
| And turn my miserable hut | στολίδι να `σαι μοναχό, |
| Into a starry bower. | στο δόλιο το τσαρδί μου. |
| | |
| For you I'll play bouzouki | Να παίζω στο μπουζούκι μου, |
| And for you I'm going to sing | για σένα τραγουδάω |
| Together with you I will do | και τη μποέμικη ζωή, |
| The grand bohemian thing. | κοντά σου να περνάω. |

Stratos Payoumtzis sang this one. The 'road' is *hidjaskiar*. The bohemian life is the rackety life, you know, dancing, partying, all that sort of thing. But of course a guy has to work first and then he'll do the bohemian life, because if he doesn't work, how's it going to happen? With work there'll be the money and everything he needs to lead this kind of life. Here's another song from this time, *M'ekapses Tsachpina mou Oraia*, (rec. 1934).

**You Burnt me Beautiful Flirt**   **Μ'έκαψες Τσαχπίνα μου Ωραία**

You burnt me beautiful flirt
Crazy flirt you burnt me.
Burnt me and I melt completely
As you kiss me very sweetly.

With that blonde hair of yours, my love,
You burnt my heart, you flighty dove.

You've burnt me, now give me a kiss.
From you I want consoling bliss.
I love you darling crazy blonde
Come into my arms so fond.

Come and heal my failing heart beat
With your kisses, for they are sweet.
I have you in my head, you flirt,
All day long, you know I hurt.

Come let fresh air into my brain
With your sweet kiss just once again.

Μ' έκαψες, τσαχπίνα μου ωραία
μ' έκαψες, τσαχπίνα μου τρελή,
μ' έκαψες και λιώνω ολοένα
με τ' ολόγλυκο σου το φιλί.

Με τα ολόξανθα μαλλιά σου, φως μου
τσαχπίνα, μούχεις κάψει την καρδιά,
μ' έκαψες κι ένα φιλάκι δός μου
θέλω από σε παρηγοριά.

Εσένα αγαπώ, τρελή ξανθιά μου
έλα στη δική μου αγκαλιά,
έλα να μου γιάνεις την καρδιά μου
με τα ολόγλυκα σου τα φιλιά.

Σ' έχω μες στο νου μου όλη μέρα
τσαχπίνα μου, το ξέβρεις πώς πονώ,
έλα για να πάρει ο νους μου αγέρα
με το γλυκό φιλί σου το στερνό.

I wrote this in 1936 and I sang it myself on a record at Odeon. Now it's been recorded again at Music Box with twelve songs, in which, again, I'm singing. So about this song: it happened that I got to know a prostitute. Her name was Marika. She had blonde hair, a beautiful woman, and she was in love with me. She was already involved though, with a cousin of mine so she kept it under wraps. She worked in a brothel and you paid over your five *talira* to climb on top of her. I held back for the sake of my cousin but me and Marika were still friends, not in a bad way, you understand? She used to go out with her boyfriend and I went along too. The next thing was, one fine day my cousin died. So then I got in there. She and I used to go round the *tekedhes.* We smoked, both of us. She liked hashish and she loved being with me, I can't tell you! We loved each other and all the *manghes* of Piraeus knew her and looked after her because she was a big-hearted woman. She liked going into the *tekes* and she'd say to the *teketzis* 'Let the boys have a smoke'. She paid too! A good woman.

How does it happen that a good woman falls in this way? It takes a lot for a good woman to go to the bad. She talked to me sometimes about how her mother had died, her father too, so she was left with a stepmother who had other kids and looked after her own but not Marika. It got so bad she just had to get out of there. So she hitched up with a guy who took her eyes out, as they say, and after that I don't know what. She told me it was all because of the stepmother. She was from Kaminia in Piraeus. I kept Marika for about seven months. Then, one day she says to me:

'Markos, I'm going to get married.'

'Do get married, Marika my dear' says I. What else could I say to her? 'What are you waiting for? Enough is enough.'

So she married this guy from Thebes. About seven or eight years went by. I forgot all about her and then one time I went to play in Thebes. She came and found me. I'd been avoiding her - since she was married what did I want with her? 'Come to my house,' she said, 'I split with my husband.' So I went there and she told me a whole heap of things all about this husband who'd left her. I've not seen her again since then. She's still alive, in the same place in Thebes, I guess. It was for her I wrote that song.

There are some pathetic low-down types in this world and what they do is destroy women. Like I told you before, however many women I've been mixed up with, I looked after them a lot, and loved them; I didn't beat them, I didn't talk ugly to them. I mean, I was okay. At any rate, I felt sorry for these dames and I still do now. The one who really *was* a whore was this piece of work, my first wife. She shouldn't have done the things she did to me. Fine, to start with we were poor, but afterwards didn't she see the good times coming? Think I didn't look after her? When I first married her I was poor and yet we were all sweetness and light. I was working in the slaughterhouse and it's not like I kept her naked and hungry. I had good parents. I had my father who, if I wasn't working because of the *bouzouki*, he held things together so neither of us went hungry, not me, not her either. But still my father was trying to tell me. My mother was worried too. She was so smart and she'd cottoned onto her. As long as I kept Zingoala poor she was fine, she wasn't looking for more. But when they called me to the studios to make records, and I began to make money and dressed her up in shoes, dresses, crosses, rings, bracelets, all those kinds of things, that's when she wanted to go find some stranger to fuck. Was that my fault? I was getting shitloads of money. I was up to the mark with two to three thousand a month. I had two or three new suits and a new overcoat every year. I was pleased with it all. Couldn't she see that our life had changed and we'd hit the jackpot? I'd accustomed her to thousands. What did this woman want now that made her do such a thing? If she'd taken a better guy than me, more handsome, I'd say to hell with it! But I was a hunk, dammit, and loads of women were chasing after me! She shouldn't have done it. But she was a no good woman, that's for sure, a right bitch of a woman.

This guy she went off with, who took her for an arm and a leg, he was laughable! A pitiful joke and nothing more! He tried to act the *mangas* but he really wasn't up to it. Waste of time. Now you'll say to me 'Why are you telling me this? Are you still fighting him?' No, I'm telling you simply the way it is. He was not the kind of guy you'd expect to cut the mustard with this woman. For sure she'll have played fast and loose with him too. You think if she wasn't getting it from him she wouldn't go elsewhere? She took this guy just as a cover. Was I to blame? No I did everything I could to make her a lady. She'd have been called Mrs Vamvakaris just like my wife is now, my proper wife. She only has to see my wife and she goes all shakey. As for me, well, what can she say? I'm in a pretty poor state now, but my wife ... she sees her and feels bad. She sees the children I have and then she's fit to burst. Damn whore, I kept her so many years! You can't imagine the curses she shoved under our door. Even now ... would you believe it? Black magic to make Vangelio die. Every possible kind of bad voodoo. Whenever she saw Vangelio walking by she'd turn and run away. She's a woman of seventy by now. But back then she was beautiful and I was in love with her. She'd got me in her power.

### I'll Come and Wake You[146]

At earliest dawn all secretly
I'll come and wake you up at three.
Your mother won't hear anything.
Come talk to me, make my heart sing.

### Θα'ρθω να σε Ξυπνήσω

Χαράματα η ώρα τρεις
θα'ρθω να σε ξυπνήσω
κρυφά από τη μανούλα σου
να σε χαρώ
να βγεις να σου μιλήσω.

---

146 Tha'rtho na se Xypniso, 1935.

No one will see, no one at all,
Just you and the moon will hear my call.
Come to your window, come please do,
And let me catch a glimpse of you.

Don't reveal our secret love
Please don't give the game away.
No matter what they do to you
Please, I beg, do not betray.

Δε θα μας δει άλλος κανείς
μόνο το φεγγαράκι
έβγα στο παραθύρι σου
να σε χαρώ,
για να σε δω λιγάκι.

Τη μυστική αγάπη μας
μην την εφανερώσεις
ότι και να σου κάνουνε
να σε χαρώ
να μην τηνε προδώσεις.

It's a nice song that. I sang it at Odeon records. A neat *chasapiko* and a refined one but I wrote it for that low-down slut. You may remember I told you that after some time went by I used to go and tap at her windows, whore that she was, just to see her. You'll say to me what was all that about? Well, I was still getting over the love sickness and that's why I wrote *Ta Ble sou Parathyria*[147] but I've not written anything else for that woman ... nothing. Why would I make her more important by writing about her? Here's a neat *Chasapiko, I Poneiri*, which went down very well in 1936 and now Michalis Chatziantoniou sang it at Music Box records four or five years ago:

| The Minx | Η Πονηρή |
|---|---|
| I'm going to get blind drunk<br>You minx! And all because of you.<br>I'm going to fight with all the folks<br>Who live around you too. | Εγώ για σε βρε πονηρή<br>θα πάω να σουρώσω<br>μες στο δικό σου μαχαλά<br>με όλους θα μαλώσω. |
| You told me I should wait for you,<br>We'd meet at seven o'clock<br>You liar! I don't understand,<br>You made me a laughing stock! | Εφτά η ώρα μου 'χες πει<br>για να σε περιμένω<br>ψεύτρα γιατί με γέλασες<br>δε σε καταλαβαίνω. |
| With all the folks that live near you<br>I'm going to pick a fight | Μέσα στη συνοικία σου<br>με όλους θα μαλώσω |

---

[147] Your Blue Windows, see chap 15 p.155.

| | |
|---|---|
| From all your folks who stitched me up, | κι από το σόι που 'μπλεξα |
| I'll soon be out of sight. | γρήγορα να γλυτώσω. |
| | |
| You and your mother hooked me up | Μ' έμπλεξες συ κι η μάνα σου |
| Because you thought me rich, | γιατ' είχα παραδάκια |
| You ruined me and watered me | σκύλα πώς με κατάστρεψες |
| With poison, filthy bitch! | με πότισες φαρμάκια. |

I brought this one out before the war with different words. I changed them later because they didn't get past the censorship. What I *used* to sing was *Thelo na Yino Ischyros*:

| **I Want to Be Strong** | **Θέλω να Γίνω Ισχυρός** |
|---|---|
| I want to be as forceful | Θέλω να γίνω ισχυρός |
| As Signor Mussolini | ωσάν τον Μουσολίνι, |
| Or tough as Mr Hitler | ωσάν τον Χίτλερ ζόρικος |
| Who's such a frightful meanie. | π'ούτε ψιλή δε δίνει. |
| | |
| Or like Kemal who made the Turks | Σαν τον Κεμάλ που έκανε |
| Into a mighty nation, | μεγάλη την Τουρκία, |
| So that the Greeks were at a loss | και κάνουν κόζι οι Έλληνες |
| And filled with consternation. | κι έχουνε απορία. |
| | |
| And you commander Stalin, yay! | Κι εσύ βρε Στάλιν αρχηγέ |
| Pride of the world and bastion, | του κόσμου το καμάρι, |
| All the workers love you since | όλοι οι εργάτες σ' αγαπούν |
| You are a mighty champion. | γιατί είσαι παλικάρι. |

How would I present a thing like this to Metaxas? So I threw it out myself and gave it the words of *I Poneiri*. Most of my songs, I just can't remember how I came to write them. *Stis Thalassas tin Ammoudhia* is another *hidjaskiar* a pre-war record. This one was a hit.

| **On the Beach** | **Στης Θάλασσας την αμμουδιά** |
|---|---|
| On the beach down by the sea, | Στης θάλασσας την αμμουδιά |
| Hey aman aman, | βρε αμάν αμάν |
| I had a little coffee shop, | είχα καφενεδάκι |
| And every morning you came by | Κι ερχόσουνα κάθε πρωί |

To vent your love and sadly sigh.
One day I stumbled on a pair
Of dusky beauties lying there.
Spread out upon the sand they lay
Drunk as lords all through the day.

Come over here you dervish dude!
Sit here, don't stand apart.
Listen to the songs we sing
They come straight from the heart.

Take your little baglama
Give us a little pleasure.
Roll up and light your cigarette
Sit and smoke at leisure.

Fill me up the arghile
I'll smoke and I'll get high.
And after that, my beauties,
The baglama I'll try.

With the finest scented leaf
I'll tamp your arghile,
There by Pasalimani
In old Yiannis' teke.

κι έσπαγες νταλκαδάκι.
Δυο χανουμάκια έμορφα,
πάντοτε μεθυσμένα
ένα πρωί τα τράκαρα
στην άμμο ξαπλωμένα.

Πλησίασε ντερβίση μου,
και κάθισε κοντά μας
κι άκου τραγούδια του σεβντά
βγαλμένα απ' τη καρδιά μας.

Πάρ' το μπαγλαμαδάκι σου
λίγο να μας γουστάρεις
άναψ' το τσιγαρλίκι σου,
και κάτσε να φουμάρεις.

Γεμίστε μου το ναργιλέ
να πιω να μαστουριάσω
ύστερα χανουμάκια μου,
το μπαγλαμά να πιάσω.

Να σου πατήσω ναργιλέ
με τουμπεκί σπαχάνι,
στου Μπάρμπα Γιάννη τον τεκέ
μες στο Πασαλιμάνι.

Nice song, which can't get in anywhere now because of the censorship. The censorship came in under Metaxas. Before that, our songs came out just the way we wrote them and we wrote whatever we liked. The censorship put the kibosh on all of that. This one now - if we ran it past the censorship they'd throw it all out. If it's a couple of bad words that have to come out then they can take them out themselves. If it's a lot, then they chuck the whole thing. The music isn't lost - they don't throw that out, only the words.

| | |
|---|---|
| **That's how I want you** | **Έτσι σε Θέλω** |
| That's how I want you, sweety pie, | Έτσι σε θέλω μάτια μου[148] |
| A flirty good time girl, | να 'σαι γλεντζού τσαχπίνα |
| The old vineyard at Rafina? | κι ας πάει και το παλιάμπελο |
| That can go to hell. | που έχω στη Ραφήνα. |
| | |
| What can I do with money? | Τι να τα κάνω τα λεφτά |
| A palace is no prize. | και τα ψηλά παλάτια |
| These things are not worth anything | τίποτα δεν αξίζουνε αμάν αμάν |
| Compared with your sweet eyes, | μπρος τα γλυκά σου μάτια. |
| | |
| And like I said the things I have, | Όσα κι αν εχω στο'χω πει |
| All of it I'll sell | όλα θα τα πουλησω, |
| To have just you is quite enough | φτάνει μονάχα ταίρι μου |
| My soul mate and my gel. | εσένα ν'αποχτησω. |
| | |
| A stolen kiss, whatever you say | Ένα φιλάκι πεταχτό |
| Is worth my empty purse | όσο κι αν πεις αξίζει |
| That's why I love you, and the world | γι' αυτό και γω σ' αγάπησα |
| Can shout at me and curse. | κι ο κόσμος ας με βρίζει. |

This one got into Columbia - I did it twice but I don't remember how it came about that I recorded it. Here's another nice *chasapiko* of that time, *Christinaki*:

| | |
|---|---|
| *Christinaki* | *Χριστινάκι* |
| Ah that smouldering glance of yours | Η φλογερή σου η ματιά |
| Your laughter that's so sweet | και το γλυκό σου γέλιο |
| It's made me want you so, | μου'χουν ραΐσει την καρδιά, |
| Christina mine | Χριστίνα μου, |
| My heart's too broke to beat. | μ'έκανες και σε θέλω. |
| | |
| You have such flirty devilry | Έχεις μεγάλη τσαχπινιά |
| You slay us with your darts. | κι όλους μας φοβερίζεις |
| With your delicious prettiness | με τη γλυκιά σου ομορφιά |
| My little flirt, | τσαχπίνα μου |
| You break a lot of hearts. | πολλές καρδιές ραγίζεις. |

---

148 *Etsi se Thelo* - Composed not by Markos but by Lazaros Rouvas and Yiorgos Petropouleas., rec.1937.

| | |
|---|---|
| The grocers in the market<br>And the fishermen you tease.<br>The butchers are the ones you like,<br>Christina mine,<br>You smile and aim to please. | Ψαράδες και μανάβηδες<br>στην αγορά πειράζεις<br>σ'αρέσουν οι χασάπηδες,<br>Χριστίνα μου,<br>και τους καλοκοιτάζεις. |
| But think, do change your naughty ways<br>And have a little care,<br>The world has changed, it's mostly bad<br>My little flirt,<br>Christina, oh so mad. | Σκέψου τη γνώμη άλλαξε<br>και πρόσεξε λιγάκι<br>γιατί ο κόσμος άλλαξε,<br>τσαχπίνα μου,<br>τρελλό μου Χριστινάκι. |

This one, *Mia Omorfi Melachrini*, (rec. 1939) I wrote in 1937 or 38 and I sang it at Odeon:

**A Brunette Beauty**[149]   **Μια Όμορφη Μελαχροινή**

| | |
|---|---|
| A brunette beauty, whimsical<br>And full of fine caprices<br>She struts and lords it over me,<br>She poses and she teases. | Μια όμορφη μελαχρινή<br>ναζιάρα και σκερτσόζα<br>τόσο πολύ με τυραννεί<br>και μου κρατάει πόζα. |
| I shall go up to her one night.<br>I'll ask her, yes I will,<br>How did you get to be so bad?<br>You're going to make me ill! | Θα τη ζυγώσω μια βραδιά<br>και θα την αρωτήσω<br>πως γίνεσαι τόσο κακιά<br>για σένα θα αρρωστήσω. |
| But oh her eyes and oh that black,<br>That curling frizzy hair<br>When all these charms are in my arms<br>They smooth out every care. | Τα κατσαρά της τα μαλλιά<br>τα μάτια της τα μαύρα<br>μες την δική μου αγκαλιά<br>θα σβήσουν κάθε λαύρα. |

---

149 *Mia Omorfi Melachrini*, rec. 1939.

A *niaventi chasapiko* that I've sung myself is: *I Boemissa*, (rec. 1940).

| The Bohemian Girl | Η Μποέμισσα |
|---|---|
| Bohemian girl you knocked me<br>   right off course,<br>With that crazy look of yours<br>With your petting and your pats<br>And your sweet little chats. | Με πλάνεψες μποέμισσα,<br>με τη τρελή ματιά σου,<br>με τα πολλά τα χάδια σου,<br>και τη γλυκιά μιλιά σου, |
| Why should I see you little one?<br>To meet you is too tiring,<br>Since you just don't know how to love,<br>I'm pretty near expiring. | Γιατί μικρό μου να σε ιδώ,<br>γιατί να σ' αντικρίσω,<br>εσύ δεν ξέρεις ν' αγαπάς,<br>κοντεύω πια να σβήσω. |
| When I tell you I love you,<br>You start to jest and grin<br>It pleases you to torture me and<br>Stick the boot right in. | Όταν σου λέω σ' αγαπώ,<br>γελάς και κοροϊδεύεις,<br>σ' αρέσει να με τυραννάς,<br>σκληρά να με παιδεύεις. |
| Bohemian girl, bohemian girl,<br>Just think how you'll grow old.<br>Like other girls, on youth and looks<br>You'll soon have lost your hold. | Μποέμισσα, μποέμισσα,<br>σκέψου πως θα γεράσεις,<br>και γρήγορα τα νιάτα σου,<br>σαν όλες θα τα χάσεις. |

I sang this one in 1936 with the Abatzi girl, I mean the sister of Rita Abatzi.[150] That's also when I wrote *I Ziliara*[151] a tortured song. I was in a terrible state when I wrote this song. It was 1935 and I was on a boat heading for Syra, the first time I went back there. After that I started going regularly to Syra. I went again and again, four, five or six times for work. Here's another one I wrote at that time. I put in the music after I got back to Athens. Didn't I say that when I'm in a bad state I write better? Who can tell me the reason why? But I'm not alone in this. I've heard other composers saying the same.

---
150 Sofia Karivali.
151 'The Jealous Woman'.

## To Hollywood[152]

I'll go off to America
And make a heap of dough
Americans and Greeks alike
I'll wow them with my show.

The wide-eyed starlets of the screen
I'll get to see them all,
I'll visit Frank Sinatra
Up in his lofty hall.

To Hollywood I'll go as well,
I'll set my foot right there
The place is strewn with gold and pearls,
A very swell affair.

If anybody wants to send
Some greetings on their part,
I'll put knots in my handkerchief
And learn them off by heart.

## Στο Χόλυγουντ

Θα πάω στην Αμερική
και πλούτη θ' αποχτήσω,
Αμερικάνους και Ρωμιούς
θα τους ευχαριστήσω.

Τ' άστρα θα ιδώ του σινεμά
με τα μεγάλα μάτια,
στου Φρανκ Σινάτρα θ'ανεβώ
τα μακρινά παλάτια.

Ακόμα και στο Χόλυγουντ
θα βάλω το ποδάρι,
που 'ναι στρωμμένο μάλαμα
και με μαργαριτάρι.

Κι αν θέλει χαιρετίσματα
κανένας να του στείλει,
κρυμμένα τα'χω στην καρδιά
και κόμπο στο μαντήλι.

I sang that before the war, a nice *niaventi* and one of my first *chasapika*. Back then I used to say I'd climb up to Annie Odra's lofty halls. She was famous at that time but these days I say Frank Sinatra's and that's better.

### For You My Black-Eyed Beauty[153]

For you my black-eyed beauty
I let my youth fly by,
You devil, you have ruined me,
Then left me high and dry.

Since I got tangled up with you,
I shunned my mother and brothers too,
Ah, sly temptress, in your arms
I lost my reason to your charms.

### Για Σένα Μαυρομάτα Μου

Για σένα μαυρομάτα μου
χαράμισα τα νιάτα μου
κακούργα με κατάστρεψες
κι ύστερα μ' απαράτησες.

Μαζί σου σαν τυλίχτηκα
μάνα κι αδέρφια αρνήθηκα,
πλανεύτρα στην αγκάλη σου
με τρέλλαναν τα κάλλη σου.

---

152 *Sto Hollywood*, rec. 1936.
153 *Ya Sena Mavromata Mou*, rec. Parlaphone 1946, *aptaliko-zebekiko*.

Every night I roam and drink,
I start to lurch and veer,
First I get sloshed, and then blind drunk
Shed many a bitter tear.

Και κάθε βράδυ ξενυχτώ
τα πίνω και παραπατώ,
εμέθυσα ξεμέθυσα
και μαύρο δάκρυ για σένα
έχυσα.

This one was a big hit and it came out with Odeon:

### My Flirt[154]

Ah you disowned me
In ruthless fashion,
All those years
when you were my passion.
You sucked me dry,
Made me your slave.
Now in the streets
I grieve and rave.

I tell you, I tell you,
I can't bear this,
Come back to my arms,
You teasing doll.
Back to our nest!
Give me a kiss.

Charming doll,
When I first knew you,
You were classy, quite the best.
You lost your mind,
And pushed me far.
Now I drink at Marios' bar.

I tell you, I tell you
I can't bear this.
I love you, I love you,
Don't play the tyrant, cruel tease,
Remember how to love, oh please.

### Παιχνιδιάρα Μου

Αχ, με αρνήθηκες,
δε λυπήθηκες,
τόσα χρόνια που σε αγαπούσα,
με μαράζωσες
και με σκλάβωσες,
μες τους δρόμους τώρα
πονεμένος τριγυρνώ.

Α! Θα στο πω! Θα στο πω!
Δεν μπορώ!
Ξαναγύρισε στην αγκάλη μου,
παιχνιδιάρικο κουκλί,
στη φωλίτσα μας,
δως μου το φιλί.

Κούκλα γόησσα,
σαν σε γνώρισα,
ήσουνα ένα κορίτσι φίνο,
ξεμυαλίστηκες
και μ' αρνήθηκες
και στου Μάριου το καπηλειό τα πίνω.

Α! Θα στο πω! Α! Θα στο πω!
Δεν μπορώ! Δεν μπορώ!
Σ' αγαπώ! Σ' αγαπώ!
Παιχνιδιάρα μου μη με τυραννάς
την αγάπη μην ξεχνάς,

---

154 *Paichnidiara Mou*, rec. 1947.

| | |
|---|---|
| *You swore to me that you would love,* | Ορκιζόσουνα πως θα μ' αγαπάς. |
| *Old age I warn you, is pretty rough,* | Πρίν τα γηρατειά, έρθουν τα σκληρά |
| *So change your mind,* | και τη γνώμη σου μικρό ν' αλλάξεις. |
| *My sweet. Enough!* | |
| | |
| *Come I beg you, while you may.* | Έλα να χαρείς, τώρα που μπορείς, |
| *Our youth slips by* | φεύγουν τα νιάτα φως μου |
| *It runs away.* | και διαβαίνουν. |

A nice *chasaposerviko, niaventi* on a record of '37 - '38.

| **When You See Me and Whistle**[155] | **Σαν με Ιδείς και σου Σφυρίξω** |
|---|---|
| *I want to see you in the night,* | Θέλω να σε βρω το βράδυ, |
| *A little moment out of sight,* | μιά στιγμούλα στο σκοτάδι, |
| *So that I can tell you a secret* | να σου πω το μυστικό μου και τον |
| *And my very painful plight.* | πόνο τον δικό μου. |
| | |
| *First I'll whistle and you'll see me,* | Σαν με δείς να σου σφυρίξω, |
| *Then you'll throw me down the door key* | πέτα το κλειδί ν' ανοίξω, |
| *I'll let you out, then face to face,* | να βγεις και να σ' ανταμώσω, |
| *In your hands a letter place.* | ένα γράμμα να σου δώσω. |
| | |
| *You want to see how I adore you?* | Θες να δείς πως σε λατρεύω, τη |
| *See I risk my whole life for you!* | ζωή μου κινδυνεύω, |
| *Sassy girl, my lady fine,* | ντερμπεντέρισα κυρά μου, |
| *I'm surely going to make you mine.* | θα σε κάνω πιά δικιά μου. |

This one is Houzam, a *zebekiko, youroukiko*. *Derbederissa* means a smart girl. In 1935 I wrote Frangosyriani for a girl in Syros. From 1936 – 39, I was writing all the time – I was on a roll. Same in 1940 - 43, only they weren't making records then because of the war and all that. I was writing all about girls, you know, love songs. What else would I write about since I was a kid? I *have* written some others but even those in the end all come back down to love affairs. I've written some about jobs people do.

---

[155] *San Me idhis kai Sou Sfirixo*, rec. 1951.

Oh butcher with the apron,     Χασάπη μου με την ποδια
Which as you tie it up behind ...     Που σαν τη δέσεις πίσω...

I don't remember the rest of that but here's another:

**In the Meat Market**     **Μεσ'στη Χασάπικη Αγορά**

The butcher's boy
In the market place
With the bushy brows
And the mole on his face,

When he sees me walk
In front of him
He stabs the block
With his knife so trim

His cheeks blush red
They kill me dead.
His beauty's made me
Lose my head.
He charms, and he enchants,
And he puts me in a daze.
I feel for him Mama - can't bear delays!

He's tall and strong and manly
Like a lamp he's all ablaze.
You have to know, Mama, that I
Can't help but love him madly.
The way that I am going
I'm afraid will turn out badly.
If I can't have him I shall die.
I'll peak and pine away.
Because of him, in blackest earth
You'll bury me one day.

Μεσ'στη χασάπικη αγορά
ένα χασαπάκι,
με την ελίτσα
και τα φρύδια τα σμιχτά,
όταν με βλέπει
και περνάω από μπροστά του,
τη μαχαιρίτσα του
στο κούτσουρο κτυπά,

Τα μαγουλά του κοκκινίζουν
και με σφάζουν,
η ομορφιά του μ'έχει
κάνει σαν τρελλή,
με γοητεύει, με μαγεύει,
με παιδεύει,
τον εσυμπάθησα,
μανούλα μου, πολύ.

Εχει ένα μπόι λεβεντιά
σαν τη λαμπάδα,
να ξέρεις, μάνα μου,
τρελλά τον αγαπώ
και όπως πάω, αν δεν τον πάρω,
θα χτικιάσω,
γι'αυτόνε, μάνα μου,
στη μαύρη γη θα μπώ.

Another from that time is 'Grousouzis' (rec. 1937):

| Loser | Ο Γρουσούζης |
|---|---|
| All night long you rotten loser | Βρε γουρσούζη, όλη νύχτα |
| You sit drinking, hopeless boozer | κάθεσαι και μπεκροπίνεις |
| With the bottle everlasting | και στο σπίτι τα παιδιά σου |
| While your kids at home are fasting. | θεονήστικα τ' αφήνεις. |
| | |
| All day long you lurch and totter | Μεθυσμένος όλη μέρα πού γυρνάς |
| Drunk as a lord, pathetic rotter | και μπεκρουλιάζεις |
| Torturing your family | και την οικογένειά σου |
| With lean and hungry misery. | απ' την πείνα την ταράζεις; |
| | |
| Have a care and change your ways | Κοίταξε ν' αλλάξεις γνώμη |
| Gather up your addled wits | να μαζέψεις τα μυαλά σου |
| Keep a few coins in your pocket | κι αν σου μείνει μια δεκάρα |
| Take some small change to your kids. | να τη φέρνεις στα παιδιά σου. |
| | |
| Go hunt for another girlfriend | Σαν εγώ δε σου αρέσω |
| Since you don't love me no more | κοίταξε άλλη να πάρεις |
| I can't stand you any longer | δεν μπορώ για να σ' αντέξω |
| Alcoholic, grumbling bore! | να 'σαι μπέκρας και γρινιάρης. |

Back then it was all smoking *arghile*, songwriting and music. That was my work all the time. Plus going out to do recordings. I didn't do anything else. When I didn't have other work I used to sit outside my house and let the pavement eat me. People used to come and find me there, just as they do now.

| I Was Once a Young Kid Too | Κάποτε Ήμουνα κι Εγώ |
|---|---|
| I was once a young kid too, | Κάποτε ήμουνα κι εγώ |
| And I was pretty cool | παιδάκι από τα φίνα |
| I had a lot of heartache | και η καρδιά μ' επόνεσε |
| For a sweet and flirty girl. | για μια γλυκειά τσαχπίνα. |
| | |
| People all would turn and look | Όταν την έπαιρνα μαζί |
| When the two of us went by | ο κόσμος με κοιτούσε |
| But then she went out on the town, | μ' αυτή μου την αμόλησε |
| To play with another guy | και μ' άλλονε γλεντούσε. |

My mind went dark and cloudy,　　Κι από το ντέρτι το πολύ
The pain it couldn't take,　　　　Θολώνει το μυαλό μου
My poor soul from lovesickness　　και η ψυχή μου η δύστυχη
Began to tear and break.　　　　σπαράζει από τον καημό μου.

And ever since, in other girls,　　Και από τότε πια και γω
I find I take no pleasure.　　　　καμιά πια δε γουστάρω
The tzoura and the arghileh　　　τη τζούρα μου πάντα τραβώ
Now take up all my leisure.　　　και αργιλέ φουμάρω.

All my first songs were c*hasiklidhika*. From 1934 when I began, they were all like that. These hashish songs came out on records but I've forgotten them now. I wrote a lot until 1936. After Metaxas took over we wrote differently. They called me up to the censorship board and said to me: 'You're not going to write about hashish anymore.' I don't know who these guys are at the Censorship[156] or what ministry they serve under. I don't know them but, for sure, they know *me* because I've been writing so many years. To start with they used to give me instructions and they'd say: 'Markos, you've got to write better. And if you can't, bring it here so we can write it for you. Some musician, Psaroudhas - good luck to him if he's still alive, and God rest him if he's dead - he said to me: 'Come on pal, you bring them here so I can fix them for you.' I didn't go to these guys. I never had any need of them. I stopped writing what wasn't allowed. I adapted. I shaped up. Instead of writing those heavy *mangas* songs, and I mean genuinely heavy mangas songs eh? ... *very mangas*, I sat down and wrote something more, you know ... I mean it was the *words* these guys were after, they didn't mind about the music. There was nothing else I could do. It was the law here. Whatever Metaxas said had to happen. Back then, just a little before the censorship began, I wrote *O Markos Ypourgos* (rec. 1936). I sang it on a record just

---

156 When Markos recorded the interviews with Angeliki Vellou-Keil, Greece was living under the Junta, the dictatorship of the Colonels which lasted from 1967-74. Censorship was severe, as under Metaxas in 1936.

before Metaxas came to power, five or six months before. I sang it just in time. This one wouldn't have got past the censorship. It was a hit. Eh ... what lay behind this song was that all these guys who rose up and became prime ministers, they kept dying! How could such a thing happen - four or five of them dying one after the other?

| *Markos the Minister* | *O Markos Ypourgos* |
|---|---|
| Kondylis died and now the next | Επέθαν' ο Κονδύλης μας |
| To go was Venizelos | πάει κι ο Βενιζέλος |
| Then Demertzis, he popped his | την πούλεψε κι ο Δεμερτζής |
| Clogs for all he tried to tell us. | που θα `φερνε το τέλος. |
| | |
| All who become prime ministers, | Όσοι γενούν πρωθυπουργοί |
| All of them will die, | όλοι τους θα πεθάνουν |
| The people drive them out for | τους κυνηγάει ο λαός |
| Those good policies they try. | απ' τα καλά που κάνουν. |
| | |
| I bet you anything that I'll | Βάζω υποψηφιότητα |
| Prime Minister become | πρωθυπουργός να γίνω |
| And eat and drink all lazily | να κάθομαι τεμπέλικα |
| And sit there on my bum, | να τρώω και να πίνω. |
| | |
| Stand up in the parliament | Και ν' ανεβαίνω στη Βουλή |
| And boss them all around | εγώ να τους διατάζω |
| Tamp their arghileh for them | να τους πατώ τον αργιλέ |
| And get them nicely stoned. | και να τους μαστουριάζω. |

A song can be chewed up by the censorship because of various words, various meanings which they don't like.

See, there's this one I've got right now at the censorship board:

| | |
|---|---|
| At Three, at Dawn | Χαράματα η Ώρα Τρεις |
| | |
| At three, at dawn | Χαράματα η ώρα τρεις |
| The world is quiet as death. | που ο κόσμος ησυχάζει |
| A mother weeps, | μια μάνα κλαίει κι οδύρεται |
| Feels pain and pants for breath. | και βαριαναστενάζει. |
| | |
| She pours out tears, | Κλαίει και χύνει δάκρυα |
| For her sick son she cries | για τ'άρρωστο παιδί της |
| Her body burns, | φωτιά ανάβει στην καρδιά |
| Her heart is lit with fires. | και καίει το κορμί της. |

I'm afraid they won't pass this one because it's a sad song. They've thrown out other ones like this:

| | |
|---|---|
| My heart is torn | Τα βάσανα πληγώνουν |
| With so much strife. | την καρδιά μου |
| No breath is left, | και μου μαραίνουν τη ζωή |
| It withers my life. | δε μου'μεινε πνοή. |
| | |
| I sit and think | Σαν συλλογούμαι |
| And never sleep at night, | τα βράδια δεν κοιμούμαι |
| My sorrows fence me in | γιατί με ζώνουν οι καημοί |
| And hold me tight. | καθ' ώρα και στιγμή. |
| | |
| Inside my cell | Μες το κελί μου, |
| My body'll waste away, | θα λυώσει το κορμί μου |
| Until, Sweet mama, | ώσπου να βρω τη λευτεριά |
| I see the light of day. | μανούλα μου γλυκιά. |

Four years ago that song was at RCA.[157] The censorship passed it, I recorded it and sang it myself, but they went to RCA and stopped it. That probably happened during Papandreou's government.

---

157 Radio Corporation of America.

I take care. The songs that are in danger of not passing the censorship, I don't submit them. I put in another word that *will* get past. It's not a problem for me. I've got used to keeping this always in mind. Why should I write a song, go through all that trouble just to have it rejected? In those first songs of mine, before Metaxas, I wrote whatever I wanted. Then, full stop. After that I wrote what I *had* to write so that I could get past the censorship. I was writing better songs.

Everything changed with Metaxas. Before that, the longest sentence for being caught in the *tekes* was two, maybe three days in prison. But after '36, '37, 38, when Greece made a pact with Turkey on the hashish question, then it turned into a very big deal. Now, when they caught you, they had to find out the source: 'Who gave it you? Where did you buy it, Markos, this hashish you're smoking?' I'd keep my mouth shut. Next thing was beatings with the truncheon, then torture. 'Will you give evidence where you got it?'

'So and so gave it to me.' They bring in the other guy.

'Tell us where you found it, who brought it to you?' And so on. They'd find the source all right. That's how it's been ever since with the 'black'. Not only with the 'black' but all narcotics. They beat people up and put them in prison for years, eh? They find the source. People can't hold out against the beatings. Eh ... there are very few guys who don't talk. They force a man. After all the tortures they put him through, he squeals. They cracked down on it hard and most people gave it up. These days they smoke spliffs. But me, I liked the *arghile*. A spliff now ... hell, you've got to be be joking! All the garbage gets in. We *chasiklidhes*, we *manghes*, didn't smoke spliffs. Hardly. The spliff wasn't good because all those 'sapphires' I was talking about get into your throat. Just think of all the greasy gunge we used to take from inside when we took the *seri* out of the *loulas* and cleaned it. With spliffs all that stuff goes into your throat, while with the *arghile* the water cleaned it up.

So with all that going on, what was I to do? I got out, I left off all this business. Later I had children. I didn't want my kids to know what I was. Now that they've grown up people say things: 'Eh! What's this? Your father … ? So many years he was like that?' I don't care. My kids see me as I am now. They're older and they understand. Now I can hang out with them as a friend. We talk about things and I always say 'Keep away from that stuff.' I say to Stelios, 'Avoid it, kid, because it's not a good thing.' He keeps company with those types, guys who know me. 'Hey,' they say to him, 'we know your dad. We did this' or 'we did that with him.' Stelios now, *he* asks me questions. He's the only one of them that does. He's a bit more of a *mangas*, this one, this Stelios. Of course I'm not saying he's not a good boy. All my kids are wonderful, all three of them but the older one and the younger one are … how can I put it? More steady. One of them is a sea captain. What would *he* be doing sitting around listening to such rubbish? Is that of any interest to him? Who would dare to go up to him and tell him about me? And the youngster, since he also does this kind of stuff, it's possible someone might say something to him, but he doesn't care. He doesn't sit there asking. He never says to me 'Some guy told me this story.' But the other one, Stelios, he *does* ask me. I can't sit down and tell my kids what I did. I mean it's not for me to do. It's not right for me to teach a kid so that he says 'Well, if my father did it, I'll do it too. It didn't do *him* any harm.' No I just keep off the subject. Sometimes this one carries on at me. 'You're going to tell me, go on, since even strangers tell me.'

'Yeah,' I say to him, 'since the others told you everything, fine. Enough said.'

## APPENDIX: INTRODUCTION (1972)
by Angeliki Vellou-Keil

With its sources hidden in the ports of the Eastern Mediterranean in the 19th century, *laiko* song, the song of the Greek working class, makes its appearance in Piraeus during the early years of the 20th century, blooms profusely from 1930 to 1950 and from that point fades. Its ghost will probably continue to haunt us until it is buried properly, allowed to decompose and fertilize a new song - a song with the power to recreate the Greek people.

An adequate study of the development of *laiko* song, or a good introduction to the life of Markos Vamvakaris, must deal with the difficult topic of dialectical relationships between the creation of the song and its acceptance and use by an ever-widening audience. Even a mere sketching out of this phenomenon takes on large dimensions. We need historical depth. For example, what was life like for Greek and non-Greek working people in the ports of Constantinople, Izmir, Alexandria? We need historical and ethnographic work not only on the ports of the Ottoman Empire but also on the growth of the Greek State, especially Piraeus and Ermoupolis, Syra. We need technical musicological analyses of the different styles, especially as these were shaped by diverse Eastern and Western influences. Finally we need to study the symbols, the language of the songs, in their relationship with the social development of the Greek people.

Of course, if we wish to understand the meaning of the development of the *laiko* song from a heavy *zebekiko* (the central dance style of classic *laika* originating with Turkish mercenaries from Asia Minor known as *zebekia*) to *syrtaki* (a synthetic dance pieced together from various styles and popularized by paid dancers in tourist night spots of contemporary Athens) and its transformation from the hash den (*teke*) to the American television advertisements of Olympic Airlines, we need to study it not only as the art par excellence of the Greek working class, but in continuous tension with the art, the needs and interests of the Greek bourgeoisie, and we must do all this in relation to Greek history and to Greece's position in the international scene at this point and in the future.

It is obvious that this work has not been done and cannot be accomplished in an introduction to one book and by one person. Why has this material not been collected and organized in this manner? Probably because we must open up to scrutiny three topics that have long frightened, if not paralyzed, Greek scholarship to date (1972).

These three topics are: (1) The nature of Greek dependence on the capitalist West; (2) The Eastern texture of modern Greek culture; and (3) The class structure of Greek society. A courageous and studious facing up to these topics is essential not only in order to study usefully the *laiko* song but also in order to see clearly who we, the Greeks, are, to understand our life yesterday and to direct our action today, dreaming of tomorrow.

# THE ERA

Our *laiko* songs, our urban centers and the Greek nation state developed almost simultaneously. It is paradoxical, even though historically easily understood, that this era, which of course starts with 1821 (the year of the beginning of the war of independence that culminated in the establishment of the Greek state in 1827) and comes up to the present, is exactly the era when the tradition of our people is being assaulted and swamped by the economic, political and military power, as well as by the methods and ideas, of the West.

From the very beginning, the Greek state considered the tradition of the people suspect because it was the tradition of slavery, material poverty and political impotence. It had no obvious relationship to the creation of a strong, modern state except as an obstacle. The power and growth were in Europe. Political and economic dependence was on the West since 1827. Coping with this dependence defined the official national stance towards Greek identity. Ideologically our ancient ancestors were considered the only element of tradition worthy of recognition and pride. Disappearance of the continuing traditional culture of the Greek peasant was necessary in order to come close to the reigning Western Civilization. By the end of the 19th century and the beginning of the 20th century it is already a given that 'progress', the creation of power, if it ever came to Greece, would come only through the means of this civilization, that is: central state administrative machinery, bourgeois ideology, technology, European education, ideas, fashions, etc. The Tricoupis government (1875-1895) marks the basic solidification of western-bourgeois influences in the development of the Greek state and society. Tricoupis exhausted revenue and foreign credit in his attempt to build an economic and administrative infrastructure that would modernize Greece. He was forced to declare bankruptcy and accept crippling dependence on England, the major creditor.

From this period forward, the literate individual who has the means to serve this profitable economic drift towards the West has every reason, every encouragement and motive, to accept the culture of the West as well. The more he understands, the more he gets hold of and uses with ease its methods, the more he will progress economically. Economic salvation and security are based not only on the acceptance but in the enthusiastic learning of Western culture. The way in which this happens is not simple. The class which swallows unchewed Western culture can, at the same time create an ideology that tries to show that this does not amount to a negation of what has euphemistically come to be called 'our heritage'. But, while celebrating heritage, treasuring grandmother's village costume or hanging folk artifacts on the wall, basic questions about the central values of the West are not asked and Westernization takes place violently on all fronts at once. Chauvinism and 'fatherland' worship simply run parallel with the destruction of the people's culture and blind us to its swift demise.

In contrast to the bourgeois, the class at the bottom of the emerging economic-social hierarchy has no immediate motive or chance to get hold of and use Western culture. Their fate, and they know it, is tied up with the coal that they shovel, the merchandise that they move on their backs, the animals that they slaughter; they are to be consumed by the monster: Western bourgeois economy. This class will feed the mechanized power, always cut off from its use and from the enjoyment of its goods. Their position in society defines their stance vis a vis the new and reigning culture. They face it through their own experience and in place of the myth of 'progress' they see what it costs them. They know that they must learn to live serving the monster and to die feeding it; there is no way out, and they face the western-bourgeois civilization as fate rather than a supreme value.

The history of the struggle of independence of 1821 and the first years of the Greek nation state shows that the peasantry was consumed by the revolutionary war without managing to impress its crying needs and demands on the state. When we consider the emerging working urban class as the historical development of the peasantry that participated in the struggle for independence, then it becomes apparent that the attitude that is being sketched out here is nothing sudden or novel. It is the result of long and bitter experience over generations. The struggle for independence was national while the resulting state ended up essentially bourgeois.

For their values, the peasants-become-workers continue to embrace the people's tradition which is shaken in its entirety and is tumbling under the onslaught of western culture. The traditional values that permeate economic institutions unravel first. Economic institutions are the immediate target of Westernization. The same process destroys the arts that are closely related to the economy, i.e. weaving, metal work, wood carving and the like. However, the values of the expressive arts (the arts that are based less on materials, but rather use the human body as their material and means of expression) not tied to the economy, remain strong and the new proletarian embraces them like the only floating plank from the shipwreck of tradition. The working class of the new cities in this particular turn of Greek history is the only social class that needs and furthers any aspect of the people's tradition. The expressive arts are the only root of the tradition that does not get sick unto death from the invasion of the West but rather can graft on Western elements successfully, pushing forth new growth and new life. This axiomatic statement may seem too absolute but I think it is true. Later in the discussion of the cities and of the *mangas* we will return to this point. My assumptions may be stated as follows:

Modern Greek culture can be divided into three streams or class traditions.

• The traditions of the functionally illiterate peasantry that are based on the institutions and social life of the village.

• The tradition of the functionally illiterate workers in the large ports of the Ottoman empire which is continually cross fertilized by Eastern and Western elements but which is based on the life cycle of the working class neighborhood and its friendship groups.

• The literate tradition of Fanari (Greek neighborhood in Istanbul) and the Greek entrepeneurs of the Ottoman empire as well as the Greek diaspora in the commercial centers of Europe. This tradition is based on the development of individual intents and concerns; the ideas and values which mythify our national inheritance, both Byzantine and Ancient and which certain individuals continually try to align with the reigning Western ideologies.

After the creation of the Greek state, bourgeois interests and style, governmental machinery and official ideology, some people tried to cover the contradictions between these three distinct streams of culture with 'nationalism'. Only after this cloak is pulled away can we examine the pile of contradictions contained within the idea of a 'Greek national character'.

The traditions of peasants and workers, taken together, form the *laiko* tradition. They share as their common antithesis a literate culture which is opposed to the complex, everyday, social life of the people. This common root is embodied in a complex of styles, methods, knowledge, sensibilities and strategies of thought that are summarized by the term 'oral tradition'. This basic difference between *laika* and literate tradition is fundamental and remains constant no matter what the rate of cross influences between them. This important difference is especially palpable and substantial on the issue of creating art, on the meaning of recreation, and in the relationship between the artist and his public, as we shall see.

The work of continuing a Greek culture and tradition, then, is done only by these people at the bottom, not because they are more virtuous and more capable than the upwardly mobile strivers, but because they are the only ones who, by their very economic constraints, are permitted certain freedoms: freedom from faith in bourgeois ideology; from illusions like 'progress'; from thrift (for everything important has been stolen) and the freedom to meet the fate of wage labouring head on - to create new songs that speak eloquently of social bondage.

So it is that the expressive arts (dance, song, shadow puppet theater, conversation) are the only roots of the people's tradition that are transplanted and live in the city, expressing the new conditions of life and capable of absorbing certain Western elements and technical influences, while remaining thoroughly Greek.

## THE NEW CITIES

How does the social space and life within it change with the flow of peasants to the cities? The cities fill up with people whose social universe was comparatively narrow but intense. The traditions, values, guiding principles were rooted in this narrow social space. In the new city even though some social institutions continue through the family, close friends and compatriots, the social universe of the village has stopped existing as a unit. The individual comes in constant contact with other individuals who have their values rooted in other 'fatherlands'. Social space becomes heterogeneous. The neighborhood tends to play the role of the village but that goes only so far. Life in the city pushes the individual to stand alone. This 'individuation' emerges out of the new economic organization. The Westernized economy levels the individual to a wage. 'People in our days weigh you with money'. The institutions through which the individual could be useful to society tend to be transferred to the center and ultimately to the state. The value of the individual used to emerge not only out of work for the production of material goods that sustain life but also out of participation in the arts, rituals and functions of social exchange and communication that kept village society in harmony and strength. Evaluation of a personality (positively or negatively) was based not only on values of productivity but also on values of participation in a locality.

In the city, contributions to groups of the sort which a good dancer, good musician, good teller of tales can make, are trivialized. The person who would spend his means to organize events, feasts, weddings, rituals where relationships can be revivified for the good of the whole community, is frustrated. Though such events continue, they lose much of their meaning because the bounded and bonded community, the village, no longer exists. This mode of contribution continues rather as a personal need and habit. These functions, with the destruction of the village community, will either unravel under economic pressures or they will be exploited by the economic system as it absorbs them: compare the festivals of Christmas and New Year in Greece today with those of twenty five, fifty, or 100 years ago.

So the values that emerge out of the factory and social organization of the modern state are:
- The value of the individual equals the value of his or her wage. The personality, the talent, the tradition of the individual are irrelevant and the wage comes out of the relation of the individual to the 'productive' machinery. In front of the machinery as in the face of necessity, individuals are equal and interchangeable.
- Time equals money.
- One must submit to, if not believe in, the center. If the worker serves faithfully his factory or everyone his post, then what we call 'progress' will come and it will better all our lives. Faith in progress, faith in the future, make the present bearable.

The new organization of production and society establishes money as the only value and replaces participation in the community with submission to the center, whether it be factory, school, state, army or prison. It is obvious that with this value system, the workers as a class are at the bottom rung of the value hierarchy. The day wage sometimes exists and sometimes cannot be secured. When it can be found it is small. The center is unapproachable by this class. The center only uses the working class.

Three stances can be distinguished vis a vis the new life, bourgeois ideology and the new conditions. Most of the workers accept, with complaints, the valuation of the bourgeois society, even though this way they cannot avoid a negative evaluation of themselves. They place their hope in 'progress' and with continuous and long hours of labour and privation they save the means to educate their children. So they hope that at least their children will escape from the tyranny of the societal bottom and move into the shopkeeper class and then the bourgeois class. Another stance involves embracing socialism, and a critical facing of the center. Basically this solution says: 'Our problems come out of the fact that the relationship of the center to us is one of exploitation. The only salvation, the only just solution is the overthrow of the center as it exists and in the organization of a center that is going to serve us and in which we can participate.' The third stance is the one assumed by the manghes. They refuse to attribute value to money. The value of the individual is not measured by his wage but by his personality. Time is not money. Rather the time, that by necessity has to be money, is limited as much as possible. The *mangas* uses the 'friendship group,' hashish, the dance, the 'pluckings', and some love-making to negate this equation. The center is an evil fate. Only the stupid ones can expect anything out of the center. The *mangas* avoids it like the devil avoids incense; he fools it, he undermines it even with danger to himself, he studiously ignores its existence. Even in prison he raises the value of personality against the absolutist center.[1]

## THE MANGHES AND THE BOURGEOIS

Who are the *manges* as a social group?

From amongst the workers emerges a group that perhaps is made up from the most intelligent, most seeking, most irrepressible and maybe most stubborn; include here those individuals with special abilities already developed within traditional styles who refuse to give up these practices. This group in the cities create a style of life that represents an opposition and resistance to the bourgeois way of life. In the history of Greece the *manghes* were such a group, and maybe before them the koutsavakidhes (with their fashions, worry-beads, canes, and a 'special walk'). This is not exclusively a Greek phenomenon. Every country at the analogous turn of its history can show us similar social groups that are opposing the new culture ideologically and personally, but not politically.

The *mangas* that I asked 'What does *mangas* mean?' knew very well 'what people think and say' and stoically gave me his own definition that is made up of two basic elements:

- The *mangas* knows how to live. That is, he likes the beautiful things: music, dance, good company, the 'black' (hashish), women, and peace from the screaming of everyday life. These constitute the concept of 'the beautiful'.
- He does not molest anyone and he does not like to be molested by anyone. This stance of tolerance towards his fellow man is not only a way to find some peace and quiet, it also is a basic value that is not traditional. It emerges out of the conditions of life in the city where you find all kinds of people rubbing elbows. It represents respect for personality, and a faith in the fulfillment that comes as a result of personal choices.

The *mangas*, choosing the beautiful things, rejects any compulsive chasing after money. Work is necessary for his own individual independence and sustenance for his family - an obligation he accepts. His family usually does not share the views and values of the *mangas* and for this reason it is not included in 'the beautiful things'. However, the family should be in order and not lack the means for life and respectability. Here is the bind, the rub: if he sacrifices everything for his passion, the beautiful things, his *meraki*, at this point he clashes with 'society' that heaps curses on him and defines him as a rotten element. The *mangas* insists. This may be the most important element of his humanity. By 'society' he has been cut off from the use of power and sovereignty. Usually he is an unskilled laborer; even if he's skilled, his power is miniscule.

In music and in dance as well as in the creation of new styles (dress, talk, walk, gestures) he is free not only to express his pain for his impotence and the hard life of the powerless, but he is free to use all his intelligence, all his patience, his inventiveness, his thirst for order, his tradition, to create art. This art exercises all his powers and gifts that the social system, exactly because it has relegated him to the bottom, insists that he does not possess. This is why his art is so forceful and strong. It is the proof of his value and the exercise of his freedom. His art is simple, measured, austere. The ritual character of this art is a common function that keeps this group alive. Very blindly the bourgeois points to the content of this art which is partly the miseries and horrors of the societal bottom and he thinks that these 'derelicts' are enjoying these horrors. The bourgeois has learned to see order, measure intelligence and beauty only on the path that leads to money, power, and security. Blindly he ignores that the manges are enjoying the severe order, beauty and measure of the music and the dance which by themselves, by their own will, they impose on the chaos and troubles bequeathed to them by society.

The *mangas* lives truly in his 'friendship group'. The *parea* is the antidote to the center. In the *parea*, as in the factory, the individual stands alone. However, his personality is not leveled as it is in front of the machine. In the *parea*, personality, with all its characteristics and peculiarities, is precisely the contribution of the individual to the entirety of the friendship group. The *parea* is heterogeneous just like the working class is heterogeneous. One comes from Koulouri, another from Syra, others from Crete, Roumeli, Thessaly, Istanbul, etc. The *mangas* that will manage to offer joy, comfort, courage, warmth, patience, hope, rhythm, song wisdom, etc pulled out of his own particular place of origin and from his own special tradition in a manner that is understandable, acceptable and admirable to the group -- that *mangas* is recognized.

This is the workshop of new styles in song and dance. The *parea* of the workers from all the nooks and crannies of Hellenism fashions in the new city those styles that are the living continuation of the art of the countryside. The countryside is denuded; it is slowly dying. Death will not come for another 50 or 100 years, however the consumption has set in. It loses its youth, it loses its materials. The decisions that create the preconditions of life are now taken in the city that reflects a foreign light. The countryside that was the workshop of all life ends up as nothing more than a warehouse of human and nonhuman material that will be consumed by the city. It is impossible for the village to continue the traditions. The arts unravel, are disappearing, don't bring forth fruit anymore.

In the city the middle class and those who aspire to it cannot create great or lasting art. The bourgeois does not have roots in the culture that he admires and he is trying to kill his own true cultural roots with his hate for his 'ex-peasant' self. His relationship to the culture of the West barely manages to sustain the creation of certain caricatures of art which do not give meaning to life and do not recreate him because they are tainted by fear and shame.

So the only art that lives is the one that is being born from the marriage of the *laiko* traditions with the new city, the *parea* of the *mangas* being the matchmaker.

In mid-twentieth century, an emerging middle class concerns itself not with the *laiko* traditions but with individual cultivation and the learning of an ideology that will help its class superiority. The middle class also spends its time and energies in the administration of the governmental and economic machinery. By and by, it starts bringing forth artists - individuals for whom, however, the traditions of the West are at least equally and sometimes even more important than Greek popular traditions. The public for these artists' work is numerically limited because this art does not represent a ritual, a function in the social space, but rather the communications of one individual to certain other individuals. This is why in the arts where the social-ritual function is impossible to separate from personal expressions (music, dance, theater) the art of the bourgeois has nothing to show worthy of any attention. It simply chews and re-chews foreign prototypes and as bourgeois Greeks we always feel some shame that we belong to an 'uncivilized' people because the public for the 'great works' is always small and sleepy.

In one or two generations the bourgeois class, embittered and lost, cut off from roots, disillusioned by the ultimate impotence of the individual, discovers as individuals and as a class, the art of the working class and they embrace it. The elements which for the creators of the *laiko* songs were the living continuations of tradition represent an unfulfillable nostalgia for this bourgeois generation. The social ground and underground that fed this art has been dismantled by now. The experience of the struggle (at times inimical and at times erotic) of East and West that stamped the character of this art is not represented in the experience of the settled bourgeois. At the most it is something exotic, something that perhaps soothes them because it echoes the general conditions of our country, but it is not their own struggle, their very own life.

When Markos and all of Piraeus were singing the Frangosyriani, the song represented an erotic rendez-vous at the publicly and personally meaningful landmarks of our home town The new love, the new meeting, adds to the meaning of the hometown, makes it more of a birthplace. Erotic love is kneaded into the landscape. Now when we hear or even sing 'In Serifos, in Kalymnos, in Nios and Santorini' the song resembles a fleeting romance between two tourists. They met on some six-day tour, they did their shopping in the boutiques and read some Seferis in translation. We have arrived at the point, where we look at our country with the eyes of the tourist.

How does Markos and his life fit this theoretical sketch of the era, the society and art? Let's look for a minute at Syra and the special tradition of Markos.

## SYRA

The island of Syra up to the end of the 18th century has nothing of special interest to show us, nothing that different from the rest of the islands of the Cyclades. Its populations from the time of the Franks to the late 18th century fluctuated between 800 and 4000 souls. The people seemed to be a mixture of local Greeks, at times refugees from other places in Greece, and of foreigners from the very beginning, while in religion almost all the Syrans were Roman Catholic with their own Bishop and schools. The island was never especially rich or important in the politics of the area. It never had the palace of a prince or Aga who ruled it. The governmental authority was almost always out of the island and in its population there were no great economic differences that could be considered class differences. Its people clustered around the walled town, their Kastro (which later was named Ano Hora, 'upper town' to distinguish it from Ermoupoli), hoping to protect themselves from the frequent incursions of the corsaires. They were left alone as long as they paid the required tax to the far-away governmental authority. The Kastro was the only town on the island. The valleys and small plains that had water were cultivated but did not sustain small villages (for fear of the pirates). Sheep and goats grazed over the whole island. The island of Syra was poor but basically self-sufficient.

At the beginning of the 19th century some change appears in this poor self-sufficiency. Textiles and jewelry and a few other items make their appearance and the population grows. Syra starts participating in the growing commerce of the Eastern Mediterranean. Then, with the sudden influx of the Orthodox Greeks because of persecutions that followed the proclamation of the Greek revolution of 1821, something entirely unprecedented happens in Syra. The refugee merchants and entrepreneurs from Asia Minor descend on Syra and create the town of Ermoupoli, a community devoted to commerce. Ermoupoli emerged full-grown and arrived out of the Greek bourgeois commercial class of the Ottoman Empire and the diaspora, like Athena out of Zeus' forehead. It is a first not only for this island but for all of Greece.

The Great Greek Encyclopedia informs us that the census of 1828 finds Ermoupoli with 14,929 citizens and 4,167 buildings:

| | | | |
|---|---|---|---|
| Chios | 4,500, | Constantinople | 1,000 |
| Roumeli | 1,000 | Peloponnese | 1,000 |
| Smyrna | 1,500 | Hydra | 200 |
| Moschonisos | 2,000 | Aegean Isles at Large | 2,850 |
| Psara | 250 | Foreigners | 200 |
| Heptanese | 500 | | |

In the same article Mr. D. E. Moustakas presents us with an amazing picture of bourgeois mentality and organizations that have no equal repeated anywhere in Greece. The transplanted entrepeneurs start schools, orphanages, theaters, clubs, printing presses, a customs house, a hygiene department, commercial college, insurance companies, banks, a steamship line, shipyards, library, chamber of commerce, etc. The city of Ermoupoli was fashioned from its inception with the values, ideas and institutions of the commercial-bourgeois class. Ermoupoli represents the embodiment of bourgeois ideology and was designed to serve bourgeois enterprises.

Vikelas (who must be 10-15 years older than the grandfather of Markos) in his short story of Philippe Marthas describes, in only two paragraphs, the nature of his birthplace, Ermoupoli:

However, if Syra knew little of horses and carriages, I think I do no wrong to any of her sister cities of Greece when I say that she led them all in European civilization. While most of the inhabitants of the capital still wore the fustanella (traditional short kilt with leggings), nearly all Syrans above the lowest grade in the social scale had adopted western dress. The historic cafe, 'La Belle Grece' was the only rendezvous of the Athenians (except the more serious minded, who preferred to exchange ideas at some fashionable pharmacy); but the merchants of Syra boasted of two very 'superior' clubs, where notable balls were given during the carnival. In a word, the visitor from any other part of Greece could see many signs of Europeanism not to be found elsewhere.

This is easily accounted for. Torn from their firesides by the storm of revolution and transplanted in a new soil, the first founders of the modern city of Syra clung to their ancient dress and customs less tenaciously than other Greeks. They belonged for the most part to the commercial class; many had travelled in foreign countries, or even had kinsfolk settled in western Europe; and they were soon able to make their island the trading-centre of Greece. To it sailing-vessels brought their merchandise, and steamboats put in at its harbor. In short, Syra was the first connecting-link between the rest of the world and the new Hellenic state.

With the establishment of Ermoupoli the Franko-Syrans stop being the center of their island world. On Syra, power is transferred from the Kastro, now characterized as Ano Chora, to Ermoupoli and even farther away to the big cities, centers of industry and commerce, of the world and especially of Europe, where the ships come from and go to.

From the very beginning the Franko-Syrans resist. The Great Encyclopedia mentions armed fights and clashes between the Franko-Syrans and the refugees; two in 1821, one in 1822, one in 1841, two in 1842, one in 1848, etc. But fighting was in vain. Ermoupoli represents the new and rising social organization. It has not only the power of the bourgeois society and its profitable economic activity, but the power of the new state that serves the power of the bourgeois society and validates it. The heretofore self-sufficient Franko-Syrans, Markos' people, almost overnight have been relegated to the position of a poor neighborhood, a 'reserve labor army', a 'favela.'

Ermoupoli is thriving and they will serve it with their labor; whether they want it or not they will turn to wage labor as the only way of life. The Franko-Syrans, 50-70 years before the rest of the islanders and peasants of Greece, were transformed almost overnight from peasantry to wage laborers without ever leaving their castled fortress. Without any special effort on their part they become the vanguard of all the fallen peasants that will soon take the roads from all over rural Greece to Salonika, Athens and Piraeus in scarch of wages.

Sometime around 1840-50 when Ermoupoli is already the recognized economic center of Greece, in the hamlet of Danakos, the first Markos Vamvakaris was born. This is the one called 'Rokos', the Grandfather of Markos the composer. A peasant with very fertile land, it seems he lost his land because he dealt in contraband sugar and tobacco. So a cousin of Markos told me. From the same source I learned that the grandmother of

Markos, Rosa, after the death of her husband, came to Ermoupoli in order to support her children working as a cook in the house of the Ermoupoli family, Raouzeon. Later she married the son of the family as her second husband.

In the short account of Markos we find the next generation, the father of Markos, Dhomenikos, a day wage laborer. His livelihood depends entirely on the commercial economic activity of the port of Ermoupoli. From this point on the fate of Markos and his family is a paradigm of the fallen peasantry that ends up as a powerless pool of workers in the West-dominated urban centers of Greece.

But what does all this have to do with the art of Markos?

When we sit down to listen to the pre-war (1930's) records of Markos (*bouzouki*, guitar, baglamas, Markos singing with another singer) and especially if we compare these records with those of composers that followed Markos, it is easy to single out certain special characteristics of his music. These characteristics can be experienced as tensions that are created by the juxtaposition and interrelationship of contradictory elements or factors.

- Simple melodies, because they are limited by the faithful following of the dhromos (path) or maqam of each song, in tension with western chords and accompaniment.
- The straight, sparse melody of the song in tension with the playfulness of the plucking (penia) of the and the baglama.
- The severity of the rhythm of the dance in tension with the passion of the lyrics.
- The voice of Markos, straight, cut at the end of a phrase, heavy, taking liberties with the basic rhythms of the song. It is as if Markos chose the style of his voice in simultaneous confrontation with the Italian Cantada vibrato and the eastern amanes melisma. Many times his singing partner represents one of these two styles and this tension is embodied in their cooperation.
- The points in the song when Markos has a singing partner almost shock our ear that has become accustomed to the tight harmony of the western choir. They appear almost as unsuccessful practice sessions rather than intended, studied style. However, if we approach them as style and not as mistakes, then we discover that a large measure of the joy and power of these songs springs from the unchecked personal freedom of the singing partners exactly as they collaborate idiosyncratically in the expression of the song.
- Finally all these forces that are released from the amazing interweaving of eastern and western elements are in tension with the obvious relationship of our *laiko* songs with our demotic songs that are the result of a perfecting process, not by one or two artists but by generations of artists.

Of course, all these characteristics are not personal discoveries of Markos. They are achievements of Syra and Piraeus which Markos embodied in his songs and later established publicly with his records.

Except for the few things that Markos tells us, we know very few details about the *laiko* culture. We need basic research in order to talk with some certainty, but if we are willing to engage in some detective work we can arrive at certain conclusions that have a good likelihood of being validated by research when it gets done.

So, when Markos describes life in the world of the *mangas* of Syra and talks about the old bouzouki players that he heard on his island, when he tells us 'this I remember from when I was in Syra', he is referring to the *laiko* culture of his birthplace as if it were the tradition of centuries. However, if we reconsider the census of 1828 that was mentioned above, it becomes obvious that this Syran *laiko* tradition is a relatively new mixture of special traditions of the workers of Ermoupoli who congregated at this port from every corner of the Greek world with a big percentage from the Greeks of Constantinople, Moskonisos and Smyrna. From what is known about Ermoupoli and from what Markos himself tells us, this *laiko* culture developed in parallel with the Western culture of the bourgeois class and it is not too adventurous to say, partly in opposition to it.[2]

Markos talks about the use of the roads (maqam) and about the different tunings (*douzenia*) that he learned on Syra and later in Piraeus. When he explains how he composes, he shows us that this *laiko* tradition gave him not only the material but at the same time the way, the method of composition. Levi-Strauss says: 'Music presents a much more difficult problem because we know nothing about the intellectual conditions under which musical creation takes place. In other words we do not understand the differences between the few minds that secrete music and the innumerable ones in which this phenomenon does not appear.'

Markos gives us very few explanations about how this takes place, but the little that he tells us is worthy of attention. 'The instrument gets hold of the song.' He does not think the song but seizes it with the hands on the strings. The 'roads' are open for everyone to take and to walk. However, he must walk over them again and again and again with desire, with stubbornness: 'I practiced a lot. I played and played until I became perfect'. 'I will master the *bouzouki* or I will cut off my hands with the meat cleaver'. Markos seeing an American holding the *baglama* gingerly said, 'If he has the desire, he will learn'. For Markos, this meant that he had learned all the 'roads' available to him and their *taximia* (ascending and descending formulas) until they jumped out of his hand automatically. When, in our first visit, we asked him if we could tape the *dromoi*, he'd play them first one by one and then he'd find the name of each one. Once he was well onto a road, he never doubted, never hesitated. Charlie Keil learned one of these roads on the bouzouki and after he played it again and again and again, he found that the melodies of the *laiko* songs emerge inexorably. He plays the well-known taximi 5-6 times, he gets bored, he starts beating his foot to the 4/4 of the hassapiko or the 9/4 of the *zebekiko* and his hands start making melodies. Of course a foreigner cannot have the *dromoi* kneaded into his hand or into the soles of his feet - he could never converse while playing as Markos very often did.

So Levi-Strauss makes a serious mistake when he says that 'in theory if not in practice every reasonably educated person could write poetry good or bad while musical creation is based on special characteristics which can be cultivated only when they are already there'. In theory and in practice, every person that learns the *dromoi* can create *laiko* melodies, good or bad, because basically the conditions under which musical creation takes place are bodily and not mental (if this distinction can be defended at all). So we should not be talking about 'the few intellects where musical creation takes place' but about the body and soul of every person who makes music through his labour on the instrument and for bread. If indeed it was not a matter of talent but passion, then we would still want to know where does this passion for musical creation springs from.

In addition to the problem of the creator, we face the problem of the public. The time that Markos was in his prime and especially in the narrow environment of the hashish den and the *manghia*, the 'audience' used to participate in the composition in the sense that they knew the *taximi* and the roads. Their relief and joy were immediately intertwined with the progress of the artist each time he managed to arrive at a new embodiment of the familiar much-trodden road.

In a clipping from Vima I found an interview with Markos where the reporter asks him, 'Why don't the new composers write good songs?' And Markos' reply: 'Because they do not keep the maqami.' In the same article the word maqam is simply translated as 'tradition' and the point stops there. However, the word maqam is not simply tradition. It is a musical term, absolutely technical and specific. Arabic makam, in Greek 'makami', are the ancient modes again, the *dhromoi* or 'roads' to good composition.

So, if we look at Markos' usage of the word 'makami' superficially as simply tradition, easily we can arrive at the mistaken conclusion that we are dealing with a crotchety old man who, like lots of conservative old men, is complaining about the progressive youth and, to impress us, using a hard-to-understand word. However, if we take this answer seriously, precise and measured in the spirit that it was given, then something different takes shape out of the few words of Markos' answer.

Markos tells us in an absolutely concrete manner about our *laiko* musical tradition, about the roads that are related to the *echoi* of Byzantine music and whose relatedness to the *taximia* of Turkish, Persian and even Indian raga, connect us with a vast musical tradition and one that is intimately related to dance.

The use of the world 'maqam' presupposes a method of composition which we discussed above and which differs from today's 'Frankish' manner based on chords. Western music has almost deluged and destroyed our music and our sensibility. Our traditional method of composition which uses the *dhromoi* is everything but simple or artless. It presupposes the dedication of a lifetime from the composer and a public which is alive and cultivated. Markos' answer should raise questions not only about our conservatories, but also about the way our national dances are taught in school, either with no music, or even worse to the accompaniment of the piano. What's the new role of western harmony in our church? Finally, if we consider the contradictory coexistence of the *dromoi* with the chords as the basis of our *laiko* songs, then we see that Markos' statement diagnoses the death of our *laiko* musical tradition.

One of the characteristics of Markos' story worthy of special attention is that he lines up everything without special emphasis as to what's more basic or less. Whatever he says has meaning for him and is indispensable. He does not stop to embellish what the basis is and to distinguish it from what is merely an example. That's why the reader, if not careful, can consider what Markos is telling us as absolutely common and of no special interest. This could be a big mistake because Markos in his thought and word was measured and serious. He knew his work and as a very intelligent person had arrived at his conclusions. But he did not have the passion of the literate man to teach, explain, say a lot of words. That's why it is important to face the little that he tells us attentively and seriously. Like his songs, it is the distillation of an expert and of a life full of hard work.

Endnotes

1 These three stances are essentially analytical categories. They do not make up exclusive characteristics of three groups within the working class, but rather three tendencies that coexist even in the same person. Otherwise how can we comprehend the *mangas* whose life's dream is to educate his children or how can we hear the song that emerges out of the hash-den, echo in the poor neighborhoods? And what labor organizer pointed out the hurts and injustices of poverty more eloquently than the *laiko* songs? The comparison between the stance of the *mangas* and that of the socialist is complicated. They both expose the conditions of life in the working class and brand those conditions criminal. The *mangas* stoically finds that he cannot change them and he retires to his *parea*. The socialist struggles with the center through unionization in order to create a just society. The *mangas* struggles to form by reworking tradition, an expression that is going to ease his pain. The figure of the *mangas* represents an ambivalent example for the entire working class and especially the youth. The *mangas* in the working neighborhoods projects a style of life that has the heroic glow of personal resistance. If the socialist movement is not strong and does not have its own heroes it is obvious that the *mangas* presents uncontested charm.

2 Syra, in the early 1970's was still an interesting research field for *laiko* song. An overnight trip left me with the impression that the *laiko* tradition of Marko's youth is still alive in Syra at the very least in the memories of the people. Workers in the market area use local proverbs, poems and songs in their speech.. In a coffee shop of Ano Hora, in the company of seven of eight men, two played *bouzouki* for me. One is a son of Vafeas the barber that Markos mentions as a

splendid Syran *bouzouki* player. The same group of people gave ten names of Syrans who play the *bouzouki*, some well and some not so well, without including two professional players who I had just met in the marketplace, Vangelis Prekas and Takis Photinias. Vangelis Prekas by his spontaneous response to a situation, planted in my mind the notion that the *laiko* classes of Syra carry on a tradition that at least in part opposes the bourgeois tradition. One citizen was talking to me about the *zebekia* (which they told me stopped in 1935) and let it be understood that the people who celebrated the carnival in this manner were of dubious character. Mr Prekas, who was following the conversation from some distance, interrupted and insisted until it was obvious that I had been convinced, that the *zebekia* represented nothing evil or immoral but that they were 'tradition'. His manner had all the marks of his decisive intent to set the record straight. In contrast to the citizen safeguarding bourgeois values, Mr Prekas wanted me to know that the *zebekia* did not represent the immoral orgies of the underworld, but rather legitimate traditional culture. Mr Prekas, like Markos and all the *manghes*, was keenly aware of the devaluation of his culture. Their stance toward their experience and their culture is a clear indication of the continuing struggle between the two cultures for the definition of modern Greek social reality.

## ACKNOWLEDGEMENTS FOR THE GREEK EDITION

I owe much to all those who supported me both in Greece and in America during the time I was engaged in this work. When I first took up the subject of laiko song, Dinos Christianopoulos lent me his archive to study. I learnt a lot from Kiki Kalamaras and especially from Nearchos Georgiadhis. The outline they first put together of Markos' writings proved an invaluable aid in my first steps. Eleni Kaloyeropoulou read my manuscript and helped me to cut and rearrange a number of passages. Katy Kazantzis gave up many hours of her free time to the typewriter. In Syra the families of Isidoros Vafeas and Artemis Katevatis, friends of Markos, received me warmly and willingly answered my questions. In Athens the family of Thanasis and Myrto Kostikas offered me hospitality and all kinds of help. Stelios Dimopoulos solved problems which would otherwise have remained eternal mysteries to me. Christina Zioudrou, with her usual cleverness, opened doors to me which I never even knew existed. Dick Blau, Steve Salamone, Jill Stanton and Liz Kennedy listened to and made comments on the introduction. The family of Markos and especially Vangelio Vamvakaris put me up and helped me as much as they could. Charlie Keil not only helped me at every stage of the work but also funded my research. The School of Fine Arts at Buffalo in New York State University funded my journey to Athens for the interviews with Markos. Finally, this work wouldn't have seen the light of day without the enthusiasm and hard work of Dimos Mavromati. Corrections, which improved every single page of the work, are due to him and to his colleagues Poppy Kamaris and Miranda Terzopoulou - Papayorghiou. As to the final shape of the book and whatever imperfections remain, the responsibility is entirely mine.

Angeliki Vellou-Keil, 1972

Lightning Source UK Ltd.
Milton Keynes UK
UKHW010734011220
374435UK00002B/486